TOO HEAVY A YOKE

Too Heavy a Yoke

Black Women and the Burden of Strength

CHANEQUA WALKER-BARNES

CASCADE *Books* • Eugene, Oregon

TOO HEAVY A YOKE
Black Women and the Burden of Strength

Cascade Books
An Imprint of Wipf and Stock Publishers
199 W. 8th Ave., Suite 3
Eugene, OR 97401

www.wipfandstock.com

ISBN 13: 978-1-62032-066-2

Cataloguing-in-Publication data:

Walker-Barnes, Chanequa.

Too heavy a yoke : black women and the burden of strength / Chanequa Walker-Barnes.

xii + 222 pp. ; 23 cm. Includes bibliographical references and indexes.

ISBN 13: 978-1-62032-066-2

1. 2. 3. I. Title.

CALL NUMBER 2014

Manufactured in the U.S.A.

For the StrongBlackWomen upon whose shoulders I stand—
my grandmother, Gwendolyn Johnson, my mother, Laquitta Walker,
and my aunts, Lunetha, Jacobina, Marilyn, Belinda, Rochelle,
Zeporia, Denette, and Linette

In memory of
Marion Walker, Erma Barnes,
and Tracey Ann Adams

Contents

Acknowledgments   *ix*

Introduction: The Personal Is Pastoral   1

1   This Thing Called Strength: A Portrait of the
StrongBlackWoman   14

2   Too Heavy a Yoke: The Pain of the StrongBlackWoman   41

3   "To Carry Your Burden in the Heat of the Day": Racism,
Sexism, and the Making of the StrongBlackWoman   80

4   Pride and Prejudice: Societal Reactions to the
StrongBlackWoman   109

5   Must Black Women Bear the Yoke Alone? The Church and the
StrongBlackWoman   130

6   "For My Yoke Is Easy": Liberating Black Women from the
Burden of Strength   160

*Appendix: The StrongBlackWoman's Twelve-Step
Recovery Program*   197

Bibliography   199

Scripture Index   209

Subject Index   210

Acknowledgments

VARIATIONS OF THE IDEAS in this text were previously published in my article "The Burden of the Strong Black Woman," in the summer 2009 edition of the *Journal of Pastoral Theology*.

A "great cloud of witnesses" has shepherded this project from its inception to its completion. I am especially grateful for my dear friends and colleagues Kathryn Broyles and Cheryl Kirk-Duggan, who have provided continual encouragement and feedback on several chapters. My writing group members—Tonya Armstrong, Tina Ndoh, and Daphne Wiggins—reviewed the book proposal and were vital in shaping the present form of the project. And my CCDA "cohort" members affirmed my voice when I still wasn't sure that I had anything valuable to say.

This project was birthed during my time as a seminarian at Duke University Divinity School. I am forever indebted to Willie Jennings, who helped me rekindle my passion for an academic career when I thought it had been snuffed out. Conversations and courses with several Duke faculty members were vital in shaping this book and my transition from clinical psychology to pastoral theology, including Esther Acolaste, J. Kameron Carter, Mary McClintock Fulkerson, Amy Laura Hall, and Tammy Williams.

Several feminist and womanist colleagues encouraged me to pursue this project when I was tempted to let it go, especially Monica Coleman, Trina Armstrong, and Pamela Cooper-White. Renita Weems gave me a healthy dose of "You are enough!" sister-medicine when I was tempted to believe that my education and credentials were insufficient for this project and for a career in pastoral theology. My understanding of intersectionality was expanded by my participation in the 2009 Spelman-NWSA Women of Color Institute. I am grateful to its organizers, facilitators, and participants, including Beverly Guy-Sheftall, Allison Kimmich, Bonnie Thornton Dill, Andrea Smith, and M. Jacqui Alexander.

Acknowledgments

I express my sincere gratitude to the Louisville Institute for their award of a First Book Grant for Minority Scholars, which funded a research leave during which much of this book was written. The feedback from my cojourners in the 2012 Winter Seminar was immensely helpful.

I am grateful for the support of my students at Shaw University Divinity School, Duke University, and McAfee School of Theology. Students in my courses on African American women at Shaw and Duke provided fertile soil for testing the ideas expressed in this book. And my students at McAfee have been incredibly supportive in the final stages of the journey, being patient with the slow grading of their newest faculty member and expressing eagerness for the project. Special appreciation goes to Sharlyn Menard for her assistance with the footnotes and bibliography and for helping ease my load generally as I completed the manuscript.

I also wish to express my appreciation for the women of the SISTERS group at Compassion Ministries of Durham, who allowed me to be a part of their healing journeys and who intersected mine.

I am eternally thankful for my husband, Delwin, and son, Micah, who have sustained me through the writing process and beyond with their love, patience, and laughter (especially their laughter!). I am more blessed by them than they could possibly know.

Introduction

The Personal Is Pastoral

The illusion of strength has been and continues to be of major significance to me as a black woman. The one myth that I have had to endure my entire life is that of my supposed birthright to strength. Black women are supposed to be strong—caretakers, nurturers, healers of other people—any of the twelve dozen variations of Mammy. Emotional hardship is supposed to be built into the structure of our lives. It went along with the territory of being both black and female in a society that completely undervalues the lives of black people and regards all women as second-class citizens. It seemed that suffering, for a black woman, was part of the package. Or so I thought.[1]

Ten years ago I came to a startling realization: I was a StrongBlackWoman, and being one was not working for me. Having recently crossed the threshold of my thirtieth birthday, I was in a state of physical and emotional crisis: high blood pressure, weight gain, chronic self-doubt, fear of making mistakes, insomnia, fatigue, headaches, frequent illnesses, low self-esteem, mood swings, and feelings of rage. On top of all that, I was lonely. Despite my constant attempts to do for and please others, I felt alienated, detached, and abandoned. I felt that there was no one whom I could count on, no one who could and would take care of me in the way that I took care of others.

I learned to be a StrongBlackWoman early in life. I am the eldest child of a single mother, with a brother eight years my junior. With my mother working long, hard hours to support us (often twelve-hour stints on the third shift), I had to step in to help take care of the family. By the age of

---

1. Danquah, *Willow Weep for Me*, 19.

ten, I was capable of waking up and getting myself and my brother dressed and fed so that we would be ready when my mother returned home from work to take us to school and daycare. By fourteen, my afterschool routine consisted of taking the city bus to pick up my brother from daycare, helping him with his homework (and doing my own), supervising while he played outside, cooking dinner, cleaning the kitchen, and getting him bathed and in bed. In child development terms, I was a full-fledged parentified child.

Over the years my caretaking tendencies expanded to include everyone around me—family, friends, co-workers. It was a natural (and expected) progression. I was constantly concerned with the needs of others, always trying to be helpful. I was so accustomed to taking care of others that I felt pangs of guilt anytime that I did something for my own pleasure or, worst yet, did nothing at all (that activity known to others as relaxation). Over-extending myself became my modus operandi. I was living in a state of serious self-care neglect. Of course, I did not call it neglect. I called it being responsible. In fact, I prided myself on being the most responsible person I knew. And my high sense of responsibility was rewarded often by others who were pleased with me and the things that I did for them.

Even as my high sense of "responsibility" began to exert a heavy physical and psychological toll, I persisted. Many times, I was so focused on the needs of other people and their situations that I paid very little attention to the symptoms that I was experiencing. And when I did, I did not imagine that they were related to the stress and role strain that I was experiencing. In my worldview, overactivity was normative. It was what Black women did.[2] Black women, after all, were strong. Proving myself capable of taking care of everything and everyone in my sphere of existence was, I thought, a rite of passage into full Black womanhood.

Then came the breaking point. I am uncertain how long the pain had been there. On the Monday following my thirtieth birthday, I awoke with a sharp, stabbing pain in my right shoulder. I had noticed some pain a few days before. But with celebrating to do and relatives in town to help me do it, I had ignored it. It could not be ignored any longer; it hurt to breathe. I called the clinic that I had visited once and begged them to fit into the morning schedule. A few hours later, I left the clinic still in pain, with a diagnosis of "Nothing's wrong. Go home and take some Tylenol." I was finally

2. My use of the term *Black* to refer to people of African descent is intentional. The ideology of the StrongBlackWoman is not limited to the United States but seems to be fairly ubiquitous throughout the African diaspora, including the Caribbean, Canada, and the United Kingdom. For example, see Edge and Rogers, "Dealing with It."

starting to listen to my body's screams, but the medical establishment was not.

A few weeks later, with the intensity of the pain lessened, I was in full swing, preparing to host Thanksgiving for my family. Earlier that year, my husband and I had decided to forego the normal Thanksgiving festivities and to spend the holiday in a bed and breakfast. We both needed some quiet time. But when my family asked us to host dinner in our new home in North Carolina, we could not bear to say no. In the week prior to Thanksgiving, we spent hundreds of dollars for food, household decorations, and kennel reservations for our dog (who was not exactly "fit for comp'ny"). By Wednesday afternoon, we had done most of the cooking for the twenty or so aunts, uncles, and cousins that we expected. That is when the phone calls started. One by one, relatives began calling to send their regrets. On Thursday, two people showed up. As they drove away the following day, I realized that once again I had allowed the desires of others to trump my own needs. Like many Black women, I had inadvertently fallen into the trap of being a StrongBlackWoman.

The Myth of Strength

Ask anyone—Black or White, male or female—to describe Black women and the most common answer is likely to be *strong*. The StrongBlackWoman is a legendary figure, typified by extraordinary capacities for caregiving and for suffering without complaint. She is a cultural myth that defines—and confines—ways of being in the world for women of African descent. While both Black men's and Black women's identities have been bound by cultural mandates to be strong, the manifestation of strength that has become normative for Black women is uniquely racialized and gendered. *Strong* is a racial-gender codeword. It is verbal and mental shorthand for the three core features of the StrongBlackWoman—caregiving, independence, and emotional strength/regulation.

My use of the phrase, "StrongBlackWoman," with the spaces omitted between the words, is intentional. The literary "scrunching" is meant to emphasize the distinction between being a Black woman who is strong and being a StrongBlackWoman. There are strong women (and men) in all racial and ethnic groups, individuals who possess a multiplicity of spiritual, emotional, and/or physical fortitudes that sustain them through periods of crisis and through journeys of struggle. This type of strength is not associated with any particular personality type, but instead exists as a component of varied and multilayered personalities, a component that may be invisible until a need for its manifestation arises. The StrongBlack-Woman, in contrast, is a particular, and fixed, way of being in the world. It is a racialized gender performance, a scripted role into which Black women are socialized, usually beginning in childhood. Rather than being a genuine expression of personality, it is a mask that stifles authenticity, subsuming multifaceted selves behind a singular wall of self-sacrifice and emotional stoicism. The StrongBlackWoman is at once an archetype, a performance, and an ideology. It is, in effect, the hegemonic black femininity.[3]

The StrongBlackWoman is the woman who constantly extends herself on behalf of others. In her intimate and family relationships, on her job, and in her church and community, she is the "go-to" woman, the one upon whom others depend when they need assistance, counsel, or comfort. Driven by a deeply ingrained desire to be seen as helpful and caring, she is practically incapable of saying no to others' requests without experiencing feelings of guilt and worthlessness. As her willingness to help repeatedly reinforces others' tendencies to ask her for help, her very nature becomes defined by multitasking and over-commitment. A modern day Atlas, she bears the weight of her multiple worlds upon her shoulders. And unfortunately, she is as incapable of saying "help" as she is of saying "no." Since childhood, she has been taught that a good woman, especially a good Black woman, is independent, a giver (and not a receiver) of help, including emotional, financial, or instrumental support. Moreover, as a woman of (usually Christian) faith, if she does need help, it should come from only one source—God. Thus, fearful of being seen as unfaithful, the Strong-BlackWoman invests considerable effort in maintaining the appearance of strength and suppresses all behaviors, emotions, and thoughts that might contradict or threaten that image. Even as the physical and psychological toll of her excessive caregiving mount up, she maintains a façade of having it all together and being in control.

---

3. While the StrongBlackWoman is the hegemonic black femininity, strength is not the universal lens through which to view Black women's lives. That is, not every Black woman who demonstrates strength is a StrongBlackWoman. In qualitative interviews with African-American women, for example, sociologist Tamara Beauboeuf-Lafontant found that fully one-third of the women in her study did not consider the type of strength associated with the StrongBlackWoman to be a motif that was applicable to themselves (Beauboeuf-Lafontant, *Behind the Mask*, 14).

A Deadly Silence

Whereas being a Black woman who is strong may be commendable, being a StrongBlackWoman may be dangerous. The mythological strength of Black women often masks the very real vulnerabilities of their lives. There is a largely ignored health crisis confronting Black women in America. Black women are experiencing epidemic rates of medical conditions such as obesity, diabetes, hypertension, and HIV/AIDS. And they have higher morbidity and mortality rates than any other racial-gender group for nearly every major cause of death. Yet while writers in secular disciplines—primarily journalism, psychology, and sociology—have begun to document the phenomenon of the StrongBlackWoman and its deleterious health effects, there has been little discussion of the issue among church leadership.

Ironically, it was in the church that the link between my personal narrative and the patterned experiences of Black women became clear. As I embarked upon a personal journey of healing, I was continually confronted by stories of StrongBlackWomen—sisters who were crumbling under the strain of doing too much for too many people and in too many places. During worship services, women were giving testimonies of suffering and issuing requests for prayer. They were calling into gospel radio programs, crying about being on the verge of a breakdown. Almost always, their stories of emotional and physical strain contained allusions to excessive caretaking and service to others. Yet rarely did any of them appear to notice the link. Neither, it seemed, did any of the pastors, ministers, or lay leaders to whom they were issuing their pleas. These testimonies, along with the stories of Black Christian women with whom I worked in my private practice as a psychologist and in women's ministry, indicated that the crisis was deeply rooted in the church.

Indeed, perhaps nowhere in society is the StrongBlackWoman more ubiquitous than in the Christian church. The church reinforces the mythology of the StrongBlackWoman by silencing, ignoring, and even romanticizing the suffering of Black women. Rather than offering a balm to heal the wounds of Black women who cry out about their pain, the church admonishes them with platitudes such as "God won't give you any more than you can bear" and "If He brought you to it, He'll bring you through it." And while the existence of the church is dependent upon the labor and participation of its largely female membership, women's leadership and decision-making authority in many denominations are limited to roles that have expectations of caregiver-based service that is neither required nor expected of men—church mother, first lady, and pastor's aide. Imprisoned within the unholy trinity of self-denial, suffering, and silence, the Christian StrongBlackWoman serves as the modern sacrificial lamb, with the church functioning as both the officiating priest and the altar of ungodly fire.

An Ideological Ancestry

While the term *StrongBlackWoman* (with or without spaces) began to appear in the literature in the last dozen years, the construct is not without ideological forebears. The twenty-first century StrongBlackWoman is the offspring of the Superwoman identified by Michele Wallace in her 1979 text, *Black Macho and the Myth of the Superwoman*.[4] Wallace described the superwoman as

> a woman of inordinate strength, with an ability for tolerating an unusual amount of misery and heavy, distasteful work. This woman does not have the same fears, weaknesses, and insecurities as other women, but believes herself to be and is, in fact, stronger emotionally than most men. Less of a woman in that she is less "feminine" and helpless, she is really *more* of a woman in that she is the embodiment of Mother Earth, the quintessential mother with infinite sexual, life-giving, and nurturing reserves.[5]

Unfortunately, Wallace's exposition of the superwoman was overshadowed by her critique of patriarchy within the Black nationalist movement. Her primary thesis, that sexism within the Black community was responsible for the demise of the Black Power movement, was met with considerable backlash from scholars as well as activists.[6] Further, her lack of data to substantiate her thesis muted its power.

Following Wallace's work, there was a twenty-year lull in which research and writing on the StrongBlackWoman was severely limited. A break

---

4. Wallace, *Black Macho*.

5. Ibid., 107.

6. In the introduction to a later edition of the book, Wallace retracted this thesis, admitting that it was shortsighted and failed to take into account the role of external forces (such as the FBI) as well as the ever-changing nature of resistance movements. She further discussed how her thesis had been shaped by then-unreconciled conflicts in her personal and family history, including her father's death by a drug overdose during her adolescent years (ibid., xvii–xxxviii).

in the silence came at the turn of the twentieth century with the back-to-back publication of two texts. In 1999, journalist and self-described "hip-hop feminist" Joan Morgan published *When Chickenheads Come Home to Roost.*[7] Part memoir and part cultural criticism, the book explicitly named the myth of the StrongBlackWoman as a hindrance to the physical and psychosocial health of Black women. The following year, psychologists Leslie Jackson and Beverly Greene published *Psychotherapy with African American Women,* an edited volume of scholarly essays on issues that impact clinical work with African-American women.[8] Written by African-American female psychotherapists, the essays—two of which explicitly focused upon the StrongBlackWoman—blend psychodynamic theory, clinical practice, and personal experience. Since then, there have been a number of articles, chapters, and books focusing upon the icon of the StrongBlackWoman, oftentimes using varying terminologies to describe the phenomenon.[9]

Regardless of the nomenclature, the literature is characterized by a common core: the StrongBlackWoman is an adaptive response by Black women that, on the one hand, enables them to cope with the very real pressures of their lives yet, on the other, places them at heightened risk for physical and psychological distress. The literature is also marked by a common set of limitations. First, rigid disciplinary and methodological boundaries have prevented authors from the type of cross-disciplinary discourse that would engender a full understanding of the features and etiology of the StrongBlackWoman. To put it simply, the authors are not talking to one another. For example, the academic texts make little to no reference to "non-academic" authors such as Joan Morgan; social science scholars overlook the contributions of scholars in the humanities and cultural studies, and vice versa. Consequently, each author's view of the StrongBlackWoman tends to be myopic. Secondly, pastoral theology and practice have rarely been part of the conversation. While several texts allude to spiritual and religious issues that may be at stake in the formation and maintenance of the StrongBlackWoman, few authors have dealt explicitly with these issues and none have explored them with any detail. If the church is involved in

7. Morgan, *When Chickenheads Come Home to Roost.*

8. Jackson and Greene, *Psychotherapy with African American Women.*

9. For example, in her ethnographic study, Kesho Scott captures a similar concept using the term "habits of surviving" (Scott, *Habit of Surviving*). Other similar concepts include Jones and Shorter-Gooden's "Sisterella Complex" (Jones and Shorter-Gooden, *Shifting)* and James' "John Henryism" (James, "John Henryism and the Health of African Americans").

constructing and reinforcing the ideology that imprisons StrongBlack-Women, it has a pronounced responsibility for setting the captives free.

Purpose and Organization of This Book

Too Heavy a Yoke seeks to heighten pastoral awareness and discourse about the inordinate burden that the demand for *strength* places upon women of African descent. The book is intended primarily for pastoral theologians, pastoral caregivers (including pastors, pastoral counselors, and women's ministry leaders), and Christian mental health professionals whose ministry and services encompass Black women. My aim is to provide these caregivers with the knowledge and skills needed to respond compassionately and effectively to Black women whose lives are constrained by the yoke of the StrongBlackWoman. *Too Heavy a Yoke* has a fourfold mission. First, it describes the beliefs, thoughts, and behaviors that are characteristic of the StrongBlackWoman and the impact of this myth upon the physical, emotional, and relational health of the women who emulate it. Second, it explains the functions of this myth in American society, providing the reader with a new understanding of how the archetype originated and how it continues to be reinforced. Third, it highlights the unique significance of this phenomenon for the Christian church and the responsibility of pastoral caregivers in confronting and alleviating its existence. Finally, it provides a model for liberative pastoral care with StrongBlackWomen.

I employ a womanist methodology in which intersectional analyses are a necessary interpretive tool for understanding the ways in which race, gender, and religion intersect to shape the lives of Black woman today. Black women's location at the intersection of race and gender predisposes them to experiences that cannot be explained solely by either race or gender. In other words, Black women experience—by sheer virtue of their Black woman-*ness*—joys and struggles that are qualitatively and quantitatively different from those of Black men, White women, and other women of color. This is no less true for the archetype of the StrongBlackWoman. Indeed, one of my chief aims in this text is to demonstrate how the intersection of race, gender, and class identity creates a lethal stronghold for Black women. And while the attributes and sequelae of the StrongBlackWoman could be exhibited by men and women of other races, what is unique for Black women is the degree to which these are prescriptive as a function of one's fixed public identity.

My own intersectional existence—as a Black female, Christian minister, clinical psychologist, and scholar who has been reared in a working class family of StrongBlackWomen—has significant implications for the approach of this book and the sources used. In this text, I privilege the lived experiences of Black women as authoritative sources. The description of the characteristics and consequences of the StrongBlackWoman presented in this book has developed primarily from the narratives of Black women that have emerged from my clinical work and ministry with women, as well as those that have been related through biographical narratives of Black women. However, while starting at the level of personal identity narratives, a womanist methodology aims to situate the lives of individual Black women within a structural analysis of race-gender-class oppression. Thus, I draw these experiences into conversation with literature in theology, psychology, and cultural criticism, as well as with original case studies and empirical research. Situating the lived experiences of StrongBlackWomen in historical and contemporary context enables pastoral caregivers to recognize that the struggles of the individual parishioner must not be reduced to individual pathology but rather are intrinsically connected to forces at play within families, churches, and society. The StrongBlackWoman is not the problem, but is a symptom of a larger problem.

This intersectional framework, which contextualizes the StrongBlackWoman against a backdrop of historical and contemporary oppression, marks a significant and important distinction between the critique in this text and the backlash against Black women's strength that is pervasive in public discourse and in the church. From public policy to viral video, the StrongBlackWoman has become patriarchy's favorite whipping girl, blamed for everything from the declining rates of Black marriage to the disproportionate incarceration of Black men. In this book, I provide what I hope to be an *empathetic critique* of the StrongBlackWoman. I take seriously the second component of Alice Walker's definition of a womanist: "A woman who loves other women, sexually and/or nonsexually. Appreciates and prefers women's culture, women's emotional flexibility (values tears as natural counter-balance of laughter), and women's strength. . . . Committed to survival and wholeness of entire people, male *and* female."[10] Thus, even as I dissect the StrongBlackWoman, I understand the archetype to be a functional and often necessary adaptation to the stresses of Black women's lives. My dual location as patient and doctor predisposes me to an empathetic,

10. Walker, *In Search of Our Mothers' Gardens*, xi.

and perhaps also sympathetic, stance, one that emerges from my concern about Black women's health and well-being, rather than a vested interest in upholding the status quo of patriarchy.

This personal and pastoral concern about Black women's well-being gives rise to a praxeological impulse. A womanist pastoral theology is intrinsically praxeological,[11] committed to both analyzing the meanings and mechanisms of injustice and to moving to direct action. Thus, my goal in this text is to move beyond illuminating racial-gender inequities that contribute to the formation and maintenance of the StrongBlackWoman ideology, to cultivating practices of transformation that liberate Black women from the burden of strength. Given the church's and society's codependency upon Black women's strength, liberative pastoral practice with StrongBlackWomen is inherently multisystemic, concerned not only with relieving the distress of individual StrongBlackWomen but also with addressing the congregational and societal practices and policies that provide life to this mythological figure of strength. It also necessitates a reflective stance on the part of the pastoral caregiver, who must be open to evaluating his or her own participation in the perpetuation of this archetype. Throughout this book, therefore, I suggest multisystemic pastoral practices for reflection and praxis.

I begin this text by elucidating the distinction between being a Black woman who is strong and being a StrongBlackWoman. In chapter 1, I articulate the defining features of the StrongBlackWoman—caregiving, independence, and emotional strength/regulation—and their implications for the lives of Black women. Drawing upon 1 Samuel, I argue that the StrongBlackWoman is an intergenerationally and culturally transmitted suit of armor that has significant advantages and disadvantages for Black women. Detailed case examples help to illuminate the inner lives and struggles of StrongBlackWomen and challenge readers to look beyond the superficial strength of Black women.

In chapter 2, I move to discussing the health consequences of this archetype. I draw a link between the StrongBlackWoman's capacity to withstand suffering without complaint and the health crisis among Black women in America. Devoting most of their time to caring for the needs of others, StrongBlackWomen have difficulty establishing and maintaining

---

11. The term *praxeological method* has typically been used in economics but has been appropriated more recently by feminist and womanist theologians, including Cooper-White and Townes (Cooper-White, *Many Voices*, 3; Townes, *Breaking the Fine Rain*, 1).

healthy lifestyle habits of exercise, nutrition, and stress reduction. Concomitantly, Black women in America experience disproportionately high rates of physical and mental health disorders, including obesity, diabetes, hypertension, HIV/AIDS, and depression. Drawing upon the findings of epidemiologic studies, I paint a comprehensive picture of the health profile of Black women in America. I propose a theoretical model of the link between embodiment of the StrongBlackWoman and health outcomes, and report studies that investigate that link. In addition to research in the social and health sciences, informal data is obtained through my experience as a clinical psychologist and minister. Some examples come from clinical cases and ministry encounters with Black women.

Following the detailed description of the primary features of the archetype and its associated consequences upon the health of Black women, the next two chapters analyze the social forces that have contributed to the evolution and maintenance of the StrongBlackWoman. In chapter 3, I argue that the etiology of the archetype is rooted in Black women's attempt to defend against the negative representations of their identities by White racism. Against the backdrop of controlling images of the Mammy, the Jezebel, and the matriarch, the StrongBlackWoman emerged as a counternarrative that highlighted the cultural strengths and achievements of Black women. The StrongBlackWoman developed as a racialized version of the cult of true womanhood—a White, middle-class ideal characterized by piety, purity, domesticity, and submissiveness.[12] The myth of the StrongBlackWoman played a prominent role in the racial uplift movement of the late nineteenth century and was promulgated through the Black church and Black women's clubs. Ultimately, the synergy between racism, sexism, and religious symbolism created an identity that locks Black women in a prison of suffering, silence, and self-sacrifice even as it pretends to guard them from attack. Black women's restrictive identities became the embodied locus of atonement for the imputed sins of the race as dictated by White racism.

In chapter 4, I examine how the discourse of strength has been employed in contemporary society. Despite society's corroboration in prolonging the myth of the StrongBlackWoman, Black women's strength has continually existed between a tension of praise and punishment in American culture. On the one hand, Black women are revered for their strength and its contribution to the maintenance of Black families, churches, and communities. On the other, Black women are reviled for their strength

---

12. Welter, "Cult of True Womanhood."

and blamed for the decay of Black marriages and families. Utilizing examples from public policy, Black nationalist ideology, and popular media, I describe the contradictory depictions of and reactions to the icon of the StrongBlackWoman in popular culture and their impact upon the psyche of Black women, who must constantly walk the tightrope between being strong without being too strong.

Having described the characteristics of the archetype, its etiology, and its utilization and function in American society, in the final two chapters I turn specifically to addressing the theological and pastoral implications of this ideology in the church. In chapter 5, I argue that the ideology of the StrongBlackWoman and the church's complicity in reinforcing this archetype represent violations of the Greatest Commandment.[13] Drawing upon feminist and womanist theology, I argue that the church's distorted theology of self-love and self-sacrifice pose serious consequences for the health and well-being of African-American women. Then I describe biblical and theological resources for healing African-American women's identities, focusing upon Trinitarian doctrine and passages from Luke's travel narrative. The final chapter, then, explores pastoral interventions for healing Strong-BlackWomen. I begin by proffering a womanist framework for pastoral care. Then, framing the ideology of the StrongBlackWoman as a form of addiction, I propose a twelve-step recovery process as the basis for pastoral intervention and describe a concrete model for pastoral intervention based upon this process.

Too Heavy a Yoke does not present an exhaustive plan for intervention. Given the multilayered constructions of race and gender identity interwoven in the StrongBlackWoman, and the problems inherent in each of those underlying constructions, the terminal point of Black women's healing journey is likely eschatological. What *Too Heavy a Yoke* seeks to do is to issue a clarion call, not simply for Black women themselves but for pastoral caregivers of every race and gender. My hope is that *Too Heavy a Yoke* will help the church to see the pain in its midst and that its collective heart will be broken to the extent that it will be moved to action.

13. Matt 22:34–40; Mark 12:28–31; and Luke 10:25–37.

Suggestions for Pastoral Practice

- As you prepare to read this book, pray that your heart will not be hardened and that you will maintain a posture of openness and non-defensiveness.

- Read and meditate upon Song of Solomon 1:5–7. Journal about the reflections and insights that you gain during your meditation.

1

This Thing Called Strength

A Portrait of the StrongBlackWoman

> Time and again the needs of others have been superimposed on
> us. The need to believe that a black woman will love you come
> rain or come shine, that no matter how heavy the burden we can
> shoulder it, that we are naturally more resilient, that mothering
> and self-sacrifice are second nature to us, that we are called to be of
> service to others, that we will bear the shield. Strong Black woman
> is the amalgam of all that and so much more. She's flesh and blood
> real, myth and fiction, fact and lie. The assumption that we African
> American females are inherently strong, as if it were woven into
> our mitochondrial DNA, is taken as Gospel by our tribe as well as
> by others.[1]

Just say "StrongBlackWoman" and nearly anyone who has significant relationships with Black women has some idea of what you are talking about.
Indeed, the word *strong* is such a frequent descriptor of Black women that
it could be argued that the term *StrongBlackWoman* is virtually redundant.
It is certainly the case that an individual can be strong, black, and a woman
without being the "StrongBlackWoman." Yet, the societal pressure to be

---

1. Gillespie, foreword to Parks, *Fierce Angels*, ix.

strong is so intense for Black women that many, if not most, embody at least some aspect of the StrongBlackWoman at some point in their lives. Black women are expected to be strong. And conversations about them—as individuals or as a collective—routinely invoke the notion of their strength.[2] It is not uncommon, for example, to hear stories like this:

> No one knows how Ms. Martha does it.[3] She lost her husband and only child in the same year. The day after her husband's funeral, she came to church. We weren't expecting to see her in worship that day. But there she was, singing in the choir and praising God! Then, that same year, her son was in a car accident that left him comatose. When she went to see him, just before leaving his side, she kissed him on the forehead and said, "If you're not here when I get back, I'll see you on the other side." He passed away a few hours later. But Ms. Martha never missed a beat. She shows up every Sunday with a smile on her face. No one has ever seen her cry. She didn't even cry at either of their funerals. What an incredibly strong woman of faith!

I heard the story of Ms. Martha while sitting in the pastor's study of a church at which I was a guest preacher. The pastor had just returned from out of town. In the hour before the worship service began, several church leaders dropped by to welcome us both and to update the pastor on the happenings in the congregation during his absence. Although he was one of my seminary students, he was not familiar with my research on the StrongBlackWoman. Thus, he could not have known that the discussion about Ms. Martha was a cultural goldmine for me. As I silently listened in on the conversation about Ms. Martha, I tried to detect any signs of recognition that there might be more behind the scenes of Ms. Martha's strength

---

2. There is wide agreement among African-American female scholars and activists that the StrongBlackWoman is the dominant model for African-American female identity (Beauboeuf-Lafontant, *Behind the Mask*, 1; Danquah, *Willow Weep for Me*, 19; Morgan, *When Chickenheads Come Home to Roost*, 83; Romero, "Icon of the Strong Black Woman," 226; M. Wallace, *Black Macho*, 107). Melissa Harris-Perry, for example, describes the identity as "a specific citizenship imperative for African-American women—a role and image to which they are expected to conform" (Harris-Perry, *Sister Citizen*). Marcia Gillespie states, "She's a staple figure in the stories we tell and the fiction others create about us, the multi-dimensional woman we often lose sight of in the midst of all the stereotypes that swirl around her" (Gillespie, foreword to *Fierce Angels*, viii).

3. Each of the case examples in this chapter is derived from actual persons and situations that I have encountered in my professional or personal experiences. In each case, I have altered the person's name and other identifying characteristics.

or that there might be some awareness that it's unhealthy not to grieve the major losses that she had sustained. Yet the praise for Ms. Martha's strength was unwavering. No one questioned whether her outward appearance of strength held up when she was alone at home, or whether it gave way to depression and despair.

Ms. Martha could have easily been a stand-in for any number of the African-American women whom I had treated in therapy over the years. These women were highly diverse, ranging in age from their twenties to their fifties. They were students at Ivy League schools, minimum wage workers who struggled to make ends meet, corporate employees, and management level professionals in university and government agencies. Some were married, with or without children; others were single. And despite their great socioeconomic diversity, they were similar in many respects. Most of them had no serious psychopathology; in fact, it was often difficult to find any psychiatric disorder for which they met the diagnostic criteria. Usually, I diagnosed them with dysthymia—a chronic, low grade depression sometimes associated with chronic stress. But the real issue that brought each of them into therapy was being the StrongBlackWoman.[4]

Each of these women was under significant stress related to a common cause—their roles as caregivers. Regardless of their age or station in life, each had a high sense of responsibility and consequently served as a load bearer. That is, they were the individuals who could be relied upon most when something went wrong in their extended families, on their jobs, and in their churches and communities. They were the women who took care of ailing family members and who were generally the first called whenever someone had a problem. At work and at church, they could be counted upon to take up the slack when someone else failed to live up to their responsibilities. Often, in fact, they foresaw the probability that the other person would fall short and they stepped up to the plate long before they were asked. They were the individuals who made sure that everything was done in its appointed place and time. They tried to be helpful to everyone who asked and even to those who did not. They rarely said no to anyone. And they hardly ever asked for help, instead relying solely upon God to be their ultimate load bearer. These women were all faithful Christians, active churchgoers. Like Ms. Martha, each possessed a strong sense of faith that

4. Psychotherapist Regina Romero notes that symptoms of depression, anxiety, and sleep and appetite disturbances are common among StrongBlackWomen (Romero, "Icon of the Strong Black Woman," 225).

was often publicly heralded by those who knew them. Indeed, it was often out of their faith that they felt both compelled and empowered to serve others so endlessly. Whenever they felt the weight of responsibility bearing upon them, they ignored it, believing sincerely that God would continue to empower them to serve.

Ironically, the more that they did, the more people asked them to do. And on the rare occasions that they did ask for help or voice a complaint, their cries were unheard, not because others were trying to be cruel to them, but because people had come to think of them as strong and capable of handling all that life threw at them. Over time, the burden of responsibility became too heavy to bear. But because they did not want to let anyone down (and because their pride would not allow themselves to be seen as persons in need of help), they kept giving, even as they felt their physical and/or emotional health giving way. They ignored the weight gain, hypertension, and migraines. They hid their chronic unhappiness and crying spells from their family and friends until finally, feeling on the verge of a breakdown, they decided to see a therapist. And in classic StrongBlackWoman style, they never told anyone that they were in therapy, not their spouses, parents, children, best friends, or pastors. Especially not their pastors.

Each of my clients, in some way, was a Ms. Martha in her congregation. She was a woman whose perceived success was lauded in her church, sometimes in a very public way, as an outworking of her great spiritual faith. During one session, for example, a young female client described her frustration at her pastor's incessant praise of her achievements:

> Client: He did it again.
>
> Me: Who did what?
>
> Client: The pastor. On Sunday, he brought me up in front of the entire congregation and began talking about what a wonderful example I am. I wish he would stop doing that. It makes me feel like such a fraud.

Often, my clients openly stated that they could not turn to their pastors or fellow church members for support precisely because those individuals expected them to do well all the time. They were afraid that any admission of difficulty or weakness would be interpreted as a sign of failure or, worse, a lack of faith. The memories of these women lurked in my consciousness as I listened to the accolades being lavished upon Ms. Martha. I wondered whether she was as strong as she appeared to be, or whether she, like my clients, was wearing the armor of the StrongBlackWoman.

Three Core Features of the StrongBlackWoman

"What's so bad about being the StrongBlackWoman?" That's the response that I receive from churchwomen and from students when I teach and preach on this subject. It is a fair question. After all, the image of the Strong-BlackWoman is an infinitely more palatable alternative to the negative stereotypes of African-American womanhood that have been propagated since our arrival on the shores of the United States: the sexually promiscuous and manipulative Jezebel, the asexual and happily oppressed Mammy, and the sharp-tongued and emasculating Sapphire. Indeed, the image of the StrongBlackWoman has become an icon precisely because it is a counter to those other images. Yet, for all its superficial positivity, this image is no more freeing than the others.[5]

To be clear, being the StrongBlackWoman is not the same as being strong, being Black and being a woman. That is, one can be a Black woman who is strong without falling into the cultural trap of the StrongBlackWoman. The StrongBlackWoman is a very specific way of being in the world, with three core features—emotional strength/regulation, caregiving, and independence. Obviously, these characteristics are not unique to StrongBlackWomen or even to Black women. Many individuals—regardless of race or gender—embody each of them to some degree. Further, these are not inherently bad attributes. Indeed, possessed in moderation, they are desirable and commendable qualities. In the case of the StrongBlackWoman, however, there is no moderation. As described below, the StrongBlackWoman possesses each of these characteristics to such an excessive degree that it interferes significantly with her physical health, her emotional and spiritual well-being, and her relationships.

A STRONG Sista

As might be expected, emotional strength/regulation is the central defining characteristic of the StrongBlackWoman. Yet while there seems to be a nearly universal consensus that Black women are strong, the meaning

---

5. Beauboeuf-Lafontant labels the expectation of African-American women's strength as a "mystique" that conceals the true material conditions of Black women's lives. "Swept under this cover story are what Black women experience disproportionately—disparagements and violations of their minds and bodies, foreclosed opportunities to experience full citizenship, and social responsibilities that fall to them as people of color, who are women, and too often also poor" (Beauboeuf-Lafontant, *Behind the Mask,* 2).

of their strength is nebulous. People use the word loosely to refer to Black women, with little to no attempt to explain what is meant. When explanation is rendered, it usually focuses upon superficial characteristics. For example, in the case of Ms. Martha, her designation as a strong woman was based upon her attendance at worship on the day after her husband's funeral and her capacity to restrain tears in the presence of others following the death of her husband and son. Rarely do people take the time to probe beneath the surface of this thing called strength and to figure out what is really happening in the life of the StrongBlackWoman.[6]

The use of the word *strong* as a distinctive descriptor for African-American women has a peculiar history. During the American slavocracy, Black women were routinely depicted as being unusually strong, possessing physical hardiness that far exceeded that of women of other races and even rivaled that of men. In contrast to the "delicate" White woman, Black women were seen as capable of performing heavy physical labor in the plantation fields and household.[7] They could work through sickness and needed little recovery time after childbirth. And they were able to endure separation from their children and families. Indeed, the "unfeminine" strength of Black women was seen as evidence of their inferior humanity. It "proved" that they were incapable of full citizenship in society and that they were suitable for little more than the menial physical and reproductive labor that were characteristic of their slave status. In her narrative *Incidents in the Life of a Slave Girl*, Harriet Jacobs narrates an incident within the plantation household where she was enslaved that well illustrates how the supposed strength of Black women was utilized to justify inhumane treatment:

6. Romero notes that the term *StrongBlackWoman* "is a mantra so much a part of U.S. culture that it is seldom realized how great a toll it has taken on the emotional well-being of the African American woman" (Romero, "Icon of the Strong Black Woman," 225).

7. The depiction of Black women as unnaturally strong played an important role in the economic system of American chattel slavery. Hazel Carby notes, "While fragility was valorized as the ideal state of woman, heavy labor required other physical attributes. Strength and ability to bear fatigue, argued to be so distasteful a presence in a white woman, were positive features to be emphasized in the promotion and selling of a black female field hand at a slave auction" (Carby, *Reconstructing Womanhood*, 25). Emilie Townes notes that "all have usually *assumed* the Black woman's capabilities. This legacy differs considerably from where the majority of white women begin. White culture does not assume that white women are capable. African-American women who have the legacy of clearing the fields, caring for the children of others as well as their own, and functioning in marginalized roles—while being called on to provide the backbone of Black values—are considered a deviation from the norm and an anomaly in United States society" (Townes, "Living in the New Jerusalem," 79).

> [The Flints] had a pet dog, that was a nuisance in the house. The cook was ordered to make some Indian mush for him. He refused to eat, and when his head was held over it, the froth flowed from his mouth into the basin. He died a few minutes after. When Dr. Flint came in, he said the mush had not been well cooked, and that was the reason the animal would not eat it. He sent for the cook and compelled her to eat it. He thought that the woman's stomach was stronger than the dog's; but her sufferings afterwards proved that he was mistaken.[8]

During and since slavery, then, the "strength" of Black women has been a backhanded compliment, a convenient rationalization for the oppressive circumstances under which Black women lived and labored. Most Americans, however, ignore the history of this particular depiction of African-American women and continue to internalize the notion that they are exceptionally strong. While our modern sensibilities reject the notion that Blacks are physically superior to Whites, we have retained the idea that Black women have an innate emotional and spiritual strength that exceeds that of Black men and individuals of other racial/ethnic groups. We only have to look as far as popular culture to find evidence of this belief. For example, in the television and film industry, where women of color are underrepresented, Black women are frequently chosen to play characters who possess emotional and spiritual wisdom in abundance. Take, for example, the role of Whoopi Goldberg as Guinan on *Star Trek: The Next Generation*. As a 600-year-old member of the "Listener" race, Guinan's presence on the show was almost totally restricted to the bar of the U.S.S. Enterprise, where she serenely dispensed drinks and wisdom as she listened to the problems of the ship's officers, while dressed in a shapeless head-to-toe uniform that left only her face and hands visible. Her near-disembodiment was sharply contrasted by the other counselor figure on the show, Deanna Troi, played by Greek actress Martina Sirtis. Genetically gifted with heightened emotional empathy, Troi was a fully-developed character with her own story lines, which included both romance and danger. Whereas Guinan (she only had one name) was a nearly stoic bartender with heightened spiritual wisdom and no life outside the bar, Troi was the ship's official counselor with a vibrant professional and personal existence. Similar Sophia characters are found in: the Oracle in *The Matrix* trilogy, portrayed by Mary Alice and Gloria Foster; CCH Pounder's role as Mrs. Frederic, the mysterious

8. Jacobs, *Incidents in the Life of a Slave Girl*, 12–13.

sage and warehouse caretaker in Syfy's *Warehouse 13*; and Alfre Woodard's character, Lt. Tanya Rice, the maternal character on TNT's *Memphis Beat*. Sophia characters are frequently unnamed (or have only one name) and often have no role or presence outside of the moments when they appear to dispense wisdom or to pronounce judgment. Yet because they represent a dramatic departure from the typically negative portrayals of Black female characters, it often goes unnoticed that they embody another stereotype.

The myth of Black women's strength is dangerously seductive in that it imbues Black women with a certain moral and emotional superiority, providing a psychic balm against the daily insults incurred from social injustice. No matter what her lot in life, a Black woman can take comfort in the fact that she is strong, that she possesses the emotional and spiritual fortitude that have enabled her foremothers to withstand suffering and that will enable her to do likewise. To some degree, this has an element of truth, as attested by Black women's survival against incredible odds of gender, racial, and class oppression. Further, the myth of strength may have an inoculative element to it: Black women who believe that they are strong enough to endure suffering may in fact be more likely to endure it. Strength, then, is not inherently negative, but can be a gift that enables life in the midst of a death-dealing environment.

For the StrongBlackWoman, however, strength takes on a particular connotation that has dangerous consequences. Specifically, strength is intrinsically linked to suffering, that is, the capacity to withstand suffering without complaint. The StrongBlackWoman, then, is supposed to be capable of enduring life's struggles without complaining. Indeed, she evinces no sign that she is under duress. Regardless of the level of chaos occurring in her life, she appears "cool, calm, and collected." She is cautious to maintain control over her emotions, especially those that reveal her vulnerability, such as sadness, grief, helplessness, hurt, embarrassment, anxiety, regret, or fear, among others. It is common, for example, for StrongBlackWomen to avoid crying, both publicly and privately, because they believe it to be an unacceptable display of weakness. In my clinical experience, Black female clients have frequently likened crying to having "a breakdown." They viewed it as a failure, rather than a normative emotional experience.[9] And

---

9. Romero describes a similar pattern. She states, "Showing vulnerability is unacceptable to [a StrongBlackWoman]. . . . Exaggerated terms are often used to describe the simple act of crying. 'Falling apart' or 'breaking down' are common references. This is not a matter of being dramatic or using colorful language. Rather, the [StrongBlackWoman]

if private crying is a breakdown, crying in front of others—including children and spouses—is a catastrophe. Kesho Scott, in her ethnographic study of four middle-aged Black women, exemplifies this with a quote from one of her participants:

> I don't believe my husband has ever seen me cry. We have been married thirty-two years and I know that it has a lot to do with me being a black woman. When I get angry with him, I will raise my voice or walk out, but I will not let him see me cry. I don't think tears get his or anybody's sympathy. I avoid tears because it is important for me to appear to have control over the situation. I don't want the person in power to know that I have lost control.[10]

This statement exposes an important element of the emotional repertoire of the StrongBlackWoman: anger is a favored emotion over sadness. In a classic "fight or flight" style, when the StrongBlackWoman cannot avoid, or flee, vulnerability, she assumes a fighter's stance, preferring the active emotions of anger, irritability, disgust, contempt, and annoyance.

Such fear of vulnerability is likely an inevitable consequence of the burden of strength. In order to reduce vulnerability, StrongBlackWomen often rely excessively upon the defense mechanisms of repression and suppression to deal with negative emotions. Despite their seemingly stoic demeanor in the face of stress, StrongBlackWomen are no more impervious to the difficulties of life than anyone else. That is, they experience fear, sadness, grief, and worry to the same extent as do other people. Indeed, given the socioeconomic, relational, and health challenges that confront Black women's lives, it could be reasonably expected that they have more opportunities to experience negative emotions than do other people. What is distinctive about StrongBlackWomen is the degree to which they suppress and repress these emotions, consciously and/or unconsciously keeping these feelings out of awareness. The StrongBlackWoman effectually creates a mental dam behind which she blocks off negative affect. Because any breaks in the dam might unleash the flood of emotionality behind it, she has to be very careful about her emotional displays, carefully restraining and controlling all negative emotions. In this regard, even her anger is subject to limited expression.

---

actually experiences crying as 'falling apart'" (Romero, "Icon of the Strong Black Woman," 227).

10. Scott, *Habit of Surviving*, 79.

While limited use of defense mechanisms such as denial, repression, and suppression can be an effective means to cope with stressful situations temporarily, long-term reliance upon them is a guaranteed recipe for emotional and physical overload. Failure to acknowledge and cope with negative emotions does not limit their impact. Instead, that impact becomes redirected, often taking its toll upon their physical health, predisposing them to stress-related health problems such as hypertension, ulcers, migraines and chronic pain, sleep and appetite disturbance, and obesity. Unfortunately, because Black women's strength has become such a cultural mandate, their suffering is often viewed as normative. And because the StrongBlackWoman bears the burden of strength to an extreme, she often does not recognize the emotional and physical distress that is a result of her stress, but takes it for granted as a normal consequence of life. In essence, she has developed an extraordinary capacity for "walking with broken feet," often unaware that she is in pain. Further, when she does become aware of her distress, she is unlikely to attribute it to role strain and is prone to associate it with weakness and insufficiency in meeting the demands that life has placed upon her. Thus, strength becomes a double-edged sword: women who suffer emotional and/or physical breakdowns as a result of repressing and suppressing stress responses believe that the solution is greater repression and suppression!

The following case example illustrates the deleterious effects of this conceptualization of strength.

Tanya was a forty-two-year-old woman whom I saw in my clinical practice. To outsiders, she seemed to have it all. She and her husband both had graduate degrees and successful careers. They owned a home in an established middle-class community, drove new cars, wore nice clothes, and had an active family life that included frequent travel. Their four children (ages three, seven, twelve, and fifteen) were well behaved and performed well in school. Tanya was considered to be a model Christian in her local church; in fact, the pastor had even used her faith as a sermonic illustration. No one knew that she had been functioning in a state of low-grade depression for years and had recently begun therapy.

Much of Tanya's depression stemmed from chronic stress in her family and professional life, and her lack of a support system. Her husband, Henry, was a senior administrator at a college that was sixty miles away from the family's home. He usually left home before the children awoke and typically did not return until nearly their bedtime. During the week, then, Tanya essentially functioned as a single parent, with sole responsibility for caring for the children and juggling their school and extracurricular activities together with her full-time job. Her only sources of social support were her parents and her two siblings, all of whom lived more than 500 miles away. She had no friends, in part due to her busy schedule but also because of her guarded demeanor. Tanya was always pleasant to other people, but she rarely shared anything about her life—either positive or negative—with others. She experienced some joy from her job as director of a math and science enrichment program, but it was not the dream of becoming a college mathematics professor that she had deferred so that her husband could finish his doctorate. Since he finished his doctorate, Henry had promised that she could pursue her own degree as soon as he settled into a job; however, his frequent and sudden job changes repeatedly derailed her plans. Just two weeks before Tanya called me to inquire about therapy, Henry had come home one day and announced that he had accepted a job offer in another state. Tanya was furious that he had not consulted her about the offer, but she said nothing, instead presenting her usual display of parental unity for the sake of the children, who were very upset about leaving their schools and friends. For weeks following the announcement, she barely said anything to Henry at all, afraid that if she broached the conversation, she would not be able to contain the years of resentment that had welled up inside her.

Tanya's mother taught her that personal and marital difficulties were private matters that should not be shared outside one's immediate (nuclear) family. On the few occasions that Tanya tried to confide her marital difficulties to her mother, she was rebuffed and told that she be grateful to have a successful and kind husband who is a good father. So for years, Tanya suppressed her feelings, redirecting her time and energy to her job, her children, and her church. Outwardly, she put on the display of doting mother and wife. But internally, she was feeling like a ticking time bomb. She frequently cried herself to sleep at night and occasionally exploded at the children over relatively minor situations. By the time that she presented for her first therapy appointment, Tanya met the criteria for dysthymia, a mild, but chronic, form of depression that typically lasts for at least two years. Notably, even as Tanya described her experiences and her symptoms, she was rarely emotional. Her affect was usually blunted. On a few occasions, she allowed herself to shed a few tears, but quickly wiped them away and resumed her emotionless display.

When Tanya first began therapy, she did not tell anyone, including Henry. After several sessions, and at my continued prompting, she divulged her secret to Henry, who, much to his credit, asked if he could attend a session with her. During their joint session, Henry expressed his surprise that Tanya was unhappy, although he admitted realizing that she was not excited about the move and that their marriage had grown distant. By the end of the session, Henry had promised to talk with his current employer about rescinding his resignation. He expressed a commitment to attending further sessions and to providing more support for Tanya at home. A few weeks later, however, Tanya abruptly ended therapy, several sessions short of our initially agreed upon term of twelve sessions. She reported that it had become very difficult to fit appointments into her schedule, which included overseeing a summer program for talented high school students, transporting her children to and from various camps, and hosting her teenaged nephew for the summer. She stated that she would contact me to continue our sessions in August, but I never heard from her.

Tanya exemplifies an important consequence of the notion of strength-as-stoicism for StrongBlackWoman, namely that it reduces emotional intimacy, including the mutuality and reciprocity necessary for developing and maintaining healthy relationships. The StrongBlackWoman's fear of vulnerability often means that she has a difficult time opening herself up to others, even those with whom she has long-term relationships. Ironically, because of her extensive involvement in family and social networks, the StrongBlackWoman can seem to be quite relational even when she feels very isolated. She may inadvertently create a vicious cycle in which because she rarely demonstrates signs of vulnerability or need, other people are often unsure how to respond when she does, thus reinforcing the sense that she cannot depend upon anyone.

The Consummate Caregiver

Tanya's case also highlights the second characteristic of the StrongBlack-Woman: she is a perpetual caretaker.[11] The StrongBlackWoman has a keenly developed capacity to discern the needs of others and to respond to them. Often, in fact, she tries to anticipate the needs before they arise. Her caregiving is not limited to those within her immediate family but includes extended family, friends, and employers. She prides herself on being helpful. She is the first person whom people call upon when they

11. Morgan, *When Chickenheads Come Home to Roost*, 87; Romero, "Icon of the Strong Black Women," 229–30; B. Wallace, "Womanist Legacy," 47.

have a problem. They want her counsel, her prayers, her assistance, and sometimes her money. They know that they can count on her to come to the rescue because she always does. Her caregiving tendencies are so well known that sometimes she receives requests for counsel or assistance from people she barely knows. If there is a sick family member, she can be relied upon to help take care of them. If she is unable to be there personally, she is expected to provide financial support. For many StrongBlackWomen, their caregiving responsibilities begin early in life. They may have been the eldest child, or at least the eldest female child, and consequently expected to help with their younger siblings. Because they demonstrated a high sense of responsibility and accountability at a young age, they were given greater responsibilities than other children their age. Their ability to handle these responsibilities well made others give them even more responsibility. Eventually, this translated into leadership opportunities. StrongBlackWomen are likely to be placed in charge of large projects at work. If the project is beyond her official duties, she is likely to be asked to "help" another staff person, with the unspoken expectation that she will make sure that the job gets done. Likewise, in congregations and community organizations, she is likely to be the chairperson of important committees or auxiliary ministries. In churches that use the "armor-bearer" tradition, she is likely to be the person. Whenever there is a church function, she will be among the first to arrive and the last to leave. Even if she is not part of the team responsible for the function, she will show up early just in case her help is needed. In some cases, her literal job role involves caregiving, which may make it difficult to see how she exceeds reasonable expectations. She is often the first to volunteer to take on a project or task. And if she does not volunteer, others will do it for her. And she will almost always accept, even if reluctantly.

Because caregiving is such a widely accepted aspect of hegemonic femininity, not only in the United States but also throughout the world, the unique caregiving functions of StrongBlackWomen are best illustrated by example. I offer several below.

Tanisha is a high-school guidance counselor who has been the primary source of emotional support for her parents since graduating college. After years of doubting herself, she finally applies to doctoral programs in clinical psychology and is accepted by her first choice, with the offer of full financial support. As she prepares for her big move, however, her excitement is dampened by the reactions of her parents and grandmother, who are distressed about her moving seven hundred miles away. When her professor calls Tanisha's name from the roster on the first day of classes, she is absent. After four months of trying to reassure her family, she has been worn down by their insistent claims that they cannot make it without her. Giving up on her dream of becoming a psychologist, she instead settles into her job at the high school. She buys a house and her parents move in with her. She counsels high school students during the day and her family at night. Meanwhile, she has no time for herself. With food as her only source of comfort, her weight steadily creeps up. Spiraling into a cycle of depression, she decides that gastric bypass surgery is her only option. Three days after the surgery, she dies from a blood clot at the age of twenty-seven.

April is a thirty-three-year-old salon owner who accumulates high telephone bills as a result of frequent collect calls from her incarcerated brother. She is her brother's main contact because he knows that she will always accept his phone calls and that she will use her telephone's three-way feature to connect him to others. Her assistance is not limited to her brother. Throughout her workday, her telephone rings constantly as family and friends in crisis seek her counsel and advice. By the time that her workday ends, she feels that she has worked two jobs—one as a hairstylist and salon owner, the second as a crisis counselor. Further, the end of her workday does not signal the end of her caregiving. In addition to caring for her husband and six-year-old son, April is the primary caregiver for her aging mother and is managing the estate of her recently deceased grandparents. She spends much of her "free" time with her mother or cleaning and organizing her grandparents' home. Moreover, as an entrepreneur and a pioneer in the fledgling natural hair-care industry, she is highly sought after as a speaker and sponsor of community events.

Teresa is a sixty-three-year-old retired teacher who holds down multiple leadership roles in her local church and in her denomination's regional organizations. Over the years, she has held every leadership position available to the laity and served as chairperson of every committee except the men's ministry. Nothing happens at the church without her involvement. At the regional level, she is widely known and is frequently called upon by denominational leaders to serve on special committees or participate in programming. Although she is retired, she works part-time as the administrative assistant for a local non-profit organization. She does not need the money, but works there because the organization needed help and she needed something to do. Teresa is married, with three adult children who have families of their own. Her eldest son is going through some marital difficulties and has recently moved back in with his parents. On weekends, his two young children come to stay with him, increasing her household size from two to five. Her husband is retired and is very supportive with managing household responsibilities, but the majority of it still falls upon Teresa.

As these examples demonstrate, it is common for StrongBlackWomen to hold multiple roles in which they assume a caregiving functioning for people or entities outside of their immediate family, often resulting in role strain. While strain resulting from multiple roles is a problem for women regardless of ethnicity, it is heightened for black women given the extended kinship structures of many black families. StrongBlackWomen are not just providing care for their spouses, children, and aging parents. They also care for siblings, aunts and uncles, cousins, friends, coworkers, and employers. The need for assistance by family members and friends may be especially heightened in black families because of their higher rates of poverty, lower job status, and a higher proportion of households headed by single females. The extended family structures of African-American families are, then, both a blessing and a curse. On the one hand, extended families can provide significant social and emotional support. But for StrongBlackWomen, having a large extended family also means having more people who are likely to call on one for support.

The legacy of the Mammy archetype is also an important factor in the caregiving tendencies of StrongBlackWomen. Originating during slavery and becoming the dominant image of black women during Reconstruction, Mammy was caricatured as eager to care for the needs of her owners/employers, even to the neglect of her needs and those of her family. While many people would reject this stereotype as an overtly negative image, it continues to contribute to the view of black women as possessing infinite resources for caregiving and for coping with adversity. Internalization of this image by Black women leads to a strong need to be nurturing and supportive of others and feelings of guilt, selfishness, and low self-worth if they are unable to provide assistance to others.

For the StrongBlackWoman, caregiving is a compulsive activity, one over which she almost has no control. She spends most of her days caring for the needs of others. Although she promises to reserve her leftover time, energy, and money for herself, there are usually no leftovers. The StrongBlackWoman often feels that she is being "selfish" anytime that she does something purely for her own enjoyment. The resulting feeling of guilt causes her to fill her days with constant activity on behalf of others. So she ends up taking care of the needs of others at the expense of her own spiritual, physical, and emotional health. She becomes tired, unhappy, not living up to her full potential, and stressed out.

Miss Independent

It almost goes without saying that independence is a heavily weighted cultural value among African-American women.[12] Indeed, if strength is the most commonly used descriptor for black women, independence may run a close second. The two constructs are related (and sometimes used interchangeably) albeit distinct. Whereas the strength of the StrongBlack-Woman has to do with her capacity to regulate affect, particularly in response to suffering or struggle, independence is about self-reliance. Again, pop culture provides extensive testimony about the independence of Black women, with hip-hop and R&B music repeatedly resounding the theme. Three songs, in particular, illumine the meaning of Black women's independence—Destiny's Child's "Independent Women Part 1" (2000), Webbie's "Independent" (2008), and Ne-Yo's "Miss Independent" (2008).

In 2000, the female trio Destiny's Child released their single "Independent Women, Part 1" as the lead track on the *Charlie's Angels* soundtrack. While the movie featured three non-Black actresses, the song was not originally written for the film and ostensibly was aimed at the trio's then largely Black audience. The lyrics of the song reveal that Black female independence is largely a financial matter. The trio enumerates their possessions—jewelry, clothing, shoes, home, and car—emphasizing that they bought each without contribution from anyone. As independent women, they pay their bills and finance their entertainment, depending upon no one. They do not accept gifts from others, choosing instead to buy what

---

12. Numerous scholars in the social sciences and humanities have identified self-reliance and independence as critical elements of Black women's self-definition. Collins, for example, traces the theme through the writing of African-American female scholars such as Maria Stewart, Gloria Joseph, and Lena Wright Myers, as well as through the works of blues and R&B singers such as Billie Holiday and Aretha Franklin (Collins, *Black Feminist Thought*, 116–17). She states, "Whether by choice or circumstance, African-American women have 'possessed the spirit of independence,' have been self-reliant, and have encouraged one another to value this vision of womanhood that clearly challenges prevailing notions of femininity. . . . These beliefs have found wide support among African-American women" (ibid., 116).

they want. In fact, they only require companionship when they feel lonely. For Destiny's Child, then, an independent woman is one who has, and utilizes, her own purchasing power. This independence has a particularly vital function in romantic relationships, where being "fifty-fifty" allows women to resist male domination and control. Because an independent woman is financially self-sufficient, she is a position to "dismiss" a romantic partner who tries to control her. The song's message was wildly successful, peaking at number one on the Billboard Hot 100, Pop, and R&B/Hip-Hop charts in 2000 and spending at least a full year on each. While it may have been written originally for an R&B audience, it's coupling with the Charlie's Angels soundtrack lent Destiny's Child crossover power that firmly launched the trio into a worldwide pop phenomenon (the song also charted in Britain, Japan, and Canada). Clearly, the anthem of female independence, written and performed by a trio of African-American women, held powerful sway in the international imagination. One can only wonder if the commercial appeal would have been the same had the song been performed by a trio of White women.

In 2008, both rapper Webbie and R&B crooner Ne-Yo issued their odes to female independence. In several respects, Webbie's "Independent" echoes the theme of financial self-sufficiency raised by Destiny's Child eight years earlier. In the chorus, Webbie repeatedly spells out the word *independent* and asks whether his male listeners understand its meaning. He then goes on to define the term as a woman who owns a home and car and works two jobs. Webbie goes a step beyond Destiny's Child in emphasizing that the economic success of an independent woman comes from her work ethic. Like Destiny's Child, however, he notes the implications for romantic partnerships, challenging would-be suitors of independent women that they need to step up their game if they plan on attracting one of these women. Independent women, it seems, are not easily impressed by trinkets such as jewelry. They neither expect nor want a man to take care of them financially, and would rather devote their time to working so that they can support themselves. Still, however, they choose their mates based upon money.

For both Webbie and Destiny's Child, then, Black female independence is about financial autonomy, particularly within the sphere of interpersonal relationships. It allows women to be selective about their choice of romantic partners and to resist dependence upon men.[13] Both suggest, moreover,

13. Ironically, even then their true "independence" is questionable given that it seems

that a woman who is independent only "needs" a man for entertainment and sex. What Destiny's Child insinuates with "When it's over, please get up and leave," Webbie makes explicit: "Only time she need a man for that good drill." While this sentiment may seem crude, it echoes a phrase commonly articulated by Black women: "I don't need a man."

Ironically, in neither song are Black women empowered beyond their capacity to resist male control within personal relationships. In contrast to these songs, Ne-Yo tries to articulate a subtler understanding of female independence. Consistent with Destiny's Child and Webbie, he asserts that an independent woman is financially self-sufficient and responsible. She can "do" for herself, pays her bills on time, and is not excessively in debt. However, Ne-Yo finds her most remarkable characteristic to be her internal sense of power and authority. An independent woman walks, talks, looks, and behaves like a "boss." Her power has an element of mystique to it in that it seems effortless and he cannot fully articulate why it draws him to her. Importantly, whereas the other artists depict an independent woman as one who is interested in male companionship primarily to meet her sexual needs, Ne-Yo characterizes her as wanting, although not needing, emotional intimacy. The only suitable romantic partner for such a woman is a man who possesses a similar sense of authority. In Ne-Yo's imagination, a woman is not exploited for her independence but is loved for it, in part because it makes the couple excel together.

These three songs illuminate three aspects of black female independence that are central to the archetype of the StrongBlackWoman: financial self-sufficiency, a strong work ethic, and socioemotional autonomy. The StrongBlackWoman is expected to be able to support herself financially without assistance from anyone—including close family and friends. Given the frequency with which African-American couples have separate bank accounts, splitting the household bills equally between partners, it seems that many StrongBlackWomen are reluctant even to be financially dependent upon their spouses. In part, I believe, this is due to the strong messages about the necessity of independence that are communicated via family and the broader culture. As evidenced by the songs above, popular culture clearly sends the message that a good Black woman is one who is not "in a man's pocket." Moreover, African-American parents often begin teaching

---

to consist solely of the purchase and consumption of material goods in an economic system largely controlled by men. In fact, Webbie's lyrics reveal that women's economic self-sufficiency can be directly beneficial to their romantic partners, whom they spoil with material gifts.

their daughters about the value of financial independence at an early age, emphasizing the importance of education and occupational achievement to a greater degree than they do for their sons.

Further, the StrongBlackWoman has a strong work ethic. She usually prides herself on being responsible, reliable, and productive. She has a high level of internal motivation and is likely to be a perfectionist. She gives maximum effort to every task, often exceeding the effort required to accomplish the task well. Her work ethic is not limited to employment settings but extends to other contexts as well, including family, church, and community. In every context in which she is involved, she is known as a hard worker. Finally, independence for the StrongBlackWoman means socioemotional autonomy, depending and relying solely upon herself to meet her needs. StrongBlackWomen have a hard time asking for help and a hard time receiving help when it's offered. Candace, a thirty-four-year-old participant in a focus group conducted by one of my seminary students, put it this way:

> I don't like to ask nobody for nothing. It has to be the last resort before I ask for help. There has to be no other way. If I am struggling financially, I wait until the very end because I feel like I should be able to do it. No matter what, I am supposed to be able to do it; I don't want to ask. I don't know if that's pride or being strong or what, but I don't want to ask. . . . I am supposed to take care of others; I don't want them taking care of me. If I'm not able to be there for everyone, then they just need to leave me alone until I can do it.

Candace's statement evokes a phrase that is common among African-American women: "I don't need anyone." Among African-American Christian women, the phrase undergoes alteration: "I don't need anyone but God." On the surface, this appears to be a bold declaration of faith. However, it is also a forceful assertion of one's ability to live without the benefit of supportive relationships with other people.

Independence is as important an attribute of the StrongBlackWoman as strength and caregiving. In fact, it is the hinge upon which the other attributes rest: the StrongBlackWoman's capacities for strength and caregiving are directly related to the extent to which she is independent and self-reliant. That is, the StrongBlackWoman is a woman who meets the needs of others without appearing to have any needs of her own, at least any needs that she cannot meet without the support of anyone else, including spouses, family, friends, or church members. This manifests itself in women's lives on a day-to-day basis. Consider the following examples:

Suzette is a thirty-four-year-old manager for a state agency. She is married with a seven-year-old son. She and her husband recently reunited after a two-year separation. Throughout the entire marriage, they have had entirely separate financial lives, including separate post-office boxes, bank accounts, and credit cards. They split all household expenditures equally, including the cost of their family vacations, despite the fact that Suzette's husband makes considerably more money than she does. Suzette is stressed by their financial arrangement, especially since her husband wants to move into a larger, more expensive home and take a luxury cruise this year. At the same time, though, she is not sure that she wants to change the arrangement since having her own accounts enables her to spend money without consulting her husband. Plus, she does not really like asking him, or anyone, for help. She likes people to think that she can handle things on her own. Just recently, for example, she stayed up all night making one hundred cupcakes for her son's school, when his teachers asked with less than twenty-four hours' notice. Her husband offered to order them from a bakery, but Suzette refused, saying that she would rather make them herself.

Jeanette is a fifty-six-year-old corporate employee and single mother of two adult children, whom she raised with virtually no financial support from their fathers. Although she does not have a college degree, she is a highly skilled worker and has often functioned in a supervisory capacity. In fact, her know-how is so valued that newly hired supervisors, often fresh out of college, are assigned to her for training. Because her lack of degree prevents her from meeting the criteria to be a supervisor, she has the responsibilities without the title, or the salary. After paying her rent and car note, she usually has very little left over. At times, she is unable to afford her utilities, or sometimes food. Yet she never asks for help; in fact, her co-workers usually come to her seeking counsel and prayer throughout the day. After leaving work on most evenings, she drives directly to her church, attending Bible study and midweek worship services, or assisting the pastor and his wife with administrative tasks. As one of the first lady's armor-bearers, she is not allowed to leave the church before the first lady. No one at the church knows that she has had little to eat all day or that she will go home to a darkened apartment, because she could not afford to pay her electric bill this month. And when her son rushes her to the hospital after she has chest pains, she swears him to secrecy. Meanwhile, at family gatherings, relatives praise her for her strength, saying that they have never heard her complain about anything.

As with strength and caregiving, then, many African-American women practice a radical independence, one that is the antithesis not only of dependency, but also interdependency. Obviously, the high valuation placed upon independence is not unique to African-American women. Independence and individualism are distinctively Western ideals. For many African-American women, however, independence takes on added meaning because they bear the burden of constantly disproving stereotypes that label them as lazy, dependent, and unwilling to earn an honest living. Nearly 150 years after the end of the slavery, the legacy of the Jezebel continues to be evoked in the rhetoric of politicians and rappers alike, who castigate welfare mothers and "gold diggers," women who supposedly take advantage of individuals and the American public by collecting money without laboring to earn it. African-American women, then, must constantly prove themselves worthy of citizenship by demonstrating their ability to support themselves without the assistance of others. This obligation is particularly cruel for StrongBlackWomen; when paired with their caregiving responsibilities, independence means that they are unable to receive the same sort of care that they extend to others.

An Ill-Fitting Suit of Armor

While each of these core features—emotional strength, caregiving, and independence—can have both positive and negative elements, in the ideology of the StrongBlackWoman they become bound together in a way that stifles authentic self-expression. In other words, the StrongBlackWoman is not an authentic identity. It does not reflect a woman's true self. Rather, it is a role that Black women play, a character that they represent, or a mask that they wear. Or perhaps most appropriately, it is a suit of armor, a protective covering worn by Black women to mitigate damage from a hostile world that constantly assaults their character with degrading images and stereotypes, and that saddles them with disproportionate rates of poverty and single-parenthood. Indeed, we might imagine the triumvirate of emotional strength, caregiving, and independence respectively as the helmet, breastplate, and shield of this suit of armor. For many women, the Strong-BlackWoman is the standard psychological defense. Donning the armor is Black women's method of suiting up for battle, preparing to defend the psyche against the attacks waged by sexism, racism, and classism. In this sense, the ideology of the StrongBlackWoman has an important adaptive function that must not be ignored: Black women have donned the armor of the StrongBlackWoman because it has been, to a considerable extent, the most effective means available for coping with the stresses of their existence. For at least two centuries, it has enabled survival, allowing black women to function by repressing grief, sadness, and anger, and by covering emotional distress with an outer façade of imperturbability, independence, and caregiving.

To be sure, there is nothing wrong with wearing a suit of armor every once in a while, especially when gearing up for battle. But there are two issues with the armor of the StrongBlackWoman that render it ultimately maladaptive. First, many Black women have become so conditioned to wearing their armor that they do not know how to remove it when they are no longer on the battlefield. Even when they are in settings of assumed safety—with family, with romantic partners or spouses, in their local congregations—many Black women have difficulty fully divesting themselves of the armor. They remain in defensive mode, guarding their emotions, refusing to rely upon or trust others, and keeping people from getting too close to them. Thus, the armor of the StrongBlackWoman shields Black women from the threat of devaluation but also keeps them from the type of authentic self-expression and intimacy that are necessary for optimal social and emotional health.

A second issue with the armor of the StrongBlackWoman is that it is not of our own making. It is borrowed armor, imposed upon Black women through processes of socialization that usually begin in early childhood. These socialization practices train Black girls to regulate negative affect, to extend themselves on behalf of others at the cost of ignoring their own needs, and to venerate independence over interdependence. While the church and broader U.S. society play important roles in reinforcing these messages, the primary site of socialization is the home, where Black mothers and fathers, frightened by the possibilities that lie ahead for Black girls who are unprepared to face the demons of racism, sexism, and classism, "gift" them with the armor that has been passed down from one generation of women to the next.[14]

14. Snorton admonishes pastoral caregivers to recognize that socialization into the role of the StrongBlackWoman begins at an early age: "The [StrongBlackWoman] developmentally represents an individual whose training is embedded in a family and cultural tradition of several generations. . . . Unlike her Euro-American counterparts,

Many StrongBlackWomen, then, are much like David in his epic battle against the warrior giant Goliath in 1 Samuel 17. Just before he goes out to face the giant, Saul—undoubtedly worried about the young guardian of sheep who had boldly accepted the challenge to fight a nine-foot professional soldier—tries to protect David in the best way that he knows: by dressing David in Saul's own armor. Most likely, Saul expected that David would be killed and thought that wearing Saul's armor would make it a less painful death. So he fully outfits David in what was probably some of the best armor ever made. But David was not used to the weight of all that metal and could not walk around in it. He might have had some protection from the blows of the giant Philistine but he could not maneuver in the way that best suited him. Like David, many StrongBlackWomen are not wearing their own armor. While the armor that is encumbering them may have been a perfect fit for some nineteenth-century ancestor, it does not allow them to move fully. Unlike David, though, many StrongBlack-Women have been wearing their armor for so long that they have learned not just how to walk around in it, but also how to live in it. They have even forgotten that they have it on. Still, though, it does not fit. Wearing it requires Black women to expend a tremendous amount of psychic energy to constantly monitor and restrict their behavior, which in turn impacts their physical, emotional, and spiritual well-being. In the next chapter, I will describe the inordinate burden that this archetype has upon the health of Black women. For now, though, let it suffice to say that I believe that embracing the StrongBlackWoman as the iconic representation of black femininity is contributing to a crisis of epidemic proportions in the health of Black women in the United States.

Despite its clearly negative consequences for the health and well-being of African-American women, the StrongBlackWoman is the hegemonic black femininity. Although there are variations in the way in which black women perform this identity, my experience has been that the majority of African-American women, especially those who are Christian, feel compelled to perform it at some point in their lives. Even those who proclaim that they do not fit its mold occasionally fall prey to it. I have known several African-American women (usually ordained or lay leaders

---

the young womanist must strive to continue the tradition of strength modeled by her elders" (Snorton, "Legacy of the African-American Matriarch," 55). Baker-Fletcher further describes it as "a kind of stoicism Black women are taught and expect from one another that is passed from mother to daughter" (Baker-Fletcher and Baker-Fletcher, *My Sister, My Brother*, 249–50).

in local congregations) who, after experiencing a serious illness or death of a loved one, declare that they have no intentions of playing the Strong-BlackWoman and, in nearly the same breath, insist that they will be able to maintain their normal personal and professional duties, sometimes including heavy travel and speaking schedules. Indeed, I must confess that even after nearly a decade of studying the plight of the StrongBlack-Woman and trying to pull myself out of its grasp, I routinely relapse into the role. On more than one occasion, I have been forced to re-assess my various commitments after a trusted colleague or friend (usually a woman of another racial-ethnic background) expressed incredulity regarding my capacity to manage so much at one time. Even more surprising is that these comments have often come at times when I think I am managing my StrongBlackWoman tendencies well!

As the hegemonic black femininity, the StrongBlackWoman dominates the worldview, behaviors, thoughts, and feelings of African-American women, shaping how they perceive and interact with the world. It is not an identity that is adopted piecemeal. Like a totalitarian regime, it demands wholesale public allegiance to each of its core features. This is what sets the StrongBlackWoman apart from an African-American woman who may exhibit one or more of the attributes to some degree, but who does not possess all three to the extent described above. The StrongBlackWoman embodies each of the core features to such an extreme that they interfere with her health and well-being. The StrongBlackWoman is also a totalitarian identity in that it seeks to eliminate any affect, behavior, or cognitions that threaten its maintenance. Remember the earlier quote from Kesho Scott? Whenever she felt the impulse to cry in front of her husband, she either left the room or became angry instead. Because crying is a behavior that indicates vulnerability and distress, it threatened her image as the StrongBlackWoman who was in control of her emotions. Faced with this threat, she automatically went into fight-or-flight mode: she fled the scene or she attacked.

The StrongBlackWoman is also a prescriptive identity in that it is not adopted as much as it is imposed. Society necessitates, demands even, that Black women conform to this model of womanhood even when it does not reflect their authentic personality and when it poses threats to their physical, emotional, social, and spiritual well-being. Black women who dare to shake themselves loose of its grip and vocalize a need for support may be greeted with condemnation of their "weakness" and admonished to "get it together." And this is especially likely to happen in the church.

One year after the birth of my son, I met with the staff-parish relations committee of my local church to seek their support and approval of my candidacy for ordained ministry. Entering the meeting, I felt relatively secure. While my activity in the congregation had been sharply curtailed over the past year, up until my son's birth, I had served as the lay leader, leading worship on a regular basis and attending nearly every committee meeting of the church. I had already graduated from seminary and had preached at the church on several occasions. And I served on four conference-wide committees at the appointment of the bishop, despite a conference rule mandating that persons serve on only one committee or board at a time. Having been licensed for ministry by a Baptist congregation several years earlier, I felt that my gifts for ministry had been well-established. I was caught off-guard when several committee members doggedly questioned my lack of involvement.

To some degree, it was a fair question. Operating in full StrongBlack-Woman mode, I was over-extended. In addition to teaching full-time on nights and weekends, I stayed at home with my son during the day. It was not uncommon for me to arrive at faculty or denominational meetings encumbered by a baby and a diaper bag. Both my husband and I were overwhelmed with the tasks of managing full-time employment, parenthood, and ministry while living hundreds of miles away from our families. We had tried to reach out to the church for assistance before, but had had little success. That night, after I tearfully communicated our situation to the committee, I noticed a surprising dynamic. On several occasions, two of the committee members asked how the congregation could better support me so that my gifts for ministry could be put to better use within the church. Each time, two other committee members interrupted and suggested that I needed to manage my time better or get more childcare. After several such interruptions, the first two members gave up. The striking aspect of this interchange was that the "supportive" committee members were both White; the "get yourself together" committee members were both Black.

After the scene repeated itself when I stood before the entire congregation for endorsement at our annual charge conference a few weeks later, I developed a hypothesis about what was happening: most likely being accustomed to StrongBlackWomen who push themselves past the point of fatigue, the African-American women and men in the congregation viewed my incapacity to seamlessly juggle my multiple roles without the support of others as a sign of personal failure. This interpretation was underscored later when a White female was endorsed for candidacy for ordained ministry with no resistance from the congregation, despite having only recently joined the church and having very limited involvement with the church due to her attendance at an out-of-state seminary.

I tell this narrative in part to illuminate a final characteristic of the StrongBlackWoman: it is a religious identity, which has a particular stronghold in the Black church. As I describe in chapter 3, the StrongBlackWoman has its roots in the Black women's club movement, a late nineteenth-century movement that was fostered by Black congregations and that sought, in part, to promulgate a positive view of African-American womanhood. While not an official theology preached by the Black church, the StrongBlackWoman has been propagated as a Christian ideal, and Scripture has been read through its lens. We have only to consider the titles of two favored hymns of the Black church to illustrate this point: "Long as I Got King Jesus . . . I Don't Need Nobody Else" and "I'm Happy with Jesus Alone." Carved out of the historical suffering of enslaved Blacks, these songs have functioned to "armor" generations of African-American Christians against the struggles wrought by racial oppression. To those who have nothing, these hymns have been a soothing reminder that they are not alone. Unfortunately, though, their lyrics have been interpreted as prescriptive rather than descriptive. Thus, rather than understanding them as assurances of God's presence among the lonely and forsaken, many in the church have mistaken them as advocating an ideal for Christian living.

It is no wonder, then, that Ms. Martha's lack of emotional responsiveness following personal tragedy was confused with strength, rather than recognized as a potentially maladaptive grief reaction. It is no surprise that Tanya was afraid to share with her pastor that she was in therapy because she was unhappy and her marriage was falling apart. And it is understandable that Jeanette could spend so much time at the church serving others while concealing her own financial and health struggles. When the church repeatedly praises African-American women for their "strength" while rebuking those who demonstrate vulnerability, it is saying "Armor up!" And for decades, African-American women have done this. Donning the armor of the StrongBlackWoman, they have carried the world's cross as well as their own, all while pretending that it does not hurt. They have borne the weight and the pain, simply adding layers of armor to obscure any signs of distress. But the burden of strength has become unbearable.

Suggestions for Pastoral Reflection and Practice

- This chapter began with the story of Ms. Martha, a woman who was praised for her strength and faithfulness because of her response following the deaths of her husband and son. How does the information in this chapter help you understand Ms. Martha's situation differently?

- Who might be the StrongBlackWomen in your congregation or ministry context? Think especially about those women who are involved in multiple leadership roles and auxiliaries, both within and beyond the church. Pray for God's guidance in helping you discern their unspoken needs and develop an appropriate pastoral response.

- If you are an African-American woman, in what ways do you see yourself reflected in the description of the StrongBlackWoman?

2

Too Heavy a Yoke

The Pain of the StrongBlackWoman

> Perhaps the superwoman syndrome is the flip side of our will to survive when taken to an unhealthy extreme. We are so accustomed to toughing it out, being self-reliant, being dependable for others, concerned with the salvation and wholeness of family, friends, community, and strangers that we become ill from lack of self-nurture and sometimes die early deaths as a result. The same will for survival that enables us to persevere through pain and oppression can also numb us to the realities of pain and illness if we are not grounded in God as Spirit who loves us, body and soul, as well as our loved ones. There is a thin line between survival and denial.[1]

"Sisters always have it together," said the African-American pastor as he explained his decision to focus on men's issues and the development of male leadership in his new church plant. The implication was that African-American women did not need specific pastoral attention upon the issues that impacted them because they were generally effective at addressing issues on their own. This was a young, progressive pastor, who was married to a highly educated woman whose income-earning potential outstripped

1. Baker-Fletcher and Baker-Fletcher, *My Sister, My Brother*, 146.

his own. He affirmed women's leadership in the church and had previously worked under the supervision of female pastors. So his comment was not an endorsement of patriarchy. Rather, it was an expression of a sentiment that has become pervasive in America: "Sisters are doing it for themselves."

To be sure, African-American women have made astonishing educational and occupational advances over the past four decades. In 1970, the average African-American woman had a tenth grade education and was employed as a domestic or service worker. Only one-quarter had a high school diploma and less than ten percent had received some level of postsecondary education. Fifty-nine percent earned incomes at or below the poverty level.[2] In 2010, in contrast, the average African-American woman had graduated from high school and had some college or technical training, was employed in a management or professional field, and earned between $25,000 and $49,999 per year. More than half (57 percent) had attended college, including 19.4 percent with bachelor's degrees and 10.2 percent with graduate degrees.[3] The rate of African-American women living at or below the poverty level had decreased to 27.5 percent; moreover, greater than twenty percent had incomes above $50,000, a nearly unthinkable possibility fifty years earlier.[4]

The achievements of Black women following the passage of the 1964 Civil Rights Act came at such a rapid pace that public discussion of their gains often drown out discourse about their struggles. For example, a March 2003 issue of *Newsweek* magazine featured a cover story about the educational and occupational gains of Black women. "Once consigned to mostly menial work," author Ellis Cose stated, "black women . . . have ascended to the professional-managerial class."[5] Cose noted that a greater percentage of Black women was working in professional occupations than their Black male counterparts. And the median income of college-educated Black women surpassed that of all working Black men as well as women of all races.[6] Five years later, sociologist Amadu Kaba went so far as to declare

2. U.S. Census Bureau, "Table 238. Years of School"; Westcott, "Blacks in the 1970s," 30.

3. U.S. Census Bureau, "Table 3. Educational Attainment of the Population"; U.S. Census Bureau, "Table 238. Years of School Completed"; U.S. Census Bureau, "Occupation of the Civilian Employed."

4. U.S. Census Bureau, "Table 13. Poverty Status of the Population"; U.S. Census Bureau, "Table 11. Earnings of Full-Time, Year-Round Workers."

5. Cose, "Black Gender Gap," 48.

6. Ibid. As laudatory as such claims seem to be, there is an important subtext: the

that Black women were a new "model minority," which he defined as a group that was formerly marginalized (educationally, economically, and socially) but that overcame its marginalization to become prosperous, admired, and even emulated.[7] Kaba based his designation based upon Black women's (1) high rates of college enrollment and graduation relative to Black men, (2) increases in life expectancies and reductions in death rates, (3) lower rates of substance use and suicidality relative to other racial-gender groups, and (4) lower crime rates relative to men of all racial-ethnic groups.

When we focus our attention solely upon indicators such as educational achievement, life expectancies, substance use, suicidality, and crime, it becomes easy to proclaim that "sisters always have it together" or that Black women are the new model minority. Such a restricted focus, however, represents a form of "statistical text-proofing" that is heavily shaped by a patriarchal lens. In other words, each of these outcomes represent issues that disproportionately affect men. Consequently, using them to argue that Black women are safe from racial-gender oppression (or safer, relative to Black men and White women) is akin to saying that racial disparities in health have been eliminated because people of color have lower rates of cystic fibrosis (a disease that largely affects Whites). If we want to view the lives of Black women, we need to focus our attention a different metric, incidentally the area most impacted by the StrongBlackWoman archetype: health.

Black Women and Physical Health: A Statistical Profile

A hallmark of the StrongBlackWoman is her capacity to withstand suffering without complaint. Consequently, the StrongBlackWoman has developed an extraordinary capacity for "walking with broken feet," often unaware that she is in pain. The symptoms of some physical and mental health disorders have become so widespread among Black women that they are no longer noticed or viewed as pathological. Instead, they are viewed as normative. Probably as a direct consequence, then, Black women in the

---

sentiment that Black women's success has outstripped, and come at the expense of, African-American men and families. The *Newsweek* cover text, for example, declared, "From Schools to Jobs, Black Women Are Rising Much Faster than Black Men. What It Means for Work, Family and Race Relations."

7. Kaba, "Race, Gender, and Progress," 310. Kaba's use of the term "model minority" is ironic given that the term was developed by Whites and applied to Asian Americans in the 1960s as a way of discrediting the civil rights movement.

United States are experiencing epidemic rates of medical conditions such as obesity, diabetes, hypertension, and HIV/AIDS, and higher mortality rates for nearly every major cause of death than any other racial/ethnic group.[8]

Obesity and Physical Activity

Only one-third (36.2 percent) of Black women report engaging in regular, sustained physical activity that increases breathing or heart rate, as compared to 45.3 percent of Black men, 49.6 percent of White women, and 52.3 percent of White men. Fully one-third (36.5 percent) of African-American women report having no leisure-time physical activity, that is, physical activity that is not required as a result of one's occupation, as compared to 28.3 percent of Black men, 23.1 percent of White women, and 19.5 percent of White men).[9]

It may be no surprise, then, that Black women struggle with weight problems more than any other racial-gender group. In 2005, 35.9 percent of adult Black women were obese, higher rates than Black men (28.3 percent), Hispanic women (31.0 percent) and White women (21.7 percent). Only one-third (30.1 percent) of Black women were at a healthy weight.[10] Many African Americans attribute these heavier weights to genetic factors, arguing that Blacks are naturally heavier than Whites. Historically, African-American men and women have tended to prefer larger body sizes, calling them "thick," "big-boned," and even "healthy." In 2011, The Washington

8. Unless otherwise noted, health statistics in this chapter are drawn from the 2005 National Health Interview Survey (NHIS), an annual survey conducted by the Centers for Disease Control and Prevention (Pleis and Lethbridge-Çejku, *National Health Interview Survey*). Participants in the 2005 survey included a nationally representative sample of 98,649 non-institutionalized children and adults living in 38,509 households; of these, 31,428 were adults. Each participant took part in a home-based interview conducted by trained personnel from the Census Bureau. Race-gender-specific data was provided for three racial groups: (1) Hispanic or Latina/o; (2) White only; and (3) Black only (p. 2). Comparative estimates for other racial-gender groups are provided when available for contextual purposes. Because the NHIS relies upon self-reporting of diagnosed conditions, the resulting frequencies are believed to be underestimates (p. 3).

9. American Cancer Society, *Cancer Facts & Figures for African Americans*, 17–18.

10. Pleis and Lethbridge-Çejku, *National Health Interview Survey*, 11, 82. In the NHIS, participants' self-reports of their weight and height were utilized to calculate their body mass index (BMI). Based upon BMI, participants were then categorized as underweight (having a BMI less than 18.5), healthy weight (BMI greater than or equal to 18.5 and less than 25.0), overweight (BMI greater than or equal to 25.0 and less than 30.0), or obese (BMI greater than or equal to 30.0).

Post and the Kaiser Family Foundation conducted a telephone survey of 1,936 Black and White adults in the United States on issues of race and gender.[11] They found that while Black women were heavier than White women, they were also happier with their bodies.[12] And health research yields convincing evidence to support Black women's conventional body wisdom. For example, in a large-scale study of the effects of obesity and lifestyle factors on cardiovascular disease, Louisiana State University researchers found that African-American women may be healthier at heavier weights than White women.[13]

Still, there is no disputing that Black women are disproportionately impacted by the national obesity epidemic. And while cultural values about body image have long inoculated African-American women and girls from societal pressures to be model-thin, when combined with structural disparities that hinder proper nutrition and exercise, they may also predispose them to life-threatening health conditions such as diabetes, hypertension and heart disease, and certain forms of cancer.

Diabetes and Circulatory Diseases

Since 1980, African Americans have consistently had higher rates of diagnosed diabetes than Whites. And for most of that period, the rates for Black women have exceeded those of their male counterparts.[14] Approximately 11.5 percent of Black women report having been diagnosed with diabetes, compared with 11.2 percent of Black men, 10.2 percent of Hispanic women, and 6.2 percent of White women.[15] It is believed that these numbers severely underestimate the true prevalence of diabetes in the U.S. as many people living with the disease are unaware that they have it. In 2010, the Centers for Disease Control and Prevention estimated that 4.9

11. *The Washington Post*, "Poll of Black Women in America."

12. Parker, "Black Women Heavier and Happier."

13. Katzmarzyk et al., "Ethnic-Specific BMI and Waist Circumference Thresholds." The study, which included a sample of 6,476 Black and White adults, found that Black women have a higher optimal threshold for body mass index (BMI) than White women (32.9 kg/m2 vs. 30 kg/m2), suggesting that the relationship between BMI and cardiovascular health (specifically hypertension and diabetes) may be weaker among Black women than among White women.

14. Centers for Disease Control and Prevention, *Age-Adjusted Percentage of Civilian, Noninstitutionalized Population with Diagnosed Diabetes*.

15. Pleis and Lethbridge-Çejku, *National Health Interview Survey*, 5–6, 30.

million, or 18.7 percent, of non-Hispanic Blacks ages twenty years or older had diabetes.[16]

While diabetes is generally understood to be a chronic disease, its deadly impact is often overlooked. Diabetes is the seventh leading cause of death in the U.S. It is a major cause of heart disease and stroke. Adults with diabetes are two to four times more likely to die from heart disease as well as two to four times more likely to experience a stroke.[17] Overall, the risk for death among people with diabetes is about twice that of their same-aged peers who do not have the disease.[18] Furthermore, diabetes is the leading cause of kidney failure, limb amputation, and blindness, and it doubles the average medical expenses for those with the disease.[19]

In addition to their high rates of diabetes, African-American women are at heightened risk for circulatory problems. Black women have the highest rates of hypertension and stroke of any racial-gender group within the U.S. One-third of adult Black women (34 percent) have hypertension, compared to 28.1 percent of Black men, 22.9 percent of Hispanic women, and 20.9 percent of White women. And four percent of Black women have had a stroke, compared to 2.8 percent of Black men, 2.0 percent of Hispanic women, and 2.2 percent of White women. The news regarding heart disease is mixed: African-American women have higher rates of heart disease (11.4 percent) than Hispanic women (8.1 percent) but comparable rates to Black men (9.0 percent) and White women (11.7 percent).[20]

Cancer

When it comes to cancer, the word for Black women is: *confusing*. In general, women of all ethnicities have lower rates of cancer than their male counterparts, and this is no less true for Black women. When compared to White women, however, the news is mixed. Overall, Black and White women have a relatively similar risk of cancer, with approximately one in three women developing invasive cancer during her lifetime.[21] However, there are some cancers that Black women have a lower risk of developing,

16. Centers for Disease Control and Prevention, *National Diabetes Fact Sheet*.

17. Ibid., 8.

18. Ibid., 7.

19. Ibid., 1, 7.

20 Pleis and Lethbridge-Çejku, *National Health Interview Survey*, 18.

21. American Cancer Society, *Cancer Facts & Figures*, 14.

others for which they are at increased risk, and still others from which they are more likely to die than White women. For example, the three most common forms of cancer and sources of cancer deaths among Black women are breast (accounts for 27 percent of all cancer incidence among Black women), lung (13 percent), and colon and rectum (12 percent).[22] While breast cancer is the leading cause of cancer among African-American women, the incidence rate is about twelve percent lower than in White women (although African-American women under forty have a higher incidence of breast cancer than similarly aged White women).[23] Yet Black women are more likely to die from breast cancer than are White women. The five-year breast cancer survival rate for African-American women is 77 percent, in contrast to 90 percent for White women. In other words, Black women are more than twice as likely to die from breast cancer within five years of their diagnosis than White women (23 percent versus 10 percent).[24]

Similar trends exist with colorectal cancer. Indeed, the higher death rates from colorectal cancer account for one-fourth of the disparities in cancer death rates between African-American and White women.[25] Further, African-American women are more likely than White women to develop, and die from, stomach, cervical, and uterine cancer.[26] The rates of cervical cancer, for example, are thirty percent higher in African-American women than in White women. And African-American women are more than twice as likely to die from the disease.[27]

Overall, African Americans have the highest death rate and shortest survival of any racial and ethnic group in the U.S. for most cancers.[28] For Black women, in particular, the death rate for all cancers combined is 18 percent higher than that of White women.[29] The racial differences in cancer morbidity and mortality have been linked to two types of disparities: (1) socioeconomic, that is, disparities in education, occupation, work conditions, income, wealth, housing, and overall standard of living; and (2) treatment, that is, economic and social barriers to early detection, pre-

22. Ibid., 2.
23. Ibid., 8.
24. Ibid., 4.
25. Ibid., 11.
26. Ibid., 4, 14.
27. Ibid., 9.
28. Ibid., 1.
29. Ibid.

vention, and treatment services.[30] For certain cancers, racial differences in mortality are largely due to the tendency of African Americans to be diagnosed at later (and thus more difficult to treat) stages of cancer and their decreased access to appropriate and timely treatment.[31] However, socioeconomic and treatment disparities are not the only factors at work. African-American women, for example, receive breast and cervical cancer screening at similar rates as White women.[32] And even after accounting for socioeconomic status, Black women have poorer outcomes from breast cancer.[33] Indeed, despite the popularly touted anecdotes about Black women advancing up the socioeconomic ladder, racial disparities in death rates from breast and colorectal cancers between Black and White women have increased, rather than decreased, over time.[34]

HIV/AIDS

It is no secret that Black women are at increased risk for HIV infection. Indeed, HIV is the third leading cause of death for Black women aged thirty-five to fifty-four.[35] In 2009, Black women accounted for 57 percent of all new HIV infections among women. In fact, the rate of new HIV infections among Black women was fifteen times greater than that of White women, and over three times greater than the rate among Hispanic/Latina women. At some point in her life, one of every thirty-two African-American women will be diagnosed with HIV.[36] In contrast to men (of all races), who are more likely to contract HIV through sexual intercourse with same-sex partners, women are more likely to become infected through heterosexual contact. The same pattern is true for Black women with HIV, 85 percent of whom contracted the disease through heterosexual intercourse.[37]

At least one study points to a possible link between risk for HIV infection and attitudes and behaviors associated with the StrongBlackWoman. In a study of gender role attitudes and HIV risk, Kerrigan and colleagues

30. Ibid.
31. Ibid., 4.
32. Ibid., 19.
33. Ibid., 8.
34. Ibid., 3–4.
35. Centers for Disease Control and Prevention, *HIV Among African Americans.*
36. Centers for Disease Control and Prevention, *HIV Among Women.*
37. Centers for Disease Control and Prevention, *HIV Among African Americans.*

found that the strain associated with the StrongBlackWoman role might encourage young women to prioritize the maintenance of a relationship over their own health and well-being.[38] Even though they were only sixteen to twenty-one years old at the time of the study, the female participants reported having significant responsibilities for providing emotional and/ or financial support to others. The young women reported that romantic intimacy provided a means of respite from their caregiving burden. Consequently, they placed high priority upon maintaining romantic relationships even when their partners were promiscuous. For these young women, being a StrongBlackWoman involved "not only being tough in the face of social adversity but also 'sticking by one's man,'" in essence prioritizing the maintenance of a relationship over their own health and well-being.[39]

Chronic Pain and Functional Impairment

Discussions of health disparities often omit significant indicators of physical and emotional well-being: chronic pain and functional impairment. And given the stressful circumstances of Black women's lives, it is not surprising that they report relatively high rates of each. One-fourth (26 percent) of adult Black women report suffering from arthritic conditions, including any form of arthritis, gout, lupus, or fibromyalgia. A similar proportion (27 percent) of Black women report having chronic joint pain, aching, or stiffness. In both cases, Black women report experiencing these problems at significantly higher levels than do Black men, Hispanic women and men, and White men.[40] Black women also report frequently experiencing migraines and other forms of pain that last for at least a full day, albeit at

38. Kerrigan et al., "Staying Strong." Participants in this study included a subsample of fifty Black youth who were participating in a larger, longitudinal study that examined risk for sexually transmitted diseases over a three-year period in a sample recruited from two health clinics in East Baltimore, including a sexually-transmitted infection clinic and a general adolescent health clinic. The subsample consisted of twenty-six females and twenty-four males (ages sixteen to twenty-one), approximately half of whom had been diagnosed with gonorrhea or chlamydia during their participation in the larger study.

39. Ibid, 178. This study extends the work of E. J. Sobo, *Choosing Unsafe Sex*, who found that low-income women were more likely to tolerate infidelity and promiscuity by their sexual partners in an attempt to conform to prevailing gender ideologies that define women's self-worth and social status by their involvement in stable monogamous relationships.

40. Pleis and Lethbridge-Çejku, *National Health Interview Survey*, 5–6, 30. Black and White women reported relatively similar levels of arthritic and chronic joint pain.

similar levels to White and Hispanic women. Approximately 18.4 percent of Black women report having severe headaches or migraines, 13.2 percent report neck pain, 28.1 percent report lower back pain, and 4.9 percent report facial or jaw pain.[41]

Further, African-American women report higher levels of difficulty with activities of daily living than do other racial-gender groups. In the National Health Interview Survey, respondents are asked to indicate whether they had difficulty performing nine physical activities without help (either from a person or from special equipment): walking a quarter of a mile; climbing ten steps without resting; standing for two hours; sitting for two hours; stooping, bending, or kneeling; reaching over the head; using one's fingers to grasp or handle small objects; lifting or carrying ten pounds; and pushing or pulling large objects. For all tasks except grasping or handling small objects, Black women consistently report higher rates of difficulty than did any other racial-gender group. One in five Black women (22.3 percent) reports having great difficulty with at least one of the nine activities (versus 13.3 percent of Black men, 17.5 percent of Hispanic women, and 17.0 percent of White women). The percentages of Black women who report having great difficulty performing, or being unable to perform, each of the nine tasks is below:[42]

Task	Having Difficulty or Unable to Perform
Walking one-quarter mile	12.4 percent
Climbing ten steps without resting	11.1 percent
Standing for two hours	14.3 percent
Sitting for two hours	4.8 percent
Stooping, bending, or kneeling	13.4 percent
Reaching over one's head	4.3 percent
Grasping or handling small objects	2.6 percent
Lifting or carrying ten pounds	9.8 percent
Pushing or pulling large objects	12.8 percent

Further, compared to Hispanic women, African-American women report significantly more days when they are confined to bed for more than half of the day due to illness or injury, an average of 7.2 days per year for

41. Ibid., 6, 34.
42. Ibid., 55.

Black women (compared to 3.8 days for Hispanic women).[43] Among employed adults, Black women report missing work an average of 5.3 days per year due to injury or illness, not including maternity leave (compared to 4.7 days for Black men, 3.4 for Hispanic women, and 4.9 for White women).[44]

Given the data presented above, it should come as no surprise that Black women generally rate their overall health as poor. Black women are less likely than their White counterparts to describe themselves as being in excellent or very good health (49.7 percent vs. 64.7 percent, respectively). Moreover, Black women are nearly twice as likely as White women to judge their health status as fair or poor (20.4 percent vs. 10.9 percent, respectively).[45] Clearly, Black women's bodies have not received the message that they are supposed to be the new model minority. For a group that supposedly always has it together, Black women's bodies seem to be falling apart. Black women have high rates of physical disease and distress, higher rates of morbidity from certain diseases, and higher rates of functional impairment. And ultimately, they have lower life expectancies than women of other races. In 2007, the U.S. Census Bureau estimated an average life expectancy of 76.8 years for Black women.[46] Further, it is projected that an African-American female born in 2010 will have an average life expectancy of 77.2 years, four to six fewer years of life than women of any other racial group.[47]

43. Ibid., 9, 50. The difference between Black and White women (5.7 days) was not statistically significant. The report does not test the statistical significance between bedridden days for Black women and Black men (4.8 days).

44. Ibid., 50. The report does not suggest that these differences are statistically significant.

45. Ibid., 9, 60. Hispanic women rated themselves similarly to Black women, with 50 percent rating their health as excellent or very good and 19.9 percent rating it as poor. While the report does not test whether there is a statistically significant difference between the ratings of Black women and men, superficially the ratings of Black men seem to be comparable, with 52.5 percent describing their health as excellent or very good and 18.7 percent describing it as fair or poor.

46. U.S. Census Bureau, "Table 102. Expectation of Life at Birth."

47. U.S. Census Bureau, "Table 10. Projected Life Expectancy at Birth." The projected life expectancies for other women were as follows: Whites, 81.3 years; Hispanics (of any race), 83.7 years; Asian Americans, 81.1 years; American Indians/Alaskan Natives, 76.6 years; and Pacific Islanders, 76.7 years.

The Mental Health Status of Black Women:
A Statistical Profile

Data on stress and mental health issues among Black women are less readily available than data on physical health disparities. Mental health professionals face several problems in the assessment and diagnosis of psychiatric problems among women of color. There is limited systemic and representative data regarding the epidemiology of mental heath disorders and the utilization of services. Few epidemiologic studies specifically examine rates of depression, anxiety, and other psychiatric disorders among African Americans, and fewer still focus on African-American women. Studies that do focus on this population tend to be exploratory in nature and to utilize small, nonrepresentational samples, limiting the generalizability of their findings.[48]

Fortunately, three national studies shed light on the rates of psychological distress among African-American women: the Epidemiologic Catchment Area (ECA) Study, the National Comorbidity Survey (NCS), and the previously described NHIS. Sponsored by the National Institute of Mental Health (NIMH) from 1980 to 1985, the ECA Study was the largest research study of the prevalence and incidence of psychiatric disorders in non-institutionalized community-based populations. It utilized a nationally representative sample of adults (N = 20,861) living in five cities located in culturally distinct geographic regions of the United States: New Haven (CT), Baltimore (MD), Durham (NC), St. Louis (MO), and Los Angeles (CA). The sample included a large subsample of African-American adults (N = 4,287). Using the NIMH Diagnostic Interview Schedule (DIS), the ECA Study examined the prevalence of several DSM-III diagnostic categories, including mood disorders (specifically mania, dysthymia, bipolar disorder, and major depression), anxiety disorders (i.e., obsessive compulsive disorder, phobia, panic disorder), substance use disorders (i.e., alcohol abuse or dependence, drug use or dependence), psychotic disorders (i.e., schizophrenia and schizophreniform disorder), antisocial personality disorder, and anorexia nervosa.[49]

Whereas the ECA Study examined the prevalence of a wide range of psychiatric diagnoses, the primary purpose of the NCS was to examine the prevalence and comorbidity of substance use and other mental

48. Barbee, "African American Women and Depression," 257.

49. National Institute of Mental Health, *Epidemiologic Catchment Area Study*.

health disorders. Conducted from 1990 to 1992 (with re-interviews held from 2001 to 2002), the NCS included a representative sample of over eight thousand noninstitutionalized persons, ages fifteen to fifty-four, in the United States, with African Americans accounting for 12.5 percent of respondents.[50] Using diagnostic criteria from the DSM-III-R, the NCS examined the prevalence of mood disorders (i.e., mania, major depression, and dysthymia), anxiety disorders (i.e., generalized anxiety disorder, panic disorder, agoraphobia, simple and social phobia, and posttraumatic stress disorder), substance use disorders (i.e., substance abuse and substance dependence), antisocial personality disorder, conduct disorder, and nonaffective psychosis.[51]

In contrast to the ECA Study and the NCS, the NHIS did not utilize structured diagnostic interviews of psychiatric conditions. Rather, participants were simply asked to describe the frequency with which they experienced selected symptoms of depression and anxiety during the thirty days prior to the interview. This data, while perhaps less rigorous, is valuable because it may be more sensitive to subclinical levels of psychological distress. Finally, because the NHIS is conducted annually, it provides more recent data than do the ECA Study or NCS. Despite the methodological variations, taken together, these three studies reveal that when it comes to emotional health, Black women experience a double whammy: they suffer from high rates of stress, depression, and anxiety, and they are less likely to seek help for their problems.

Stress and Distress

It is broadly believed that African-American women have higher rates of stress than White women.[52] This consensus is based, at least in part, from Black women's membership in two demographic groups that consistently have high rates of psychological distress: African Americans and women. Across gender and socioeconomic status, African Americans generally have higher rates of psychological distress than Whites.[53] Across socioeconomic status, women have higher rates of psychological distress and stress-related illnesses than men. This is largely due to women's greater susceptibility to

50. Brown and Keith, "Epidemiology of Mental Disorders," 26.
51. Ibid.
52. West, "Mammy, Sapphire, and Jezebel," 460.
53. Williams and Lawler, "Stress and Illness in Low-Income Women," 63.

relational stressors (such as the death of a spouse) and vicarious or network stress (that is, stressors experienced by people in one's social network). Indeed, the impact of vicarious stress is heightened among low-income women, who have increased exposure to community stressors and who typically utilize large social networks as coping resources.[54]

Given their race, gender, and disproportionate poverty, it is reasonable to expect that African-American women would have higher rates of distress than Black men or White women. Indeed, African-American women disproportionately experience a number of stressful conditions and events that are linked to the development of mental-health problems, including low-wage employment, caregiver and multiple role strain, medical problems and disability, social isolation, bereavement, exposure to traumatic events, and poor access to health care.[55] They also experience greater morbidity from stress and stress-related illness (i.e., coronary heart disease, cardiovascular disease, diabetes, and hypertension) than do White women.[56]

Stress and distress impact health via both direct and indirect pathways. Stress is associated with a wide array of negative health outcomes among women, including headaches, stomachaches, sleep and eating disturbances, and depression, symptoms which, in turn, exacerbate existing health problems or facilitate the development of new symptoms or diseases. Further, women who feel stressed or overwhelmed are less likely to engage in health-promoting behaviors (e.g., proper nutrition, exercise, good sleeping habits).[57]

Depression

It has been well-documented that there is a strong cultural stigma against depression, and mental illness broadly, among African Americans.[58] For a long time, many Africans Americans characterized depression as a "White disease" and viewed it as a sign of personal weakness.[59] A public opinion poll conducted by the National Mental Health Association in the late 1990s

54. Ibid., 62.

55. Ward and Heidrich, "African American Women's Beliefs."

56. Townsend, Hawkins, and Batts, "Stress and Stress Reduction," 570.

57. Ibid.

58. For further discussion on the cultural stigma against mental illness among African Americans, see Danquah, *Willow Weep for Me*; Head, *Standing in the Shadows*; Poussaint and Alexander, *Lay My Burden Down*; and Williams, *Black Pain*.

59. Jones and Shorter-Gooden, *Shifting*, 131.

found that 63 percent of African Americans believed that depression was a personal weakness; only 31 percent viewed it as a health problem.[60] Further, because of the cultural expectation of Black women's strength, Black women who suffer from depression may be especially prone to being labeled as weak. In her memoir about her personal struggles with depression, Meri Nana-Ama Danquah writes,

> Stereotypes and clichés about mental illness are as pervasive as those about race. I have noticed that the mental illness that affects white men is often characterized, if not glamorized, as a sign of genius, a burden of cerebral superiority, artistic eccentricity—as if their depression is somehow heroic. White women who suffer from mental illness are depicted as idle, spoiled, or just plain hysterical. Black men are demonized and pathologized. Black women with psychological problems are certainly not seen as geniuses; we are generally not labeled "hysterical" or "eccentric" or even "pathological." When a black woman suffers from a mental disorder, the overwhelming opinion is that she is weak. And weakness in black women is intolerable.[61]

It is likely the strength of this stigma that leads to the common misperception that African-American women are less vulnerable to depression than are White women.

In contrast to these cultural beliefs, there is growing, albeit still inconsistent, evidence that Black women experience depression at similar or higher levels than other racial-gender groups.[62] Generally, rates of depression are higher among women than men. This is no less true for African-American men and women. In both the ECA Study and NCS, Black women were significantly more likely to suffer major depression than Black men. The diagnosis of a major depressive episode requires the consistent presence of at least five of nine possible symptoms, one of which must be a depressed mood, for at least two consecutive weeks.[63] In the ECA Study, Black women were nearly five times more likely than Black men to have experienced a major depressive episode within a year, with 4.9 percent of Black women meeting the diagnostic criteria compared to 1.0 percent of Black men. Further, the rates of major depression were similar between

60. Ward and Heidrich, "African American Women's Beliefs," 2.

61. Danquah, *Willow Weep for Me*, 20.

62. Scarinci et al., "Depression in Black Women"; Barbee, "African American Women and Depression," 257; Beauboeuf-Lafontant, "You Have to Show Strength."

63. American Psychiatric Association, *DSM-IV-R*, 356.

Black women and their White counterparts, 4.6 percent of whom met the criteria for major depression within a year.[64] The NCS, in contrast, found that while Black women had twice the likelihood of a major depressive episode during a twelve-month period than Black men (10.99 vs. 4.99 percent, respectively), their rates were significantly lower than those of White women (12.68 percent).[65]

The ECA Study and NCS also found conflicting results with regard to racial-gender differences in dysthymic disorder. Dysthymia is distinguished from major depression in that, while the criteria involve fewer symptoms, they must be present for a longer period of time. To meet the criteria for dysthymic disorder, a person must experience three of seven possible symptoms, one of which must be having a depressed mood more days than not for a two-year period. Both studies found similar rates of dysthymia among African-American women: the one-year prevalence rate of the disorder was 3.6 percent in the ECA Study and 3.82 percent in the NCS. In both cases, the rates for Black women exceeded those for Black men (1.2 percent in the ECA and 2.26 percent in the NCS). However, whereas Black women had significantly higher rates of dysthymia than White women (2.83 percent) in the NCS, they had significantly lower rates than White women (4.2 percent) in the ECA.[66]

In the NHIS, participants were asked to report the frequency with which they reported four symptoms of depression within the thirty days prior to the interview: sadness, hopelessness, worthlessness, and feeling that everything was an effort, the latter possibly being a manifestation of psychomotor fatigue or exhaustion. One of every five Black women (19.8 percent) reported feeling that everything had been an effort during all, most, or some of the time, higher than did Black men (9.2 percent), Hispanic women (15.8 percent) or White women (14.4 percent). Further, Black women were more likely to report experiencing significant feelings of sadness (17.7 percent vs. 11.8 percent of Black men and 12.2 percent of White women), hopelessness (8.1 percent vs. 5.9 percent of Black men and 6.7 percent of White women), and worthlessness (6.2 percent vs. 5.0 percent of Black men and 5.5 percent of White women). Hispanic women generally had similar or slightly higher levels of sadness, hopelessness, and worthlessness than Black women (17.5, 10.4, and 7.4 percent, respectively).[67]

64. Brown and Keith, "Epidemiology of Mental Disorders," 27.
65. Ibid., 29.
66. Ibid., 27, 29.
67. Pleis and Lethbridge-Çejku, *National Health Interview Survey,* 43. The NHIS

Several authors have made a connection between depression and the cultural mandate for women to be strong (or silent) in enduring suffering. Dana Crowley Jack's conceptualization of the roots of depression in women may have particular relevance for the StrongBlackWoman.[68] In particular, Jack posits that women suffering from depression often describe their experience in terms of a "loss of self" or "silencing." Often, this involves women's loss of capacity to express their feelings, thoughts, and beliefs as they seek the approval of others.[69] And while "silent" is not often a descriptor attributed to StrongBlackWomen, it aptly describes the process by which African-American women suppress and repress feelings of vulnerability as they attempt to live up to the myth of strength. Further, as Jack notes, "women lose themselves as they try to fit into an image provided by someone else—the husband, parental teachings, the culture."[70] Internalizing the myth of the StrongBlackWoman forces African-American women to subsume their authentic selves as they try to fit into a culturally constructed stereotype of who they ought to be.

Several authors have explicitly linked the StrongBlackWoman to depression. For example, Roberta Waite and Priscilla Killian found that the strength motif was a significant factor in women's denial about depression and resistance toward treatment. As one woman stated, "I always believed that I was strong enough to deal with this pain and emptiness and get over it."[71] And in their book *Shifting: The Double Lives of Black Women in America*, journalist Charisse Jones and psychologist Kumea Shorter-Gooden identify the "Sisterella complex" as a racial-gender-specific manifestation of depression among African-American women.[72] Notably, their description of Sisterella shares much in common with the StrongBlackWoman:

> Much like the classic Cinderella character, Sisterella is the Black woman who honors others but denies herself. She achieves in her own right—indeed, she may overachieve—yet she works tirelessly, sometimes masochistically, to promote, protect, and appease others. She is trying so hard to be what others want and need that she has lost control of the shifting process. It's overtaken her. . . . She has lost sight of her own gifts as well as her own needs. Her

---

report does not specifically test the statistical significance of these differences.

68. Jack, *Silencing the Self.*

69. Ibid., 32.

70. Ibid.

71. Waite and Killian, "Health Beliefs about Depression," 191.

72. Jones and Shorter-Gooden, *Shifting*, 124.

> identity is confused, her personal goals are deeply buried, and she shrinks inwardly. She becomes depressed, sometimes severely so.[73]

Based upon the authors' description, we might think of Sisterella complex as a depressed StrongBlackWoman, one whose proclivities for taking on too much have finally become overly burdensome. For Jones and Shorter-Gooden, depression—whether as a temporary case of the "blues," an experience of depressive symptoms, or a diagnosable disorder—is a natural, perhaps even unavoidable, outcome of African-American women's attempts to live into the myth of strength. The irony of the Sisterella complex, however, is that "the very selflessness that characterizes [it] may lead clinicians and researchers to overlook the prevalence of depression in Black women."[74] Likewise, StrongBlackWomen suffering from depression may go unnoticed because they do not clearly exhibit the traditional clinical picture of depression, that is, a person who is fatigued, lethargic, or gloomy. Indeed, the level of constant activity that characterizes the StrongBlackWoman may obscure the presence of depression because it counters the widespread clinical understanding of enervation as a primary symptom of depression. Moreover, StrongBlackWomen may not appear depressed because of the great importance placed upon managing affect and appearing to be in control. Thus, even when she is experiencing deep suffering, the StrongBlackWoman will often go to great lengths to appear as though she is not. And more often than not, others—including pastoral leaders—are fooled by her performance.

Anxiety Disorders

Anxiety disorders are the most common psychiatric disorders in community-based samples. The DSM-IV distinguishes between several forms of anxiety disorders, many of which involve fear of specific situations or objects, whereas others involve more general feelings of nervousness. It is ironic, but research indicates that a population routinely described as "strong" has significant problems with fear and anxiety. While racial-gender differences in prevalence rates vary based upon the particular research study and the specific anxiety disorder under investigation, epidemiologic studies often find that African-American women have higher rates of anxiety disorders than Black men and Whites.

73. Ibid.
74. Ibid.

The most consistent differences are found with respect to phobias, which involve a marked and unreasonable fear of a specific object or situation. Indeed, in the ECA study, phobia was the single most common mental disorder among Black women. Approximately one of every five Black women (18.2 percent) experienced a diagnosable phobia within a one-year period, as contrasted with 10.2 percent of Black men and 10.9 percent of White women.[75] Similar results were found in the NCS, which examined three forms of phobic conditions: (1) simple/specific phobia, which focuses upon a specific object or situation (e.g., fear of spiders, flying, the dark); (2) social phobia, in which a person has excessive fear about being exposed to social interactions in which she may be scrutinized, such as conversations and public speaking; and (3) agoraphobia, in which a person fears or avoids particular places (e.g., open spaces, crowds, public transportation) because she worries that escape is impossible, that help will be unavailable in the event of an emergency, or that she might have a panic attack.[76] Again, simple phobia was the most frequently occurring mental disorder among Black women (14.85 percent), who had higher rates of the disorder than Black men (3.56 percent) and White women (12.10 percent). Black women also had the highest rates of agoraphobia (8.56 percent), as contrasted with 1.18 percent of Black men and 4.68 percent of White women. Finally, Black women's rates of social phobia (8.97 percent), while not significantly different from those of White women (9.09 percent), were higher than those of Black men (2.92 percent).[77]

The ECA and NCS studies found discrepant results with regard to generalized anxiety disorder, which involves the consistent presence of excessive worry even when there is no fear-inducing stimulus present.[78] The ECA found that Black women had higher rates of generalized anxiety disorder (6.6 percent) than Black men (5.5 percent) or White women (4.7 percent).[79] The NCS, in contrast, found that Black women had higher rates of generalized anxiety disorder than Black men (2.73 percent vs. 1.74 percent), but lower rates than White women (4.50 percent).[80] The discrepant findings with regard to generalized anxiety disorder parallel those of the NHIS, in which participants indicated the frequency with which they

75. Brown and Keith, "Epidemiology of Mental Disorders," 27.
76. American Psychiatric Association, *DSM-IV-TR*, 443, 450–51, 432–33.
77. Brown and Keith, "Epidemiology of Mental Disorders," 29.
78. American Psychiatric Association, *DSM-IV-TR*, 472–73.
79. Brown and Keith, "Epidemiology of Mental Disorders," 27.
80. Ibid., 29.

had experienced two symptoms of anxiety: nervousness and restlessness. Black women reported lower levels of nervousness as did women from other racial/ethnic groups (15.7 percent, as compared to 18.3 percent of Hispanic and 18.7 percent of White women). But they reported higher levels of restlessness, with one in five Black women (20.7 percent) stating that she felt restless all, most, or some of the time during the thirty days prior to the interview, compared with 14.5 percent of Black men, 17.3 percent of Hispanic women, and 18.8 percent of White women.[81]

Despite the discrepancies, when taken together, these studies demonstrate that African-American women suffer from a wide range of anxiety disorders and at higher levels than do their Black male and White female counterparts.[82] Yet if one were to poll Black Christian women about their experiences with anxiety, few women would openly acknowledge having problems. Many, in fact, would deny it, perhaps countering with quotations of Scriptures such as Phil 4:6, "Do not worry about anything, but in everything by prayer and supplication with thanksgiving let your requests be made known to God." How do we reconcile the resistance to disclose anxiety with the high rates of these disorders in mental health research? To some degree, the high rate of anxiety disorders, particularly phobic conditions, may effectively disguise them. When being afraid of specific objects or having "bad nerves" are so commonplace in a population, it may become difficult to identify such problems as conditions indicating the need for treatment.[83]

81. Pleis and Lethbridge-Çejku, *National Health Interview Survey,* 48.

82. Neal-Barnett and Crowther, "To Be Female." Small, community-based studies further demonstrate that anxiety disorders are not restricted to low-income African-American women. In a study of panic disorder among fifty middle-class African-American women who were recruited from community sources (e.g., physicians, churches, community festivals, local radio and newspaper advertisements), Neal-Barnett and Crowther found high, and relatively similar, levels of anxiety and mood disorders among their panic-disorder and non-panic-disorder groups. Consistent with the results of the national epidemiologic studies, the researchers found that the most frequently occurring anxiety disorders were general phobia, followed by social phobia and generalized anxiety disorder. The most common types of simple phobias were animals/insects (reported by 56.5 percent of the sample), small enclosed places (39.1 percent), heights (34.8 percent), driving (30.4 percent), air travel (21.7 percent), and blood and injury (8.7 percent).

83. Kirmayer and Young, "Culture and Somatization," 424. Kirmayer and Young suggest that "nerves" may be a somaticized form of anxiety and depression.

Violence and Trauma

A particularly significant finding in the NCS was that Black women had higher rates of posttraumatic stress disorder (PTSD) than did Black men or Whites (6.96 percent vs. 1.68 percent of Black men and 4.41 percent of White women).[84] PTSD is a pattern of symptoms that occurs after exposure to a traumatic event that involved a threat to physical integrity or a risk of injury or death, such as natural disaster, rape, or violence. The traumatic event may be directly experienced or witnessed; it may also be learned about in the case of a family member or close associate.[85] This finding is not surprising given that African-American women are more likely to be victimized by intimate-partner violence, sexual assault, and childhood abuse than women from other ethnic groups.[86] There is consistent evidence that African-American women are significantly more likely to be victimized by intimate partner violence than are non-Hispanic White women.[87] A national study, for example, found that 20 percent of Black women report being victims of domestic violence by their husbands or live-in boyfriends, three times the rate reported by White women.[88] Similarly, nearly one in five Black women have experienced an attempted or completed rape at some point during their lives.[89] Another study found that a substantial number of Black women carry histories of childhood abuse, with 43 percent reporting being verbally or emotionally abused as children, 20 percent reporting a history of physical abuse, and 22 percent reporting a history of sexual abuse.[90] Ironically, while churches and nonprofit organizations have devoted substantial attention to the issue of violence among African-American males, far less advocacy and education has focused upon the forms of violence that are ubiquitous among Black women.

84. Brown and Keith, "Epidemiology of Mental Disorders," 29. The ECA Study did not include post-traumatic stress disorder.

85. American Psychiatric Association, *DSM-IV-TR*, 463.

86. Neal-Barnett and Crowther, "To Be Female," 131.

87. Nicolaidis et al., "'You Don't Go Tell White People Nothing,'" 1470. It should be noted that racial disparities in intimate partner violence have been largely attributed to economic disparities.

88. Field and Caetano, "Longitudinal Model Predicting Partner Violence."

89. Centers for Disease Control and Prevention, *Sexual Violence: Facts at a Glance*.

90. Black Women's Health Imperative, "The Impact of Psychosocial Factors on Health."

Somatization

While somatization is closely related to stress and anxiety, it deserves special mention given the challenge that it poses to diagnosing and estimating mental-health problems among African-American women. In its original use in psychodynamic theory, the term *somatization* described a process by which psychological conflict was transformed into bodily distress.[91] Over the years, the term has come to be used in two interchangeable ways. First, the term is used to describe a pattern of symptom manifestation in which emotional distress and social problems are channeled, either partially or exclusively, into physical ailments.[92] The link between stressful events and illness is often not a conscious process and occurs through mediating mechanisms that occur outside the individual's awareness. Consequently, it is possible that a clinician or pastor might suspect a link between stress and health even when the individual does not acknowledge it or actively denies it.[93] Somatic complaints are relatively common within outpatient settings, accounting for a quarter to half of clinical presentations, and frequently include headache, dizziness, gastrointestinal discomfort, and/or pain in the neck, shoulders, back, and chest.[94]

Second, the term may be a "catch-all" phrase used to refer to any of the psychiatric disorders in the DSM-IV category of somatoform disorders, which include somatization disorder, hypochondriasis, undifferentiated somatoform disorder, and pain disorder.[95] Whereas somatic complaints are frequent in primary and secondary care settings, diagnosable somatoform disorders are relatively rare (with the ECA estimating a rate of 0.01 percent of the general population).[96] Yet it is significant that Black women experience significantly higher rates of somatization than other racial-gender groups. The ECA Study, for example, found that the one-year prevalence rate of somatization disorder—which involves multiple, recurring, and frequently changing complaints of physical distress over a period of at least two years—was eight times higher among African-American women than their male counterparts (0.8 percent vs. 0.1 percent) and four times the rate

91. Kirmayer and Young, "Culture and Somatization," 420.

92. Ibid. See also Jones and Shorter-Gooden, *Shifting*, 141.

93. Kirmayer and Young, "Culture and Somatization," 424.

94. Mayou et al., "Somatoform Disorders"; Tsai, "Factor Analysis," 160.

95. Kirmayer and Young, "Culture and Somatization," 420.

96. Ibid., 421.

of White women (0.2 percent).[97] The NCS did not include somatization disorder.

Barriers to Treatment

Even moreso than physical-health problems, African-American women face a number of barriers to detection, diagnosis, and treatment of mental-health problems. Cultural stigma against mental-health issues and help-seeking have often been cited as the primary barrier to treatment. For example, it has been said that African Americans believe that people of color are less susceptible to mental illness and that therapy is a "crutch" for Whites (and possibly for people of color who are unstable, "crazy," or "weak").[98] In essence, the belief is that African Americans, especially African-American women, are too strong to be saddled with emotional problems or to require professional treatment for those problems. Then, too, there is the *dirty laundry* phenomenon, specifically a cultural stigma—common among people of African descent—against sharing personal information with people outside one's home or immediate family.[99] Long before Las Vegas tempted tourists with the promise, "What happens in Vegas stays in Vegas," African-American children learned from their parents, "What goes on in this house stays in this house." The good news, however, is that concomitant with societal shifts in the perception of mental illness over the past few decades, African-American women's beliefs about mental illness and coping strategies are shifting as well. In particular, greater numbers of Black women report a willingness to seek help for mental-health problems.[100] Still, however, given the burden of mental-health problems among African-American women, their utilization of mental health treatment services is low.[101]

A Vicious Cycle: Health and the StrongBlackWoman

When the data on Black women's health outcomes are considered, it becomes difficult—daresay impossible—to make claims that "Black women

97. Brown and Keith, "Epidemiology of Mental Disorders," 27; American Psychiatric Association, *DSM-IV-TR*, 486.

98. Jones and Shorter-Gooden, *Shifting*, 131.

99. Edge and Rogers, "Dealing with It," 22.

100. Ward and Heidrich, "African American Women's Beliefs," 9.

101. Ibid., 1.

are the new model minority" or that "sisters always have it together." Such claims reveal themselves as evidence of viewing the lives of Black women through a racist-sexist lens that renders blatant health disparities invisible. The data are clear that Black women suffer disproportionately from a wide range of physical and mental-health problems, including obesity, diabetes, hypertension, HIV/AIDS, cancer mortality, chronic pain, functional impairment, stress, post-traumatic stress disorder, phobias, somatic complaints, and physical and sexual assault. Yet the soothsayers proclaim peace.[102]

Further, on the occasions when Black women's health disparities are acknowledged, it is done with a "blame-the-victim" approach, that is, with an almost exclusive focus upon obesity and its concomitant health risk behaviors (specifically, diet and exercise), treating these issues as resulting from individual pathology (i.e., laziness) rather than a confluence of systemic factors that hinder—and in some cases, undermine—African-American women's capacity to develop and maintain good health. Take, for example, Alice Randall's op-ed in the *New York Times*, "Black Women and Fat," in which the author makes the controversial claim that "many black women are fat because we want to be."[103] Randall's argument, for which she provides no support, is based upon her erroneous conflation of a cultural aesthetic that preferences curvaceous bodies and ample butts (as opposed to rail-thin bodies and ample breasts) with an intentional choice to be obese. Randall chooses not to contextualize Black women's obesity in the context of the nationwide epidemic in the U.S. She issues a call to arms for Black women to take control of their waistlines, but she does not discuss race/gender-based barriers that may impede that difficult goal. She does not discuss how the factors most commonly cited as barriers to proper diet and nutrition by Black women—lack of time and access to resources—are also indicators of the economic and relational stresses that constrain their lives.[104] Instead, she recapitulates the disdain that health-care professionals

---

102. Cf. Jer 6:14, "They have treated the wound of my people carelessly, saying, 'Peace, peace,' when there is no peace" (NRSV).

103. Randall, "Black Women and Fat."

104. Lynch et al., "Obese African-American Women's Perspectives." Using focus group methodology, the authors found that obese African-American women cited time and money constraints as the largest factor preventing weight loss. Specifically, the women reported that their time was limited by work, family, and social responsibilities, that their food choices were limited by economic resources, and that they lacked access to exercise facilities, classes, and equipment.

demonstrate for African-American women when we fail to hear the oft-repeated refrain of their lives: "I do not have the time or money to care for my health."

Professional caregivers—pastoral or otherwise—who desire to respond compassionately and effectively to the needs of African-American women must hear the "no time, no money" refrain and recognize it for what it is—a telltale sign of a woman who has been caught in the structural web of the StrongBlackWoman. Further, they must understand that the ideology of the StrongBlackWoman is strongly implicated in the health epidemic facing Black women. Many StrongBlackWomen are caught in a vicious cycle between stress and physical/mental distress that very often leads to disease.

Ecosocial Model of StrongBlackWoman-Health Connection

In contrast to the approach typified by Randall, which examines Black women's health outcomes in isolation from the conditions that shape them, I proffer an ecosocial model of the impact of the StrongBlackWoman upon physical and emotional health outcomes.[105] This model can be depicted visually as follows:

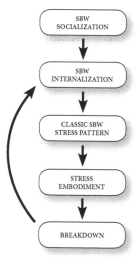

105. Krieger, "Embodiment." Ecosocial theory is prominent in epidemiological and health research, in which it is used to examine how social and structural contexts impact population patterns of health, including health disparities.

First, usually beginning in childhood, Black females learn via direct instruction and modeling that the StrongBlackWoman is a cultural norm that they are expected to embody as adults. The socialization process is multisystemic and unending. While much of it occurs within family and other intimate relationships, as I describe in chapters 3 and 4, churches and mass media also figure prominently in training Black girls and women in the three core features of the StrongBlackWoman throughout the course of their lives. Second, individuals who internalize these norms begin to personify the three core features of the StrongBlackWoman in their patterns of affect, behavior, and cognition: chronically prioritizing the needs of other people and institutions over their own; assuming excessive responsibility within their families, workplaces, churches, and communities; having difficulty asking for help and support from others; and repressing normative emotional responses to stress; and so on.

Third, over time women begin to experience the classic StrongBlack-Woman stress pattern: overload and role strain, and the embodiment of stress. Role strain is a particularly important element of the StrongBlack-Woman stress response. Carolyn West states:

> Not only are [Black women] required to function in numerous roles, such as that of worker and family caretaker, this expectation is frequently extended to community and church activities. Moreover, these roles are often performed without the benefit of economic security and partner support since Black women disproportionately earn less and are more likely to be single parents.[106]

As perpetual caretakers, StrongBlackWomen spend most of their time and energy caring for the needs of others, promising to reserve the leftovers for themselves. Usually, however, there are no leftovers and the cumulative role strain gives way to the experience of stress, that is, a lack of fit between resources and demands.[107]

Eventually, the combined effect of role strain and poor self-care results in the embodiment of stress. Embodiment is a central concept in ecosocial theory and helps us to understand how stress is translated into health problems. Among StrongBlackWomen, embodiment is the usually unconscious process by which women's bodies become the repositories of the stresses

---

106. West, "Mammy, Sapphire, and Jezebel," 459.

107. Townsend, Hawkins, and Batts, "Stress and Stress Reduction," 569. The authors provide a classic definition of stress as resulting "when the personal and situational demands placed on a person exceed their resources."

and strains resulting from their personification of a socially constructed role.[108] Extending, and closely paraphrasing Nancy Krieger's explanation, I suggest that the concept of embodiment makes two essential claims about the relationship between the StrongBlackWoman and the health status of Black women. First, Black women's bodies tell stories about the social and structural conditions of their existence, conditions that are constrained by the intersection of racism, sexism, and classism; and their bodies cannot be studied apart from these conditions. Second, Black women's bodies tell stories that they may be incapable of telling, in large part because of the myth of strength and its unrelenting demand for composure in the face of crisis, which encourages Black women to ignore, suppress, or conceal symptoms of physical and mental distress.[109] StrongBlackWomen commonly experience a mismatch between their outward appearance and inner reality. The myth of strength effectually creates a dissociative disposition, such that StrongBlackWomen manage to ignore or dismiss the symptoms of physical distress.[110]

Stress is associated with a wide array of negative health outcomes among women, including headaches, stomachaches, sleep and eating disturbances, and depression. In addition to the pain distress that they themselves cause, each of these symptoms is capable of exacerbating existing health problems or facilitating the development of new symptoms or

---

108. Beauboeuf-Lafontant, *Behind the Mask*, 7.

109. This re-articulation differs from Krieger, who identifies three critical claims of embodiment: "(1) bodies tell stories about—and cannot be studied divorced from—the conditions of our existence; (2) bodies tell stories that often—but not always—match people's stated accounts; and (3) bodies tell stories that people cannot or will not tell, either because they are unable, forbidden, or choose not to tell" ("Embodiment," 350). In my clinical and ministerial experiences, the extent of repression and denial among StrongBlackWomen often results in stated accounts that differ significantly from the stories that their bodies tell. For example, in response to the question, "How do you feel?" a StrongBlackWomen is likely to respond with "Blessed and highly favored!" even as she is overweight, hypertensive, diabetic, and experiencing chronic migraines brought on by the stresses of caring for others.

110. Extending her notion of the myth of strength as a discourse, Beauboeuf-Lafontant asserts that StrongBlackWomen lack even the language to express their distress: "Without the support and the language to express the turmoil within, strong Black women's discrepant feelings become embodied as distresses, but rarely gain the status of such given the racialized framing of eating problems and depression as white women's illnesses. Furthermore, these distresses are too often denied by the women themselves and thus rendered into another burden to carry, yet another act in one's performance of strength" (Beauboeuf-Lafontant, *Behind the Mask*, 67–68).

diseases.[111] Black women's disproportionately high rates of somatization suggest that embodiment is a particularly pronounced process among this population. As the psychological impact of role strain and overload mount, Black women are especially likely to ignore, deny, and repress their distress, which becomes embodied in recurrent and unexplained physical problems such as chronic pain, stomach problems, fatigue, and sleep disturbance.[112] It would be an injustice, however, for clergy and health-care professionals to assume that the psychological basis of these symptoms implies that they are "not real" or "in the head." For StrongBlackWomen, somatic complaints function as "idioms of distress"; that is, they are "cultural styles of expressing distress . . . that are influenced not only by cultural beliefs and practices but also by familiarity with health care systems and pathways to care."[113] They reflect a nosology that does not sharply distinguish between psychological and physical complaints, one in which diagnostic categories blend physical and emotional symptoms.[114] And they provide a language of suffering that other people—including clergy, family, and health-care professionals—will more readily accept as valid indicators of distress among women whom people generally expect to be indomitable.[115]

In addition to directly resulting in symptoms of physical and emotional disease, stress is further embodied via poor coping and self-care behaviors. Women who feel stressed or overwhelmed are less likely to engage

111. Townsend, Hawkins, and Batts, "Stress and Stress Reduction," 570.

112. Beauboeuf-Lafontant, *Behind the Mask,* 108. Several of Beauboeuf-Lafontant's interviewees spoke of processes of embodiment by which they managed their reactions by allowing their bodies to "absorb" the emotional impact of their overwhelming responsibilities and stresses. And in a 1974 study, Carter found that the presence of multiple somatic symptoms was the most commonly occurring clinical finding in diagnosing depression in African Americans (Barbee, "African American Women and Depression," 261).

113. Kirmayer and Young, "Culture and Somatization," 420.

114. Ibid., 422, 424. The authors further note that "equating somatization with primitive thinking or communication is based on several doubtful premises: that greater psychological insight necessarily results in fewer somatic symptoms; that psychological idioms are inherently more 'advanced' than somatic idioms; that somatic idioms are 'less differentiated' and inarticulate; and, finally, that psychological (and by analogy, cultural) development moves along a one-dimensional continuum from primitive to advanced. In fact, the use of a bodily idiom may say more about the social and cultural context of communication than it does about the cognitive limitations or psychological defensiveness of the individual" (426).

115. Ibid., 424.

in health-promoting behaviors.[116] Among StrongBlackWomen, the multiple and frequently competing demands of their lives prevent them from establishing and maintaining healthy lifestyle habits of nutrition, exercise, sleep, and stress reduction. In lieu of these, they may have a tendency to overutilize compensatory strategies that provide an immediate sense of relief but no real amelioration of symptoms: binge eating, compulsive shopping, and excessively focusing upon their physical appearance. A number of scholars have identified eating practices, in particular, as an embodied form of protest among women.[117] It is estimated that anywhere from 8 to 34 percent of Black women have problems with binge eating.[118] Further, the behavior is a common response to trauma and appears to be a particularly common problem among depressed Black women, almost twice as prevalent as in White women.[119] Women who internalize the StrongBlackWoman are at heightened risk for binge eating because it enhances their capacity to achieve one of the three core features of the identity: affect regulation. Indeed, a prevailing theoretical model of binge eating is the affect regulation model, which hypothesizes that binge eating is "a maladaptive attempt at regulating and managing negative affect . . . [that serves] functions such as self-soothing, emotional numbing, avoiding negative affect, or escaping aversive self-awareness."[120] Among women who internalize the StrongBlackWoman, emotional eating may be a self-soothing strategy to deal with the effects of the types of trauma that Black women disproportionately experience. It may also be a means of coping with present-day stresses concomitant with the caregiving, excessive activity, and emotional repression that characterize their lives as StrongBlackWomen. The use of binge eating as a compensatory strategy is multiply reinforced because it (1) has relatively little financial or relational cost; (2) temporarily reduces the presence, level, or intensity of negative affect; and (3) does so without challenging the myth of strength.[121] Even though binge eating often results

116. Townsend, Hawkins, and Batts, "Stress and Stress Reduction," 570.

117. Beauboeuf-Lafontant, *Behind the Mask,* 50. Beauboeuf-Lafontant, for example, notes that "for many women . . . eating practices are creative and intentional acts of self-protection in the face of trauma, such as childhood sexual abuse."

118. Harrington, Crowther, and Shipherd, "Trauma, Binge Eating, and the 'Strong Black Woman,'" 469.

119. Jones and Shorter-Gooden, *Shifting,* 132.

120. Harrington, Crowther, and Shipherd, "Trauma, Binge Eating, and the 'Strong Black Woman,'" 470.

121. Ibid., 470, 475–76; Beauboeuf-Lafontant, *Behind the Mask,* 52.

in obesity, a visual marker of the physical distress caused by personifying the StrongBlackWoman, it does not challenge the myth itself. Beauboeuf-Lafontant explains, "Venting through eating is inadequate, not simply because a woman's anger is not voiced directly to others, but also because overweight on Black women is often viewed as a physical marker of their strength or their ability to endure."[122] Obesity as a consequence of binge eating is not only normalized; it is appropriated as reinforcement of the myth of strength.

In *Shifting*, Jones and Shorter-Gooden argue that shopping and an excessive focus on physical appearance may be additional compulsive behaviors utilized by StrongBlackWomen to cope with the emotional strain of personifying the role:

> In many cases Sisterella is an emotional overeater. She uses food as a way to fill the emptiness inside, as a strategy to garner the comfort and solace that seem unachievable through relationships, work, and other pursuits. Alternatively, Sisterella may attend almost obsessively to her outward physical appearance, worrying incessantly about her hair and her clothing, and she may spend an inordinate amount of her time and resources shopping—trying to distract herself from the depression by focusing on remaking herself.[123]

It is important to note that not all StrongBlackWomen spend copious amounts of money and time upon cosmetics, beauty products, or clothing. For those who do, however, this functions as an important strategy of impression management.[124] Looking good helps to preserve the StrongBlack-Woman's image of "having it all together."

---

122. Beauboeuf-Lafontant, *Behind the Mask*, 116.

123. Jones and Shorter-Gooden, *Shifting*, 126. What Jones and Shorter-Gooden identify as the "Sisterella complex" is a racial/gender-specific manifestation of depression resulting from extended "shifting," the process whereby African-American women continually sacrifice their needs and sense of self in order to accommodate the needs of others (ibid., 6–8). Sisterella can be understood as a woman who exhibits depression as part of the classic StrongBlackWoman stress pattern (ibid., 124).

124. Black women spend more money on cosmetics and beauty products than any other group of women in America. To some degree, this may be an attempt to "measure up" to a White middle-class standard of beauty. However, as Jones and Shorter-Gooden note, it is also a form of coping: "Many of them seem to sense that by creating an outward guise of beauty, comfort, and financial security, they will be able to camouflage the profound pain and insecurity they feel inside" (Jones and Shorter-Gooden, *Shifting*, 135).

The emphasis upon physical appearance as a means of impression management points to an important, yet easily overlooked, element in the classic StrongBlackWoman stress pattern: the erosion of relational health. One of the costs of the continual emotional regulation and impression management performed by the StrongBlackWoman is the loss of authentic relationships. For many Black women, the public personification of strength contaminates intimate relationships, inhibiting the development and maintenance of reciprocal relationships within which they can display emotional vulnerability, express personal needs, and ask for support.[125] As a result, StrongBlackWomen experience relational impairment across a wide variety of interpersonal bonds, perhaps most keenly in romantic relationships. Both Beauboeuf-Lafontant and Woods-Giscombé found that difficulty in romantic relationships was a common problem for women who personify the myth of strength.[126] In addition to the loss of intimacy, personification of the myth of strength has deleterious effects upon the individuals with whom StrongBlackWomen are in relationship. As StrongBlackWomen assume excessive responsibility for the lives of other individuals, those persons are less likely to be responsible for their own lives. Perhaps more importantly, those individuals are less likely to develop the capacity to discern and respond to the StrongBlackWoman's distress. This lack of reciprocity is further compounded when Black women socialize their daughters in the myth of strength. As the primary environment in which Black women learn to accommodate to the StrongBlackWoman, the mother-daughter relationship may also be one of the relationships most fundamentally altered by the strength discourse. In teaching their daughters to be strong, Black mothers "[demonstrate] little outward compassion for their daughters' mistakes . . . [and encourage] them to learn hard life lessons." Moreover, they emphasize that it is foolish to expect help and compassion from others.[127]

125. Beauboeuf-Lafontant states, "The discourse of strength effectively leaves no space in which a woman . . . can admit woundedness" (Beauboeuf-Lafontant, *Behind the Mask*, 78).

126. Ibid., 97; Woods-Giscombé, "Superwoman Schema," 13. One of Beauboeuf-Lafontant's interviewees, for example, stated, "I'm not very easy to *share* information. I even have to, um, work on that with my *husband*, because it's very hard to be a certain way all the [time] at work, and then come home and be this person that opens up and shares. . . . I have a problem of keeping a whole lot inside. . . . Weaknesses. Anything about us that could be perceived as a weakness" (Beauboeuf-Lafontant, *Behind the Mask*, 97).

127. Beauboeuf-Lafontant, *Behind the Mask*, 79–80. Beauboeuf-Lafontant further notes that teaching Black girls to be constantly vigilant for the needs of others serves a

Almost invariably, women who exhibit the classic StrongBlackWoman stress pattern reach a point of breakdown. The notion of breakdown appears fairly commonly in the narratives of clinicians and researchers who work with StrongBlackWomen, and I have frequently heard women describe it (even utilizing the term) in my ministerial work and clinical practice. And while the specific contours vary from woman to woman, breakdowns usually involve distinct and periods of incapacity to fulfill one's usual roles, often accompanied with acute emotional and/or physical distress. In her interviews, for example, Beauboeuf-Lafontant states that several participants acknowledged the occurrence of breakdowns among the StrongBlackWomen whom they knew: "As sudden and dramatic periods of retreat from their responsibilities to others, breakdowns took the form of leaving home for hours or days, staying in bed, committing suicide, and dying in one's sleep."[128] In her study of the health effects of the Superwoman role, Woods-Giscombé noted that college-educated women in the twenty-five- to forty-five-year-old age group were particularly likely to discuss feeling physically and mentally overwhelmed by stress to the point of "having breakdowns," "blowing up," or "exploding," often directing their frustration toward other people.[129] Yet, while the demands of the childbearing years may render women more susceptible to reaching the point of breakdown, women's narratives of older relatives who were admired for their strength also reveal the malignant underside of being a StrongBlackWoman. One woman, for example, reflected upon her grandmother's "strength" and the impact that it might have had on her health problems, which included obesity, diabetes, breast cancer, and a "nervous breakdown":

> But about this strong woman thing, I never saw my Nana cry. . . .
> I mean, my Nana had gone through a lot of physical pain. It wasn't
> until I was older, I was able to look back and evaluate her life af-
> ter she passed, that I realized that a lot of these things that she
> had gone through, might not have happened if she would have
> learned to cope with what she was going through. . . . So, then I
> thought about it, like, was that really a strength, if it weakens you
> physically?[130]

---

patriarchal function in that it "reassures boys and men that the girls and women in their families will provide them with a safety net of unconditional support to cushion them from the consequences of their behavior" (ibid., 83).

128. Ibid., 125.

129. Woods-Giscombé, "Superwoman Schema," 14–15.

130. Ibid., 15.

Unfortunately, for many StrongBlackWomen, reaching the point of emotional and/or physical breakdown does not necessarily lead them to question or break away from the imperative of strength. Perhaps the most pernicious aspect of the ecosocial model is its cyclical nature, wrought mainly by a process of appraisal through which women who have been socialized into the myth of strength continually evaluate their performance. Because strength is considered a hallmark of racial-gender authenticity as well as faith, when women who personify the StrongBlackWoman begin to experience breakdown, they interpret their suffering not as an indication of the injustice or lack of fit of the role, but rather as a sign of their insufficiency in adhering to the role.[131] This perception of failure is accompanied by shame, guilt, low self-esteem, and even depression.[132] Their response, very often, is to "double down" on personification—to work harder at suppressing affect, repressing needs, caring for others, and taking on additional responsibilities. Further reinforcing this process is the scrutiny of others, particularly other women who have been similarly socialized. One of Beauboeuf-Lafonfant's participants, for example, reported that older African-American women were particularly critical of her failure to "[measure] up to their views of what a strong and dutiful daughter should do" when she had difficulty managing the burden of being the sole caregiver for two terminally ill parents.[133]

Consequently, breakdowns are often followed by an apparent return to functioning. In fact, because breakdowns are frequently unobserved by others, they can serve a homeostatic function for StrongBlackWomen. That is, they allow a woman to put the façade of strength on hold temporarily so that she can release the pent-up frustration, depression, anger, and fatigue that the mantle of strength does not allow her to express. When the breakdown is over, she is able to return to her performance.[134] Beauboeuf-Lafontant labels this a form of "pseudo recovery" and warns against the

131. This pattern is consistent with the concept of gender ambivalence, which posits that when women begin to develop awareness of the consequences of their socialization, rather than critiquing the norms, they increase self-monitoring to heighten adherence to the norm. "In other words, one fights femininity with femininity, using the disciplinary tools of being a good woman to hold oneself in check when one's excess beyond such expectations becomes evident" (Beauboeuf-Lafontant, *Behind the Mask*, 48).

132. Harrington, Crowther, and Shipherd, "Trauma, Binge Eating, and the 'Strong Black Woman,'" 470.

133. Beauboeuf-Lafontant, *Behind the Mask*, 129.

134. Ibid., 127.

cultural (often religious) notion that Black women can utilize strength to fight depression and other mental-health problems. In particular, she advises health-care professionals to be cautious in accepting the word of Black women who claim to need only strength and faith, rather than treatment, to battle depression: "embracing the same behaviors that occasioned the depression episode would not lead to healing but to a 'pseudo recovery' characterized by presenting an image of composure to others 'in an effort to keep things stable and familiar.'"[135]

A significant implication of the secrecy surrounding breakdowns and health crises among StrongBlackWomen is that it may be difficult for pastoral caregivers and other health-care professionals to detect when a woman is suffering the adverse health effects associated with the ideology. StrongBlackWomen suffer in silence. More often than not, they do not appear distressed because it is important to their self-image to appear in control. This is particularly the case with depression and other mental-health issues, which they may attempt to counter by increasing activity and taking on additional responsibilities. Further, StrongBlackWomen suffering from depression may go unnoticed because they do not clearly exhibit the traditional clinical picture of depression, that is, a person who is fatigued, lethargic, or gloomy.[136] The attempt to counter mental- and physical-health problems with increased adherence to the myth of strength often results in delayed help-seeking among StrongBlackWomen as well as symptom underreporting and minimization when they do finally seek treatment.[137] Such delays can prove to have serious, perhaps even deadly, consequences when they prevent screening and early detection of potentially fatal diseases that are treatable if caught in the early stages, such as breast and colon cancer.[138] In addition, they may have difficulty complying with treatment since taking care of oneself requires acknowledging that one has a self that is worthy of care. The irony of the classic StrongBlackWoman response pattern, then, is that the very factors that cause it—selflessness, overactivity, and excessive self-sufficiency—may also cause clinicians and researchers to overlook it.[139] And they may drain Black women of strength when they need it most—when facing serious health crises.

135. Beauboeuf-Lafontant, "You Have to Show Strength," 46.

136. Jones and Shorter-Gooden, *Shifting*, 128, 130.

137. Harrington, Crowther, and Shipherd, "Trauma, Binge Eating, and the 'Strong Black Woman,'" 476.

138. Woods-Giscombé, "Superwoman Schema," 17.

139. Jones and Shorter-Gooden, *Shifting*, 124.

Emerging Evidence of the StrongBlackWoman and Health Connection

Given the centrality of the myth of strength in the lives of Black women and its impact upon their health, the StrongBlackWoman may be one of the most understudied topics in health research.[140] To date, there are few empirical studies examining the relationship between adherence to the StrongBlackWoman and health outcomes. Some of the earliest work in this area has been done by Cheryl Woods-Giscombé. In her unpublished doctoral dissertation, Giscombé found that 24 percent of a sample of African-American women felt that "it is best for me to deny or hide personal conflicts or difficulties to present an image of strength for my family, friends, and community." Women who endorsed this item reported higher levels of distress, greater difficulty stopping negative thoughts or ideas, more emotional eating, and higher levels of extreme obesity.[141]

In a separate study, Woods-Giscombé used focus group methodology to develop a framework that operationalizes the Superwoman/StrongBlack-Woman role and to develop an assessment instrument to measure it and examine its impact on health.[142] Participants identified five themes as central to the StrongBlackWoman role: (1) obligation to demonstrate strength, (2) obligation to suppress emotions, (3) resistance to being vulnerable or dependent, (4) determination to succeed despite limited resources, and (5) obligation to help others.[143] The women in the focus groups clearly perceive the pressure to be strong to be both external and burdensome, saying

140. Woods-Giscombé, "Superwoman Schema," 15. Woods-Giscombé points out that much of the health research on the StrongBlackWoman has been incidental, with researchers effectually stumbling upon the phenomenon in the process of investigating other issues related to physical and psychological health.

141. Ibid., 18.

142. Ibid., 4–6. Woods-Giscombé utilized a community-based sample of forty-eight African-American women recruited via flyers posted at local colleges, clinics, hair salons, libraries, recreation and cultural centers, and government agencies. The sample ranged in age from nineteen to seventy-two years (mean = thirty-four) and was diverse with respect to education (18 percent did not complete high school but 31 percent had at least a four-year degree), employment (64 percent were employed; 40 percent were current students), and marital status (60 percent single, 10 percent married, 15 percent in committed relationship, and 15 percent divorced, separated, or widowed). Most (65 percent) were mothers. The median annual household income was $26,000–$50,000 (34 percent); however, 41 percent of the sample earned less than $15,000 annually. Eight focus groups were conducted, each comprised of five or six participants and lasting two hours.

143. Ibid., 6.

"they were expected to be strong even when they didn't feel like doing so."[144] Some women reported being able to compartmentalize the obligation of strength, performing it only in work settings.[145] Others, however, stated that they felt particular pressure to perform the StrongBlackWoman role within family relationships. This was particularly true for women who were older than 45 and college-educated, who reported feeling the need to present an image of strength for the sake of their children, parents, and other family and friends.[146]

Participants in Woods-Giscombé's study identified three negative consequences to the StrongBlackWoman role: strain in interpersonal relationships; increase in stress-related health behaviors; and increase in somatic symptoms.[147] They connected the StrongBlackWoman's tendencies toward overwork with several stress-related health behaviors, including lack of sleep, emotional and binge eating, and smoking. For example, one participant stated that being so busy during the day often caused her to skip meals until nighttime, when she ate enough "to make up for the two or three meals that [she] missed during the day." Another actually expressed guilt over sleeping during periods of stress: "Cause I feel like, while I'm asleep I could be doing this, this, and this."[148] There were significant developmental and class differences in women's experiences of the negative consequences of adhering to the myth of strength. Postponement of self-care was especially pronounced among two groups of women: (1) college-educated and professional women in the twenty-five- to forty-five-year-old age range; and (2) and women over the age of forty-five who did not have a college education. These women were especially likely to report feeling physically drained because they were constantly taking care of others, feeling guilty when they took time for themselves, and feeling that they were losing themselves.[149] Woods-Giscombé's findings also pointed to the impact of trauma in the lives of StrongBlackWomen. Many of the women reported having no one whom they could depend upon when

144. Ibid., 7.

145. Ibid.

146. Ibid., 6. This finding is particularly important in that it is one of the first to illuminate how developmental processes may impact conformity to and the effects of the StrongBlackWoman role.

147. Ibid., 13.

148. Ibid., 13–14.

149. Ibid., 14.

growing up. Others reported being victimized, or witnessing their mothers' victimization, in romantic relationships. Women without college education were especially likely to describe such experiences.[150]

The role of traumatic experiences was also pronounced in a 2010 study conducted by Harrington, Crowther, and Shipherd. In what is likely the most rigorous empirical examination of the StrongBlackWoman, the authors examined whether and how personification of the role mediates the relationship between trauma and binge eating among African-American women.[151] Harrington and colleagues suggested that Black women who are trauma survivors may be at particularly heightened risk for suffering the deleterious effects of the role since the image does not allow Black women to experience or express vulnerability or distress.[152] In a sample of African-American female trauma survivors, the authors tested a culturally specific model of binge eating in which they hypothesized that: (1) trauma exposure/distress would be positively associated with internalization of the StrongBlackWoman ideology; (2) such internalization would be positively associated with emotional inhibition, self-silencing, and prioritizing others' needs over one's own; and (3) emotional inhibition, self-silencing, and prioritizing others' needs would be associated with binge eating.[153] The data provided support for their model.[154] Harrington and colleagues

150. Ibid., 11–12.

151. Specifically, the authors suggest that women who have experienced trauma "may cling even more firmly to [the StrongBlackWoman's] dictates as they struggle to find culturally sanctioned ways to cope with traumatic experiences" (Harrington, Crowther, and Shipherd, "Trauma, Binge Eating, and the 'Strong Black Woman'" 470).

152. Ibid.

153. Ibid., 471–75. Participants included 179 African-American women who reported a lifetime experience of at least one traumatic event. Participants were recruited from multiple sites, including a hospital-based internal medicine clinic, undergraduate courses, faculty/staff mailings, and word of mouth. The sample was well educated (77.4 percent had attended some college or earned a trade school or associate's degree) and largely single (68.0 percent had never been married). However, almost half (46.6 percent) reported annual household incomes below $25,000. Participants reported an average of 6.02 traumatic events, with the most common exposures being witnessing family violence before age sixteen (reported by 44.1 percent of the sample), sexual harassment (34.1 percent), emotional abuse/neglect (27.4 percent), serious accident or accident-related injury (26.8 percent), and abuse/physical attack by an acquaintance (24.0 percent). Participants completed self-report surveys that included measures of trauma exposure and distress, binge eating, emotional regulation, self-silencing, and adherence to the StrongBlackWoman ideology.

154. Ibid., 476. Specifically, their data found that trauma exposure/distress

summarize: "The results suggest that emotional regulation difficulties and using eating to fulfill psychological needs are crucial mechanisms through which [StrongBlackWoman] ideology impacts African-American trauma survivors' binge eating. These women appear to use binge eating to manage negative affect associated with their traumatic experiences."[155]

Taken together, these results provide convincing, albeit preliminary results for the ecosocial model of the StrongBlackWoman. They suggest that social relationships and environmental factors are pivotal in socializing Black women into the role of the StrongBlackWoman. Personification of this role is accompanied by significant role strain and distress, which not only diminish health behaviors but also encourage the development of maladaptive coping strategies, including emotional and binge eating. Over time, this pattern results in the embodiment of stress via physical and emotional health problems. Finally, because women interpret these problems as evidence of insufficient role fulfillment, they cling even more firmly to the ideology in hopes of better managing their distress.

Suggestions for Pastoral Practice

- Because minimizing the appearance of distress is a central element of the StrongBlackWoman role, pastoral caregivers may find it difficult to discern parishioners who are in need of care. How, then, can pastors be proactive in identifying and addressing this issue in their congregations?

- When presented together, the data on Black women's health issues are overwhelming, perhaps even depressing. Often, when we become overwhelmed by the magnitude of social concerns, we become paralyzed. Fortunately, the church has a rich history of the practice of lament, especially in the Scriptures in the Hebrew canon. Consider drawing upon this history to develop individual and/or corporate rituals of lament for the health crisis among African-American women. Some possibilities include writing a psalm of lament or holding a candlelight vigil in which people can call out the names of women

---

significantly increased Black women's adherence to the StrongBlackWoman ideology, which consequently led to increased emotional regulation and self-silencing. Emotional regulation, in turn, increased the likelihood of emotional eating and consequently binge eating.

155. Ibid., 474–75.

who are battling the negative health consequences of internalizing the StrongBlackWoman. It is important that our practices of lament recognize the systemic forces of racism, sexism, and classism that result in the burden of the StrongBlackWoman, rather than simply blaming the health crisis upon the sins of Black women.

3

"To Carry Your Burden in the Heat of the Day"

Racism, Sexism, and the Making of the StrongBlackWoman

> In addition to combating the damage imposed on their communities, oppressed people often try to develop and instill values that differ drastically from those communicated by the dominant culture, especially when they recognize the role that values play in the social world of their oppressor. Sometimes oppressed people must create roles that do not exist in the societies that oppress them, and sometimes they must radically reorganize the content of roles that already exist. In the African-American experience, such innovation and resistance has been a response to the constant pressure to devise "a way out of no way."[1]

America prides itself on its individualism, particularly the notion that "we are what we make of ourselves." American nationalist rhetoric heavily emphasizes the virtues of liberty and freedom of conscience.

1. Gilkes, "*If It Wasn't for the Women . . .*," 143–44.

This emphasis obscures what scholars of race and gender studies take for granted: individual identity—especially as it relates to race and gender—is not formed in a vacuum, but is heavily dependent upon cultural constructions of what it means to be human, to be male or female, and to be Black, White, or Latina. In this chapter, I will discuss the historical and contemporary factors that have shaped the StrongBlackWoman as the dominant ideological model of identity for African-American women. After all, given the clearly negative consequences of the ideology of the StrongBlackWoman, two questions that beg to be asked are: How have Black women come to uphold this model of identity? Further, why do they socialize their daughters into its precepts? In chapter 1, I suggested conceptualizing the StrongBlackWoman as a suit of armor, in particular because it illuminates the archetype's defensive function. A person does not don a suit of armor unless she is under attack or she expects that she is vulnerable to attack. For African-American women, the StrongBlackWoman functions as a collective defensive strategy designed to mitigate the cultural assault of White patriarchal racism, an assault that has deemed Black femininity as deficient, immoral, unattractive, and altogether inferior to the hegemonic ideal of White femininity.

In this chapter, I describe the cultural assault that has resulted in the evolution and reinforcement of the StrongBlackWoman. Specifically, drawing upon Patricia Hill Collins' conceptualization of stereotypes as controlling images, I argue that the StrongBlackWoman is a controlling image developed in large part by African-American women as a photonegative of the historically dominant images of Black femininity. Further, using womanist historians' analyses of Black women's organizing within and beyond the church, I describe the systematic efforts of the Black women's club movement and Black churchwomen to "spread the gospel" of Black women's strength.

Racism's Cultural Assault against Black Women

A crucial feature of White racism has been its assault on the character and identities of Black men and women through the development and promulgation of negative stereotypes.[2] Throughout much of their history, Afri-

2. Gilkes argues that "African-American women have been the victims of the longest, most sustained cultural assault experienced by any racial-ethnic-gender group" (ibid., 197).

can-American women's identities have been popularly portrayed by three derogatory, and interconnecting, stereotypes: the Jezebel, the Mammy, and the matriarch. Originating during slavery, these images were not cultural outliers but were central to the American popular imagination and were buttressed by artistic imagery. By the early twentieth century, bolstering racist images was a standard function of "'technologies of power' at the everyday level—films, school textbooks, art, newspapers—[that] produced and disseminated a 'rhetoric of violence' . . . in the form of negative caricaturing and stereotyping."[3] A classic example is D. W. Griffith's 1915 film, *The Birth of a Nation*. Negative images such as these were not simply descriptive, that is, they did not function only to describe how Whites viewed Blacks. They were also prescriptive; that is, they influenced White expectations and perceptions of Black women—including their behavioral and moral attributes and their capacities to function as "good citizens" of a democratic society—and they ultimately lent justification to the unequal treatment of Blacks.

In her classic text *Black Feminist Thought*, Patricia Hill Collins refers to racial and gender stereotypes as "controlling images," illuminating the fact that they functioned to legitimate the oppression and brutal treatment of African-American women:

> As part of a generalized ideology of domination, stereotypical images of Black womanhood take on special meaning. Because the authority to define societal values is a major instrument of power, elite groups, in exercising power, manipulate ideas about Black womanhood. They do so by exploiting already existing symbols, or creating new ones. . . . These controlling images are designed to make racism, sexism, poverty, and other forms of social injustice appear to be natural, normal, and inevitable parts of everyday life.[4]

Collins further argues that much of the power of controlling images comes from their self-perpetuating capacity: "Even when the initial conditions that foster controlling images disappear, such images prove remarkably tenacious because they not only subjugate U.S. Black women but are key in maintaining intersecting oppressions."[5] Thus, the stereotypes about African-American womanhood perform a critical function in maintaining the societal status quo.

3. Higginbotham, *Righteous Discontent,* 189.

4. Collins, *Black Feminist Thought*, 69.

5. Ibid.

Jezebels, Mammies, and Matriarchs

The stereotypes of Black femininity are not mutually exclusive but are closely interconnected and often overlapping. Fundamental to each stereotype are myths about Black women's hypersexuality. The maintenance of the American slaveocracy depended upon White slaveowners' power to control and manipulate Black women's reproductive capacities, in essence, their power to turn women into breeders of human commodities. And because a distinguishing feature of Western race-based slavery was the intergenerational transmission of slave status from mother to child, maximizing profit in the slave economy depended, at least in part, upon maximizing childbearing by enslaved Black women. Given the control that White men had over Black women's bodies, it is no wonder then that a prominent characteristic of the American slave economy was the widespread sexual abuse of enslaved Black women.[6] While sexual assault of Black women usually took place in secret, its consequences were highly visible, most notably in the proliferation of children who clearly bore the imprint of their slave masters. The increased need for social and legal sanction of White male rapaciousness gave birth to the Jezebel image.[7]

In the Hebrew canon, Jezebel was a Phoenician princess who married Ahab, the king of Israel. Perhaps the preeminent "bad girl" of the Bible, Jezebel was notorious for her cunning, deceit, and immorality. Under her influence, Scripture notes, Ahab did more evil than any other Israelite king: "Indeed, there was no one like Ahab, who sold himself to do what was evil in the sight of the Lord, urged on by his wife Jezebel" (1 Kgs 21:25). Not content to maintain her cultural worship of Baal as an individual, she led the king, and hence all of Israel, to do the same. Further, she directly challenged the authority of YHWH, killing the Lord's prophets, likely instigating the epic battle between Elijah and the prophets of Baal, and defying the divinely instituted rules surrounding land ownership (1 Kgs 18:4; 18:15–46; 21:1–16). Jezebel remained unrepentant to the point of death;

---

6. For an extensive treatment of enslaved Black women's experiences of rape, see the work of Clinton, including "'With a Whip in His Hand'" and "Caught in the Web of the Big House."

7. Clinton notes, "Members of the southern planter class who recorded their critiques of slavery did not often attack the immorality of owners. Most bemoaned the immorality of slaves. The few who acknowledged that male planters could and did fall from grace treat the matter casually, offering a variety of lame excuses ranging from *black female promiscuity* to protection of white women from sexual licentiousness" (Clinton, "'Caught in the Web,'" 22; my italics).

she confronted her death by painting her eyes and adorning her head and taunting Jehu, then king of Israel (2 Kgs 9:30–37).

Within the American slaveocracy, the Jezebel label was quickly applied to the Black women whose enslaved status prevented them from conforming to the Victorian standards of femininity. In a culture that prized female modesty, Black women were deemed deficient because they gathered their skirts around their legs while performing physical labor, thus exposing their naked ankles and lower legs. But the most damning charge against Black femininity was their persistence in conceiving and giving birth to children out of wedlock, a phenomenon that could only be explained as proof of their immorality. Just as in the biblical narrative, the Jezebel stereotype positioned enslaved Black women as societal scapegoats, in this case as manipulative, immoral seductresses who possessed an extraordinary capacity to overwhelm the moral sensibilities of otherwise good (and often married) Christian White men and to coerce them into illicit sexual encounters. The Jezebel image functioned "to relegate all Black women to the category of sexually aggressive women, thus providing a powerful rationale for the widespread sexual assaults by White men typically reported by Black slave women."[8]

This depiction of Black women was neither incidental nor innocuous. Melissa Harris-Perry explains it this way: "Hypersexuality was more than a demeaning and false stereotype; this inaccurate portrayal was intentional. Myth advances specific economic, social, and political motives. In this case, sexual lasciviousness was a deliberate characterization that excused both profit-driven and casual sexual exploitation of black women."[9] The Jezebel stereotype was the first and most predominant image of Black womanhood in the United States precisely because it was critical to maintaining not only the American slave economy, but the ideology of White supremacy and Black inferiority as a whole. It reinforced the oft-cited justification for slavery, namely that enslavement was a way to "tame the savage, sexual nature of Africans, who, some thought, sank so low as to mate with orangutans."[10] Both during and following slavery, the notion of Black women's hypersexuality helped to reinforce the notion of White moral superiority by justifying—and indeed, rendering invisible and unnameable—the immorality, cruelty, and brutality of the U.S. racial hierarchy.[11]

8. Collins, *Black Feminist Thought*, 81.

9. Harris-Perry, *Sister Citizen*, 56.

10. White, *Too Heavy a Load*, 13.

11. Melissa Harris-Perry writes, "The idea that black women were hypersexual beings

Representations of the Jezebel stereotype were not simply relegated to oral folklore, but were buttressed by the emerging mythmaking technologies of the era. By the early twentieth century, popular media had been profoundly successful in their depiction of Black womanhood as the epitome of moral pathology, as is well typified in a 1904 newspaper quote of a White woman: "Negro women evidence more nearly the popular idea of total depravity than the men do. . . . When a man's mother, wife and daughters are all immoral women, there is no room in his fallen nature for the aspiration of honor and virtue. . . . I cannot imagine such a creation as a virtuous black woman."[12] In other words, it was not only that Black women themselves were immoral; they were responsible for the deviance of the race.

However, the successful dissemination of the Jezebel stereotype created a problem for slaveowners. After all, the same Black women who were accused of being inherently licentious were also vested with the responsibility of caring for White households: preparing their meals, cleaning their homes, nursing and rearing their children. There was a vast disjuncture between White society's belief in the moral turpitude of Black women and their utter dependence upon these women to care for their families and homes. A second controlling image was needed to mitigate the character defects of the Jezebel: the Mammy. Usually depicted as an older, overweight, dark-skinned woman, Mammy was an idealized caregiver for White families. Indeed, her central characteristics were caregiving and deference to White authority.[13] The Mammy was maternal, submissive, loyal, obedient, amiable, and non-threatening, even if sometimes sassy. She was utterly devoted to her owners/employers and eager to care for their needs, even to the neglect of her own family if necessary. In contrast to the Jezebel's conniving and promiscuity, the Mammy was often religious, asexual, and devoid of any personal desires that might tempt her to sin. Beyond her domestic duties, she was a confidante and moral guide, keeping her young charges in line. In essence, as Harris-Perry describes, Mammy was trustworthy enough to be given the responsibility for taking care of the most intimate needs of White children and families:

> Unlike the bad black woman who was aggressively sexual, Mammy had no personal needs or desires. She was a trusted adviser and confidante whose skills were used exclusively in service of

---

created space for white moral superiority by justifying the brutality of Southern white men" (Harris-Perry, *Sister Citizen*, 55).

12. Higginbotham, *Righteous Discontent*, 190.

13. Collins, *Black Feminist Thought*, 74.

the white families to which she was attached. Mammy was not a protector or defender of black children or communities. She represented a maternal ideal, but not in caring for her own children. Her love, doting, advice, correction, and supervision were reserved exclusively for white women and children. Her loyal affection to white men, women, and children was entirely devoid of sexual desire.[14]

Originating during slavery, the Mammy became the dominant image of Black women during reconstruction. In the South, in particular, it was critical in revisionist efforts to reinterpret, and legitimate, the legacy of chattel slavery and racial oppression. In 1923, for example, a Mississippi senator and the United Daughters of the Confederacy proposed the erection of a statue on the National Mall memorializing "The Black Mammy of the South."[15] Yet there is considerable evidence that, like the Jezebel, the Mammy was a figure that existed almost exclusively within White racist imaginations and had very little basis in reality. Harris-Perry, for example, notes that domestic servants were most often teenagers or young women, not "grandmotherly types. . . . It was white supremacist imaginations that remembered these powerless, coerced slave girls as soothing, comfortable, consenting women."[16] Further, Collins' observation that the life expectancy of enslaved women was 33.6 years affirms that Mammy was a largely mythical figure with little basis in the lived experiences of Black women.[17]

Nevertheless, the Mammy remains a highly romanticized figure within the American popular imagination. While modern racial sensibilities have increased awareness about the racist implications of the image, vestiges of the Mammy endure in portrayals of Black women as nurturing, good caretakers, strong, supportive, and selfless. In popular culture, the Mammy figure is a ubiquitous character in advertising, television, and film, from the smiling face of Aunt Jemima to the headless Mammy Two-Shoes character in the *Tom and Jerry* cartoons to the sassy yet supportive character that many African-American actresses play relative to White stars (such as Miranda Bailey in *Grey's Anatomy*, Ivy in Disney's *Good Luck Charlie*, and Mercedes in the hit series *Glee*). The Mammy is such a widespread representation of African-American women that Andy Warhol included a painting of the icon in his 1981 *Myths* series, along with mythological

14. Harris-Perry, *Sister Citizen*, 72–73.

15. "Unique Monument for Commemorating Virtues of 'Mammy.'"

16. Harris-Perry, *Sister Citizen*, 72.

17. Collins, *Black Feminist Thought*, 51.

and folklore characters such as Santa Claus, Superman, and Mickey Mouse. In her book *Mammy: A Century of Race, Gender, and Southern Memory*, Kimberly Wallace-Sanders writes,

> "Mammy" is part of the lexicon of antebellum mythology that continues to have a provocative and tenacious hold on the American psyche. Her large dark body and her round smiling face tower over our imaginations, causing more accurate representations of African American women to wither in her shadow. The mammy's stereotypical attributes—her deeply sonorous and effortlessly soothing voice, her infinite patience, her raucous laugh, her self-deprecating wit, her implicit understanding and acceptance of her inferiority and her devotion to whites—all point to a long-lasting and troubled marriage of racial and gender essentialism, mythology, and southern nostalgia.[18]

While both the Jezebel and the Mammy stereotypes had unique roles in maintaining the slave economy, when taken together they provided powerful justifications for the brutal treatment of Black women:

> If Black slave women could be portrayed as having excessive sexual appetites, then increased fertility should be the expected outcome. By suppressing the nurturing that African-American women might give their own children which would strengthen Black family networks, and by forcing Black women to work in the field, "wet nurse" White children, and emotionally nurture their White owners, slave owners effectively tied the controlling images of jezebel and mammy to the economic exploitation inherent in the institution of slavery.[19]

By relegating Black women to two roles, reproduction and domestic labor, which were deemed to be their "natural" functions, the combined effect of the Jezebel and Mammy stereotypes was to underscore Black women's lack of fitness for citizenship in the new nation.[20] Genetically incapable of upholding the societal standard of what it meant to be a "true" woman (which

18. Wallace-Sanders, *Mammy*, 2.

19. Collins, *Black Feminist Thought*, 81–82.

20. Harris-Perry notes that the Jezebel myth was particularly important to the emerging identity of the new republic. "The idea of black women's sexual wantonness was important to late nineteenth- and early twentieth-century nation-building efforts. Race and gender science informed public ideas of who was capable of citizenship as the country reestablished the basis of political participation following the Civil War" (Harris-Perry, *Sister Citizen*, 57).

I explain below), Black women's usefulness to society was deemed to be limited to their roles as breeders and caregivers, roles that they best fulfilled when under the control and direction of "responsible" White citizens. Thus, slavery—and later sharecropping and Jim Crow segregation—was considered the best way for Black women's co-existence with "civilized" society.

While vestiges of the the Jezebel and Mammy stereotypes persist even today, by the mid-twentieth century, the power of both images had begun to wane. After slavery ended, the myth of Black women's promiscuity no longer played the same role in maintaining the economic and social order.[21] And while the myth of the devoted, asexual servant was important to an economic system in which Black women were most freqently employed as domestic laborers in White households, by itself the Mammy image provided insufficient control over Black women's behavior.[22] Thus, a third image—the matriarch—was born. The Mammy and the matriarch are closely related, but distinct in important ways. "While the mammy typifies the Black mother figure in white homes, the matriarch symbolizes the mother figure in black homes. Just as the mammy represents the 'good' Black mother, the matriarch symbolizes the 'bad' Black mother."[23] The matriarch is, in essence, "a failed mammy."[24] She possesses significant domestic skills and devotes much of her time to taking care of others. But her caregiving has a sharp edge. She is quick-tempered, aggressive, argumentative, domineering, unfeminine, and emasculating, particularly towards her Black male counterparts. The matriarch is also often known by other names, including the sapphire, named after the character of Sapphire Stevens on the *Amos and Andy* radio and television show and, more recently, the "angry Black woman."[25]

The notion of the matriarch began to emerge through the writings of E. Franklin Frazier and W. E. B. Du Bois, both of whom described relationships between Black female-headed households, the centrality of women

21. Ibid., 71.

22. Collins, *Black Feminist Thought*, 74.

23. Ibid., 75.

24. Ibid.

25. Derived from stereotypic portrayals of African Americans, *Amos and Andy* was initially created, written, and voiced for radio by two White men beginning in the late 1920s. When the show premiered on television in 1951, it featured the recurring female characters of Sapphire Stevens and her mother, Queen, both of whom embodied the matriarch stereotype. Sapphire was loud, nosey, argumentative, and combative toward men. Her mother was domineering and aggressive.

in Black family networks, and Black poverty.[26] As Collins notes, however, both of these authors believed that matriarchal family structures were the result, not the cause, of racial oppression and poverty.[27] This understanding shifted during the 1960s, when "what began as a muted theme . . . grew into a full-blown racialized image."[28] A critical event was the publication of the Moynihan Report in 1965, wherein the matriarch first received scholarly attention. I will describe this report, and its impact upon public perceptions of African-American women, in more detail in chapter four. I mention it here solely to point out its importance in shaping a new national stereotype of African-American women's identities. It seems that just as African Americans made tremendous gains in accessing opportunities for educational, occupational, political, and social advancement, U.S. culture was also giving shape to a new controlling image by which to constrain African-American women's identities.

A number of scholars, including Collins and Harris-Perry, have illuminated how the matriarch stereotype functions to uphold the status quo of racial-gender oppression in the U.S. In particular, the matriarch plays an important role in masking oppression by attributing political and economic inequalities to Black mothers' failure to provide sufficient attention and nurture to their children and to model appropriate gender behavior.[29] As Harris-Perry notes, the matriarch is essentially a silencing technique: "The angry black woman myth renders sisters both invisible and mute."[30] It obfuscates the real, structural causes of the economic, health, and interpersonal struggles of African-American women by displacing blame onto Black women themselves. And it prevents many Black women from speak-

---

26. For example, in his essay "The Damnation of Women," Du Bois states, "As I look about me today in this veiled world of mine, despite the noisier and more spectacular advance of my brothers, I instinctively feel and know that it is the five million women of my race who really count. Black women (and women whose grandmothers were black) are today furnishing our teachers; they are the main pillars of those social settlements which we call churches; and they have with small doubt raised three-fourths of our church property. If we have today, as seems likely, over a billion dollars of accumulated goods, who shall say how much of it has been wrung from the hearts of servant girls and washerwomen and women toilers in the fields? As makers of two million homes these women are today seeking in marvelous ways to show forth our strength and beauty and our conception of the truth" (308).

27. Collins, *Black Feminist Thought*, 75.

28. Ibid.

29. Ibid., 76–77.

30. Harris-Perry, *Sister Citizen*, 88.

ing up about the true realities of their lives due to concerns that they will be labeled "angry." This, in turn, functions as a warning to women of other racial/ethnic backgrounds. Collins notes that the matriarch image played a particularly important role in controlling White women in the post-World War II era, a period in which White women were entering the labor market in increasing numbers and thus challenging their long-proscribed roles as subordinate helpmates. "In this context, the image of the Black matriarch serves as a powerful symbol for both Black and White women of what can go wrong if White patriarchal power is challenged. Aggressive, assertive women are penalized—they are abandoned by their men, end up impoverished, and are stigmatized as being unfeminine."[31] Further, Collins notes that the stereotype of the matriarch has a pronounced negative effect on heterosexual relationships. The image functions to shape Black male desire, in that it maintains the image of White womanhood as the feminine ideal. "The matriarch or overly strong Black woman has also been used to influence Black men's understandings of Black masculinity. Many Black men reject Black women as marital partners, claiming that Black women are less desirable than White ones because we are too assertive."[32]

Fallen Women and True Women

The stereotypes of Black women's identities did not develop in isolation. Rather, they were part of a complex system of racial and gender ideology. Consequently, it is impossible to consider the images of the Jezebel, the Mammy, and the matriarch—or African-American women's defensive reaction against them—without discussing cultural constructions of White womanhood. During the antebellum period, the dominant model of femininity for upper-class and middle-class White women was what is known as the cult of true womanhood.[33] The dominance of the cult of true

31. Collins, *Black Feminist Thought*, 77.

32. Ibid.

33. The term *cult* does not refer to a religious sect but rather points to the level of veneration held by society for this model of womanhood. A number of authors have identified the cult of true womanhood as the hegemonic femininity of the nineteenth century. Hazel Carby, for example, labels it "the most popular social convention of female sexuality" (Carby, *Reconstructing Womanhood*, 21). Michelle Wallace alleges that "the cult of true womanhood and the republican family ideal were actually two sides of the same coin, for an appropriately behaved woman was seen during this period as the cornerstone of a stable home, and by extension, a stable nation" (Wallace, *Black Macho*, 7).

womanhood refers to both its popularity and its control. Not only was it the model of femininity most frequently ascribed, it was also the clear standard by which women were evaluated and judged to be, or not to be, feminine.[34] From the 1820s until the Civil War, the cult of true womanhood defined the boundaries of appropriate female behavior, both within and outside the home.[35] Driven by northern industrialization and the ensuing development of the middle class, it was the means by which middle-class White women could aspire to upperclass ladyhood.[36] As Hazel Carby has stated, "the ideology of true womanhood was as racialized a concept in relation to white women as it was in its exclusion of black womanhood."[37] According to the standards of White patriarchal racism, Black womanhood was "fallen" inasmuch as it departed from the ideals of true womanhood.

Barbara Welter has conducted the most thorough analysis of the cult of true womanhood. Surveying women's literature, cookbooks, and hundreds of religious tracts and sermons published between 1820 and 1860, Welter documents the extent to which the ideology was embedded within U.S. culture.[38] Welter identifies four cardinal virtues of true womanhood: piety, purity, submissiveness, and domesticity.[39] Religious piety was the central pillar of the cult of true womanhood. It was considered the source of women's strength, which was demonstrated largely through suffering.[40] The writer of *Godey's Lady's Book*, for example, admonished that "to suffer and to be silent under suffering seems the great command [woman] has to obey."[41] Further, beyond sustaining women through their suffering, religious piety was valued because it helped to tranquilize women, preventing restlessness and unhappiness, and also because it did not compete with

34. Carby, *Reconstructing Womanhood*, 23.

35. Ibid.

36. Giddings, *When and Where I Enter*, 47; Riggs, *Awake, Arise, and Act*, 68.

37. Carby, *Reconstructing Womanhood*, 55.

38. Welter, "Cult of True Womanhood," 151. Welter's survey of women's literature included magazines (almost all of the magazines that were published for more than a three-year period as well as a sampling of magazines published for less than three years); all the gift books cited in Ralph Thompson's *American Literary Annuals and Gift Books, 1825–1865*; hundreds of religious tracts and sermons in the American Unitarian Society and the Galatea Collection of the Boston Public Library; and the collection of cookbooks housed in the New York Public Library and the Academy of Medicine of New York.

39. Ibid.

40. Ibid, 152.

41. Quoted in Welter, "Cult of True Womanhood," 162.

women's domestic responsibilities.[42] Purity was also particularly essential to the true womanhood ideology. Its absence was both "unnatural and unfeminine. Without it she was, in fact, no woman at all, but a member of some lower order."[43] The sexual innocence of the true woman was explicitly posited over and against the sexual immorality of the Jezebel. "The cult of true womanhood relied upon this backdrop of black female 'non-women' in order to more clearly define true womanhood as white, frail, and virtuous—everything that black women supposedly were not."[44] Even the thought of losing one's purity was considered sufficient to reduce a woman to tears. Madness or death was thought to be the fate of any woman who was impure.[45]

Another defining feature of the true woman was domesticity, which refers not only to women's supposed skills and abilities but also to the social location in which they were to exercise those skills. The gender norms of the antebellum period took seriously the notion that "a woman's place is in the home." Public space was the domain of men, specifically White men. Women, in contrast, were largely confined to the home, a confinement so severe that several scholars liken it to imprisonment.[46] "The true woman's exclusive role was as homemaker, mother, housewife, and family tutor of the social and moral graces. Isolated within the home, women 'raised' men above lusty temptation while keeping themselves beyond its rapacious grasp. Women's imprisonment in the home virtually guaranteed piety and purity."[47] Likewise, women's confinement to the domestic sphere, and their consequent dependence upon male financial support, also helped to assure the fourth cardinal virtue of the cult of true womanhood, submissiveness. "Submission was perhaps the most feminine virtue expected of women. Men were supposed to be religious, although they rarely had time for it, and supposed to be pure, although it came awfully hard to them, but men

---

42. Ibid., 153.

43. Ibid., 154.

44. Jenkins, *Private Lives, Proper Relations*, 7.

45. Welter, "Cult of True Womanhood," 151.

46. Welter states, "Woman, in the cult of True Womanhood presented by the women's magazines, gift annuals, and religious literature of the nineteenth century, was the hostage in the home" (ibid.).

47. Giddings, *When and Where I Enter*, 47.

were the movers, the doers, the actors. Women were the passive, submissive responders. The order of dialogue was, of course, fixed in Heaven."[48]

A true woman, then, was one who was innocent, passive, incapable of navigating the outside world, and utterly dependent upon men for financial support and protection. She was one who maintained a semblance of perpetual childhood.[49] In other words, she was weak, especially when viewed against the backdrop of the perceived physical and emotional strength of Black women. The women's literature of the nineteenth century suggested that a woman who failed to live up to the attributes of true womanhood was prone to tragedy, madness, and even death. After all, the fact that the religious literature of the era championed the cult of true womanhood signified that its tenets were divinely ordained. Indeed, "if anyone, male or female, dared to tamper with the complex of virtues which made up True Womanhood, he was damned immediately as an enemy of God, of civilization and of the Republic."[50]

The combined effect of the negative stereotypical images of Black womanhood and the idealized image of White femininity in the cult of true womanhood placed Black women in a very complicated position. On the one hand, they were vehemently opposed to popular misperception of them as "fallen" women, that is, as Jezebels, mammies, and matriarchs. Individually and collectively, they worked to counter these images. On the other hand, Black women did not want to wholeheartedly aspire to the cult of true womanhood. Their exclusion from the cult had left them with an oppositional gaze toward it.[51] Like others, they had internalized the notion of White women's weakness and they wanted no part of it. Indeed, they did not believe it possible for Black women to be weak. They were, after all, survivors of the most brutal system of genetically transmitted chattel slavery in world history. If there was anything that Black women could salvage about

48. Welter, "Cult of True Womanhood," 158–59.

49. Ibid., 160.

50. Ibid., 152.

51. The term "oppositional gaze" was coined by bell hooks to describe a strategy of resistance whereby oppressed peoples learn to critique the worldview of the powerful. She states, "Spaces of agency exist for black people, wherein we can both interrogate the gaze of the Other but also look back, and at one another, naming what we see. The 'gaze' has been and is a site of resistance for colonized black people globally. Subordinates in relations of power learn experientially that there is a critical gaze, one that 'looks' to document, one that is oppositional. In resistance struggle, the power of the dominated to assert agency by claiming and cultivating 'awareness' politicizes 'looking' relations—one learns to look a certain way in order to resist" (hooks, *Black Looks*, 116).

their personal identities from the legacy of slavery, it was that they were strong, infinitely stronger than the White women whom they perceived as pampered, entitled, and incapable of managing their own lives without the support of White men and Black women. Still, Black women were not immune to the powerful influence of the cult of true womanhood. According to Collins, Black women's reactions to the controlling images have always involved a mixture of conformity and resistance.[52] Despite their exclusion from the model, they wanted to prove that they too embodied morality and virtue, that they were in fact ladies. And thus they set out to craft a model of Black femininity that at once subverted and appropriated the cult of true womanhood: the StrongBlackWoman.[53]

The Birth of the StrongBlackWoman

The model of identity that we now know as the StrongBlackWoman had its genesis in the racial uplift movement of the late nineteenth and early twentieth century. In the post-Reconstruction era, the demeaning stereotypes of African Americans gained new traction as southern Whites attempted to regain control over Black labor. To lend support to the newly developing Jim Crow laws and legislation to disenfranchise Black voters, southern Whites and their allies launched a virulently racist propaganda campaign depicting African Americans as morally, intellectually, and physically depraved and thus incapable of good citizenship.[54] The racial uplift movement was a response to this new assault. A precursor of the Civil Rights movement,

---

52. Collins, *Black Feminist Thought*, 97.

53. The twin themes of Black women's accommodation and resistance to stereotypical images are echoed in the works of several scholars. Harris-Perry, for example, notes that "sister politics is also about challenging negative images, managing degradation, and resisting or accommodating humiliating public representations" (Harris-Perry, *Sister Citizen*, 45). And Carby's central thesis in *Reconstructing Womanhood* is that Black woman writers "addressed, used, transformed, and, on occasion, subverted the dominant ideological codes" of racial-gender identity within their works (20–21).

54. Higginbotham, *Righteous Discontent*, 4; White, *Too Heavy a Load*, 39–40. The period between 1880 and 1920 is commonly known as the "nadir" of the Black experience in the United States because of the widespread and vicious system of economic, political, and social oppression carried out against Blacks. This included lynchings and lynch mobs (more than twenty-five hundred recorded lynchings took place between 1884 and 1900); the effective peonage wrought by sharecropping laws; disenfranchisement through literacy, poll taxes, and grandfather clauses; whitecapping and mobs that forced Blacks to abandon businesses and lands; and the convict lease system.

the racial uplift movement took place from the late 1880s to 1914.[55] Led primarily by Black middle-class leaders such as W. E. B. DuBois, a critical aim of racial uplift was to "defend the image and honor of black men and women."[56] As Victor Anderson explains, they did this by formulating and disseminating the "cult of Black genius," a philosophy of racial consciousness developed in response to the negative depictions of Blacks by White racial ideology.[57] In other words, the cult of Black genius, which Anderson also calls "ontological blackness" was a counter-discourse aimed at *disproving* White racist notions of Black identity. Anderson notes that this counter-discourse had four features. First, it rejected categorical racism and its negative depictions of blacks. Second, it argued that the moral failures associated with Blacks should and could be explained historically rather than categorically. Third, it regarded Black racial identity as commensurate with civic republican humanism. Finally, it called for racial uplift as evidence of Black cultural genius and civilization. What this counter-discourse did not do, however, was attack the species logic that undergirds European racial ideology. Rather, it appropriated it. Consequently, categorical racism gave rise to a Black racial apologetics that was designed to nullify the negative definition of Black racial identity posited by White racial discourse and to replace it with a positive definition. The cult of European genius is mirrored by a discourse of Black genius, in which Black identity is defined as heroic, creative, morally masculine, revolutionary, and self-determined; in other words, strong.[58]

The "race men and women" of the late nineteenth and early twentieth century sought to advance a "politics of responsibility," whereby the personal identities and behaviors of individual African Americans were subsumed under a collective identity of strength.[59] Respectability demanded that every individual in the black community assume responsibility for behavioral self-regulation and self-improvement along moral, educational, and economic lines. The goal was to distance oneself as far as possible from images perpetuated by racist stereotypes."[60] Ironically, then, respectability,

55. Gaines, "Racial Uplift Ideology."

56. Ibid.

57. Anderson, *Beyond Ontological Blackness.*

58. Ibid., 52, 79–87.

59. For an analysis of the strength motif among African-American men, see Neal, *New Black Man.*

60. Higginbotham, *Righteous Discontent*, 196.

the hallmark of White, Western identity, became the hallmark of authentic Blackness.[61] Under the demands of the cult of Black genius, African Americans were encouraged to construct public identities that would refute the negative images of White racial ideology and prove Blacks as worthy of respect.[62] This required the suppression and denial of any weaknesses, shortcomings, or vulnerabilities that might confirm or underscore racial stereotypes. It was, in essence, to construct and maintain a public façade. The StrongBlackWoman directly continues that legacy.

Indeed, the StrongBlackWoman is the gendered manifestation of the politics of respectability that began to be advanced during the racial uplift movement. For the middle-class Black female spokespersons and activists in the racial uplift period, the goal for African-American women was not only to prove themselves strong, but also to prove themselves ladies. In other words, they wanted to prove themselves as worthy of both the cult of Black genius and the cult of true womanhood. Thus, they constructed a public persona of a new Black womanhood—the StrongBlackWoman— that would consciously and overtly disprove the characteristics of the fallen femininities of the Jezebel, the Mammy, and the matriarch: hypersexuality, excessive emotionalism, moral and intellectual weakness, lack of loyalty to Black men and families, self-centeredness, and anger. The StrongBlack-Woman was, and is, effectively a shame management strategy.[63] As Harris-Perry notes, "Though we seldom think of it this way, racism is the act of shaming others based on their identity. Blackness in America is marked by shame. . . . This collective racial shaming has a disproportionate impact on black women, and black women's attempts to escape or manage shame are part of what motivates their politics."[64] In the archetype of the Strong-BlackWoman, then, "race women" sought to undo the shame of the racist depictions of African-American women by articulating a model of Black womanhood that was without fault or blemish (cf. Eph 5:27). Intertwining Black genius with true womanhood, the StrongBlackWoman developed as an identity with three defining attributes: caregiving, emotional strength/ regulation, and independence. As Blacks, StrongBlackWomen were to be spiritually and emotionally strong, financially and emotional independent, and committed to the uplift of Black families and communities. As

61. Jenkins, *Private Lives, Proper Relations*, 29.

62. Higginbotham, *Righteous Discontent*, 195.

63. Harris-Perry, *Sister Citizen*, 22.

64. Ibid., 109.

women, they were to be consummate caregivers, morally upright, selflessly devoted to the needs of others, and capable of enduring struggle without complaint.[65]

The StrongBlackWoman, then, embodies a tension between submission and resistance toward racist and sexist images of African-American women. On the one hand, the archetype refutes patriarchal and white supremacist ideologies that depict women as dependent and overly emotional and Blacks as indolent and immoral. On the other hand, it capitulates to these same ideologies by "trying too hard" to disprove them.[66] Further, the combination of the cult of true womanhood with the cult of Black genius in the StrongBlackWoman yields an identity that is defined by suffering (i.e., by continual self-sacrifice on behalf of others and by suppression of personal needs) and that offers no hope or means for transcendence above this suffering.[67]

The New Propaganda

Like the negative images of Black women's identities in White racial ideology, the StrongBlackWoman was neither an obscure nor an incidental ideology. It was a descriptive and prescriptive model of Black women's identities that was deliberately disseminated via the work of Black women's clubs and missionary societies that were founded at the turn of the twentieth century, such as the National Association of Colored Women (NACW), the National Council of Negro Women, the Ladies Auxiliary of the Brotherhood of Sleeping Car Porters, and the Woman's Convention of the National Baptist

65. Viewing the image in this way may help explain its prevalence throughout the African diaspora. Colonialism—with its attendant racism and patriarchy—becomes the common denominator, the standard against which Black men and women develop models of identity.

66. Higginbotham notes that this tension is inherent in the politics of respectability as a whole, as it embodies a tension between submission to and transformation of negative racial images (Higginbotham, *Righteous Discontent*, 191).

67. Townes ("Living in the New Jerusalem") and Riggs ("A Clarion Call") provide alternate perspectives of how racial and gender ideology combine to form the images of Black women in white popular culture. For both authors, the images of Black women are bound by the cult of true womanhood and the ideology of the Black child-savage. For Riggs, this results in the myth of the "bad black woman." For Townes, however, it results in a more complicated image that is beset with contradictions. Namely, the Black woman is seen as promiscuous and immoral yet also contented, self-sacrificing, loyal, and capable of providing care for White babies and children.

Convention, U.S.A.[68] Indeed, it can be argued that the cultural assault on Black women's identities was the catalyst for the Black women's club movement. In 1896, James Jacks, a White man who was president of the Missouri Press Association, sought to silence the Ida B. Wells' antilynching campaign by casting doubt upon the moral integrity of Black women. In a letter to British abolitionists, Jacks defended lynching and stated that most Black women were prostitutes, thieves, and liars. The NACW was organized the same year.[69]

In her review of the work of Black women's clubs, Deborah Gray White asserts that a significant majority of club activities were devoted to elevating the public image of African-American women by teaching women to embrace the values, behavior, and manner of appearance consistent with middle-class privilege.[70]

> The defense of black womanhood united [NACW women] as did no other single cause. Both conservatives and activists believed that black women were beset with both a race problem and a woman problem. . . . What hurt most were the charges assailing black women's morals. To club leaders it seemed that all the shortcomings of the race were being traced to the black woman's alleged failures—failure to be pure, pious, submissive, and domestic, the failure to raise future generations of blacks to be good citizens, and the failure marked by continued sexual connections with white men. Clubwomen wanted the world to know that all the allegations impugning the black woman's character were false.[71]

Through the work of local and national women's clubs, African-American women undertook an extensive campaign to advance a politics of respectability that would prove wrong the type of slander that was waged against them by the likes of James Jacks.[72] They wanted to undermine popular assumptions about Black women's sexuality, morality, and cleanliness. Thus, their programs included activities such as: conducting Sunday School and

---

68. Ironically, the same period known as the Black nadir is also known as the "women's era" because of the unprecedented political and social organizing done to advance women's rights. Black women's organizing, in both religious and secular organizations, existed in the tension between these two realities (Higginbotham, *Righteous Discontent*, 4).

69. White, *Too Heavy a Load*, 22.

70. Ibid., 69.

71. Ibid., 52–53.

72. Ibid., 53.

other educational and social events for community children; sponsoring lectures on subjects such as temperance, personal hygiene, moral improvement, and female suffrage; providing free kindergarten; conducting cooking and sewing classes; establishing reading rooms and donating books by Black authors to public libraries; teaching women how to buy land and build houses; giving scholarships; and providing food and financial assistance to individuals and families.[73]

Through these activities and through club members' personal embodiment of the characteristics that they hoped to instill in others, African-American clubwomen hoped to replace the negative stereotypes of Black womanhood with the notion that they were as capable as, in fact more capable than, White women.[74] Twenty years after the publication of Jacks' letter and the founding of the NACW, Mary Church Terrell, the organization's first president, delivered a speech, titled "The Modern Woman," at Mt. Zion A. M. E. Church in Charleston, South Carolina, in 1916.[75] Wearing a pink evening dress and long white gloves, her hair impeccably groomed, Terrell began by pointing to Black women's commonalities with other women in their roles as wives, mothers, daughters, and sisters. She then described the responsibility of educated Black women "to do more than other women. Those of us fortunate enough to have education must share it with the less fortunate of our race. We must go into our communities and improve them; we must go out into the nation and change it."[76] At the conclusion of her speech, Terrell pointedly asked her packed audience of Black churchwomen, "WHO OF YOU KNOW HOW TO CARRY YOUR BURDEN IN

---

73. Ibid., 28–30.

74. White's analysis also reveals that club leaders believed that Black women were more capable as leaders than were Black men. Effectively, club leaders believed that Black women were superior to Black men in matters of morality and equal in all other respects. NACW leaders, in particular, believed that women's more "nurturing, moral, and altruistic" natures better equipped them for social welfare work than men, who were innately "belligerent, aggressive, and selfish." Some leaders, such as Anna Julia Cooper and Frances Ellen Watkins Harper, publicly voiced their sentiments that men would easily sell the interests of the race for personal gain (ibid., 36–37). The clubwomen's public criticism of Black male leadership was a source of much conflict in Black gender relations and was sometimes a cause of dissent within the clubs themselves. White notes that later members of Black women's organizations, such as National Council of Negro Women presidents Mary McLeod Bethune and Dorothy Height, were careful to avoid comments and actions that could be construed as criticisms of Black men (ibid., 155).

75. Ibid., 21.

76. Cited in ibid., 22.

THE HEAT OF THE DAY?"[77] White notes that the speech had its intended effect, galvanizing its attendees, many of whom were already active in community work, to join and establish women's groups dedicated to working against poverty.[78] Terrell's speech has clear echoes of the three core features of the StrongBlackWoman. She highlights women's roles as caregivers (i.e., their responsibility to family and community), their autonomy and heightened responsibility, and their possession of the wherewithal to accomplish more than other women.

Black clubwomen espoused a view of womanhood that affirmed traditional views of femininity while also embracing women's public leadership. That is, they believed that women ought to be the primary caretakers in the home but that they could also be educated, self-sufficient career women who were politically active.[79] "In a period when white women were often compelled to choose between a career and marriage, activist clubwomen insisted that black women could both save the race and build model homes; they could do all that a man could do and all that a woman should."[80] In other words, they believed that Black women could and should "do it all." The emphasis upon productive activity as a marker of a "good" woman was a notable departure for African Americans' conceptualization of femininity.[81] By the turn of the century, among Whites, leisure had become a significant marker of one's social standing. African-American women—even educated, married Black women of the north—could generally not afford to be idle. Notably, then, rather than succumbing to fatalism based upon their inability to embody a life of leisure, Black women crafted a model of womanhood that elevated industriousness and personal achievement.

77. Ibid., 23.

78. Ibid.

79. Giddings notes that, in contrast to their White counterparts, Black clubwomen did not view domesticity to be incompatible with work outside the home or social/political action. Maria Stewart, for example, lauded Black women for their role as mothers and submissiveness to men even as she exhorted them to economic self-sufficiency (Giddings, *When and Where I Enter*, 52). And in her examination of Harriet Jacobs' *Incidents in the Life of a Slave Girl*, Hazel Carby argues that central to Jacobs' reimagining of Black female identity was defiance: "Conventional feminine qualities of submission and passivity were replaced by an active resistance. . . . Thus, Jacobs developed an alternative set of definitions of womanhood and motherhood in the text which remained in tension with the cult of true womanhood" (Carby, *Reconstructing Womanhood*, 56).

80. White, *Too Heavy a Load*, 54.

81. Giddings, *When and Where I Enter*, 47.

Moreover, Black women were expected not to evince any sign of struggle or weakness with their multiple responsibilities. Maintaining an outward appearance of "effortless perfection" was a mandate for clubwomen: "Wanting the race to be judged by its best women, they had to become their own persuasive argument for the cause of race and black female advancement."[82] White stresses that emotional regulation and impression management came with the territory of being a Black woman, particularly when dealing with Whites: "All NACW leaders had to rein in their emotions and put on an artificial face before whites. Being their own best example usually meant being to whites something other than what they really were. Only in their private correspondence and in their diaries do a few Association leaders let go of 'the cause' and express their feelings."[83] Clubwomen, thus, were very practiced in the arts of dissemblance or shifting that are characteristic of the emotional fortitude of StrongBlackWomen, consciously putting forth an image of moral rectitude that suppressed any behaviors that might be construed as evidence of vulnerability, incapability, or immorality. And while they were especially careful to maintain this image in public, it also pervaded their private lives.

It may be tempting to dismiss the Black women's club movement as a largely secular movement. Indeed, White's account primarily depicts it thusly, with very little information about the role of the Black church in its evolution. In *Righteous Discontent*, Evelyn Higginbotham demonstrates that the Black Baptist church was a formidable ally of the racial uplift movement in general and the Black women's club movement in particular. Cheryl Gilkes makes a similar argument in her study of Black women's organizing within the Holiness and Pentecostal traditions, arguing that the uplift movement was "the specialized political arm of black church women."[84] Marcia Riggs, moreover, describes the club movement as "a *socioreligious* movement against the interaction of race, gender, and class oppression in the lives of Black women while working for the advancement of all Blacks."[85] As the only institutions under the purview of Black authority during a period when segregation denied Black access to public facilities, Black churches came to operate as public spaces that provided facilities and programs far beyond their membership. "The church served as meeting

---

82. White, *Too Heavy a Load*, 88.

83. Ibid., 98.

84. Gilkes, *"If It Wasn't for the Women . . ."*, 85.

85. Riggs, *Awake, Arise, and Act*, 70.

hall for virtually every large gathering. It held political rallies, clubwomen's conferences, and school graduations. It was the one space truly accessible to the black community."[86] It is not surprising, then, that the context of Terrell's 1916 "The Modern Woman" speech was an A. M. E. congregation and that her audience consisted largely of churchwomen. Black churches did more than provide physical space for community gatherings; they were also the venues through which racial ideology was shaped and disseminated. "Through the institution of the church, male and female leaders attempted to transform the race-conscious ideas and values of the poor, unlettered, and politically powerless black masses into an assertive collective will. . . . The black Baptist convention movement formed part of an emergent black nationalism that resonated throughout the African-American population and invoked feelings of racial pride and self-determination."[87]

Within the ranks of the Black church were thousands of women who had been trained in organizing and leadership skills through their church and denominational activities. In addition to forming their own denominational organizations, Black churches established schools, newspapers, and other institutions of racial self-help, efforts that were often made possible by women's labor and financial support.[88] The same women likely constituted the bulk of the membership in the women's clubs. Higginbotham argues, "The club movement among black women owed its very existence to the groundwork of organizational skill and leadership training gained through women's church societies. . . . More than mere precursors to secular reform and women's rights activism, black women's religious organizations undergirded and formed an identifiable part of what is erroneously assumed to be 'secular.'"[89] Indeed, Higginbotham effectively demonstrates that African-American women engaged in similar racial uplift activities within the women's clubs and within the church. In particular, she chronicles how the women of the National Baptist Convention, U.S.A., contested ideological and institutional racism through organized anti-lynching and desegregation campaigns, fund-raising, and promotion of a politics of respectability. Founded in 1895, just one year prior to the NACW, the National Baptist Convention, U.S.A., evolved into the largest organized body—religious or

86. Higginbotham, *Righteous Discontent*, 7.
87. Ibid., 48.
88. Ibid., 49–50.
89. Ibid., 16.

secular—of African Americans in the country.[90] At the local and national level, Black Baptist women formed auxiliaries that represented their interests. In some cases, they even formed separate state conventions whose organizational structure was similar to the clergy-dominated conventions.[91]

Like clubwomen, Black Christian women undertook a campaign to advance a politics of responsibility that was heavily influenced by the middle class ideals of the leadership of the women's convention movement, which was predominated by teachers and ministers' wives. Through their emphasis on respectable behavior, they attempted to promote a photonegative of the images of Black pathology that were dominant in White racial ideology. They were especially concerned with public behavior, as it wielded the greatest power to confirm or refute prevailing stereotypes of Black deviance.[92] According to Higginbotham, educated Black Christian women constituted a "Female Talented Tenth"[93] that deliberately sought to disseminate middle-class values to the masses: "Organized black church women disseminated throughout the black community the assimilationist message implicit in respectability, and they endeavored to implant middle-class values and behavioral patterns among the masses of urban blacks who retained rural folkways of speech, dress, worship, and other distinct cultural patterns. . . . This evangelical message, like the historic work of Home Missions among other ethnic and racial groups, sought to bring black America in line with both the religious and class values of the dominant society."[94]

90. Ibid., 2. While Higginbotham's work focuses on the Black Baptist church, it should be noted that women in other denominations were similarly involved in the racial uplift movement. Cheryl Townsend Gilkes, for example, argues effectively that African-American women of the Holiness and Pentecostal traditions "were as militantly pro-black, pro-woman, and pro-uplift as their Baptist and Methodist sisters were, and their political consciousness was fueled by spiritual zeal" (Gilkes, *"If It Wasn't for the Women . . .",* 46).

91. Higginbotham, *Righteous Discontent*, 73.

92. Ibid., 196.

93. The Talented Tenth was an essential element in W. E. B. Du Bois' strategy for achieving racial equality (Du Bois, "The Talented Tenth"). Higginbotham argues that within this group, women were deemed to have unique significance. Because of their roles as caregivers and teachers, women were believed to have a "more direct and pervasive role in spreading 'correct' values throughout black communities" (Higginbotham, *Righteous Discontent*, 28).

94. Higginbotham, *Righteous Discontent*, 195–96. Higginbotham identifies the church as having "the single most important role in influencing normative values and distinguishing respectable from non-respectable behavior among working-class blacks during the early twentieth century" (ibid., 204).

Also similar to clubwomen, the politics of respectability advanced by African-American churchwomen included an understanding of Black womanhood that is consistent with today's StrongBlackWoman. They merged conservative and radical elements, blending the traditional Victorian ideals of the cult of true womanhood with a public activism that previously had been associated with masculinity. On the one hand, through the churches' institutional structure, teachings, and missional activities, Black churchwomen emphasized women's traditional duties as caregivers and guardians of morality. They lauded women's roles as mothers, wives, sisters, and daughters. They instructed women and girls in proper etiquette, morality, temperance, personal cleanliness, and sexual purity, and in maintaining orderly and disciplined homes.[95] Conversely, they openly criticized women who were perceived as bringing shame upon the race, that is, those who did not meet their standards of chastity, moral integrity, and domestic prowess. At times, they prompted the church to censure or even expel members who did not conform to the code of conduct.[96]

On the other hand, while Black Christian women believed that women should be consummate caregivers, they also articulated an ideal of womanhood that contradicted the dominant culture's expectations of women, emphasizing independence, self-reliance, strength, and autonomy.[97] They explicitly rejected the notion that women's roles were confined to the private sphere of home and family.

> Black women expressed their discontent with popular conceptions regarding "woman's place" in the church and society at large. They challenged the "silent helpmate" image of women's church work and set out to convince the men that women were equally obliged to advance not only their race and denomination, but themselves . . . They articulated this viewpoint before groups of men and women in churches, convention anniversaries, and denominational schools, and in newspapers and other forms of literature.[98]

While they prioritized their roles as wives and mothers as ordained by God, they did not view these roles as incompatible with working outside the home, as so many Black women had been required to do out of necessity.[99]

95. Ibid., 193; Gilkes, "If It Wasn't for the Women . . .", 80.

96. Higginbotham, *Righteous Discontent*, 200–201.

97. Gilkes, "If It Wasn't for the Women . . .", 45.

98. Higginbotham, *Righteous Discontent*, 120–21.

99. Ibid., 136.

Indeed, managing multiple roles was seen as a marker of one's strength and fortitude. Industriousness and busy-ness were highly esteemed characteristics among Black Baptist women and a significant portion of the annual meetings of the Woman's Convention was devoted to highlighting the industry, faithfulness, and achievements of its members.[100] In her column in the *National Baptist Union*, Nannie Helen Burroughs reported:

> As far as the Woman's Convention was concerned, idleness or activity contrary to productive labor repudiated racial self-help. The rhetoric of the WC extolled all forms of honest labor, no matter how menial, and in the discourse of respectability admonished: "Don't be idle. Don't scorn labor nor look with contempt upon the laborer. Those who encourage Negro women to loaf, rather than work at service for a living are enemies to the race."[101]

Indeed, Black churchwomen believed that the needs of the African-American community necessitated that they become agents of community and social change. In contrast to the cult of true womanhood, where women's roles as teachers and helpers were to be confined to their immediate family, the Black churchwomen considered women's primary obligation to be to God rather than to their husband and children. Thus, they affirmed women's public roles as prophets and teachers of the gospel, and they believed that missionary service to their church, community, and society could take precedence over domestic responsibilities.[102] These Black Christian women rejected the notion that women's submissiveness required them to be frail, weak, or passive. Black women, they argued, were not victims; they were saving forces, self-disciplined and self-sacrificing agents of social transformation.[103]

Conjointly, the activities of the women's clubs and the Christian women's organizations formulated a powerful defense against the cultural attack upon Black women's identities. In response to White racism's depictions of African Americans as sexual and moral deviants, submissive servants, and sharp-tongued usurpers of the masculine role, they publicly reimagined authentic Black womanhood. As twin arms of the racial-uplift movement, Black clubwomen and churchwomen developed, embodied,

---

100. Ibid., 191.

101. Burroughs, "Chips from Our Woodpile," quoted in Higginbotham, *Righteous Discontent*, 211.

102. Higginbotham, *Righteous Discontent*, 130.

103. Ibid., 121.

and disseminated a model of Black womanhood that emphasized moral respectability, duty to the race, and affective strength. A "real" Black woman was a StrongBlackWoman—autonomous, industrious, reliable, and capable, a devoted and selfless worker on behalf of Black families, churches, and communities, always emotionally composed and prepared to serve as a representative for the race. Wholly devoted to advancing the image and the needs of the race, she took on her people's burden as her own, and she was ready and willing to carry it "in the heat of the day."

In the midst of a extremely hostile racial environment in which African-American women were widely depicted as deficient as women, and consequently as human beings, the "race women" at the turn of the century embarked upon the evangelical mission of spreading the gospel of the StrongBlackWoman. In doing so, they inadvertently locked Black women's identities in the grips of yet another, albeit seemingly positive, controlling image. Collins explains the problems inherent in such an approach: "Replacing negative images with positive ones can be equally problematic if the function of stereotypes as controlling images remains unrecognized. . . Seen in this light, it makes little sense in the long run for Black women to exchange one set of controlling images for another even if positive stereotypes bring better treatment in the short run."[104] Under the guise of presenting a corrective to deleterious images of African-American women, the "race women" at the turn of the century developed and reinforced a model of Black womanhood that continues to conceal the authentic experiences and needs of Black women, that encourages women to deny and ignore themselves and to maintain a façade of imperturbability at the expense of personal health and well-being. A full century later, this model of identity—the StrongBlackWoman—has contributed to a health crisis among African-American women that reinscribes the very racial-gender disparities that the women's clubs and Christian women's conventions worked hard to dismantle.

In large part, the ideology of the StrongBlackWoman has escaped significant criticism by African-American cultural and social institutions because it is a controlling image that was developed and promulgated by those very institutions. Moreover, because its controls are seemingly benign (that is, influencing behavior in directions understood to be positive), it is overlooked as a source of control that is predicated upon negative images of Black womanhood. However, as Collins asserts, controlling images

104. Collins, *Black Feminist Thought*, 114.

must be challenged regardless of whether they were developed outside of or within African-American communities.

> Confronting the controlling images forwarded by institutions external to African-American communities remains essential. But such efforts should not obscure the equally important issue of examining how African-American institutions also perpetuate these same controlling images. Although it may be painful to examine—especially in the context of a racially charged society always vigilant for signs of Black disunity—the question of how the organizations of Black civil society reproduce controlling images of Black womanhood and fail to take a stand against images developed elsewhere is equally important.[105]

Given the positive intentions of Black club and churchwomen and the oppressive circumstances under which they labored, it is tempting to simply focus upon the positive dimensions of the StrongBlackWoman as a defense against the Jezebel, the Mammy, and the matriarch. As one of my undergraduate students once remarked, "If my choices are to be Jezebel, Mammy, Sapphire, or a StrongBlackWoman, I'm going to choose the StrongBlackWoman." For far too long, African-American woman have lived, loved, and labored under the illusion that those were their only choices, indeed, under the illusion that a choice had to be made. And unfortunately, as we will see in the next chapter, U.S. society continues to advance the notion that the StrongBlackWoman is the yoke that African-American women must bear.

Suggestions for Pastoral Practice

- Spend some time observing modern popular culture, including television, film, music, and music videos. In what ways are the stereotypes of the Jezebel, the Mammy, and the matriarch still operational today? Where do you see signs of progress?

- Talk with African-American women regarding their opinions about how Black women are represented in popular culture. Where do they see problematic images, and in what ways do they feel impacted by these images? Where do they see signs of progress? Keep in mind that women from different age groups and socioeconomic backgrounds may have varying perceptions.

105. Ibid., 86.

- We might argue that the Black female activists at the turn of the century were caught between a rock and a hard place when it came to their attempts to use the StrongBlackWoman to defend against the negative images of African-American women. How does today's context differ? What factors might help explain the StrongBlackWoman's continued appeal as the standard of femininity for African-American women?

- In this chapter, I have demonstrated that other racial-gender groups are complicit in the ideology of the StrongBlackWoman. What are your reactions to this? What are the implications for the church?

4

Pride and Prejudice

Societal Reactions to the StrongBlackWoman

> Elijah then came near to all the people, and said, "How long will you go limping with two different opinions? If the Lord is God, follow him; but if Baal, then follow him." The people did not answer him a word. (1 Kgs 18:21)

Nearly 150 years following the cessation of race-based chattel slavery in the U.S., the stereotypical images of the Mammy, the Jezebel, and the sapphire have not disappeared from the country's collective imagination, but continue to predominate in popular culture's representation of African-American women.[1] Yet while the Black women's club movement may not have been able to eradicate these images, the largely church-based movement was remarkably successful in proliferating the icon of the StrongBlackWoman as a culturally viable and acceptable alternative. Even womanist theology suffers under this legacy. The notion of Black women's superhuman strength is embedded in Alice Walker's definition of a womanist: "Traditionally capable, as in: 'Mama, I'm walking to Canada and I'm

---

1. See Collins, *Black Sexual Politics,* for an effective summary of modern variations of the stereotypical images of Black femininity.

taking you and a bunch of other slaves with me.' Reply: 'It wouldn't be the first time.'"[2] Now at the dawn of the twenty-first century, the image of the StrongBlackWoman has come to receive widespread cultural approbation as the exemplar of Black womanhood, both within and without the church. Indeed, the message that Black women have extraordinary capacities for emotional strength/regulation, caregiving, and independence is repeated across such a wide range of cultural forms (including music, television, and film) and genres (including drama, science fiction, R&B, and hip-hop) that popular culture often functions as an extension of the church in evangelizing African-American women and girls into the cult of strength. In chapter 1, I utilized examples from R&B and hip-hop songs to demonstrate how popular music reifies the image of the StrongBlackWoman. In this chapter, I demonstrate that the task of crafting Black women's identities is not simply confined to institutions or art forms that are controlled by African Americans. Moreover, the image, while ubiquitous, is also paradoxical, alternately (and sometimes simultaneously) revered and castigated. From public policy to Black gospel theater to television dramas, reproducing, praising, and punishing the StrongBlackWoman have become an American enterprise.

The Myth of Black Matriarchy

It would be hard to discuss the popular reaction to the myth of the Strong-BlackWoman without mention of the 1965 U.S. Department of Labor Report, *The Negro Family: The Case for National Action.*[3] More commonly called the Moynihan Report, it was written by Daniel Patrick Moynihan, a sociologist who then served as Assistant Secretary of Labor and who would later be elected as the U.S. Senator for New York. Moynihan believed firmly in the cause of civil rights and believed that, following the momentous occasion of the passage of the 1964 Civil Rights Act, the next stage in the struggle for Black liberation was to progress beyond securing civil rights to achieving "equal results" with other racial/ethnic groups. He was dismayed, then, to note that despite improvements in income, education, and standards of living for African Americans, their circumstances were actually deteriorating relative to other racial/ethnic groups:

2. Walker, *In Search of Our Mothers' Gardens*, xi.
3. Moynihan, *The Negro Family.*

The harsh fact is that as a group, at the present time, in terms of ability to win out in the competitions of American life, they are not equal to most of those groups with which they will be competing. Individually, Negro Americans reach the highest peaks of achievement. But collectively, in the spectrum of American ethnic and religious and regional groups, where some get plenty and some get none, where some send eighty percent of their children to college and others pull them out of school at the 8th grade, Negroes are among the weakest."[4]

The goal of Moynihan's report, then, was to identify the factors that would jeopardize continued Black progress. He readily identified continuing racial discrimination as a challenge for African Americans, stating that he expected racism to exert a negative impact for at least another generation.[5] Quickly, however, he turned his attention to what he identified as the primary problem of Black progress: a fundamental deficiency in the structure of Black families, as evidenced by the lower rates of marriage among African-American women and the higher rates of out-of-wedlock births, female-headed households, and welfare dependency. Indeed, Moynihan went so far as to identify the instability of Black families as "the nation's oldest, and most intransigent, and now its most dangerous social problem."[6] In contrast to White families, which he saw as having achieved a high level of coherence and stability, he believed that the families of low-income Blacks were highly unstable and at risk of complete dissolution.[7]

Largely ignoring historical and systemic forces such as slavery, political and social disenfranchisement, economic oppression, and lack of educational opportunity, Moynihan attributed racial disparities to the failure of African Americans to develop and maintain patriarchal family

4. Ibid.

5. Grounding Moynihan's argument was his assumption that the systemic inequalities impacting African Americans would eventually be solved by several major political, administrative, and legal events of the prior decade, including Lyndon B. Johnson's election to the presidency and his subsequent cooperation with the civil rights movement, the passage of the Manpower Development and Training Act of 1962 (which was to facilitate equality in the labor market), the passage of the Economic Opportunity Act of 1964 (which was to reduce poverty), the passage of the Civil Rights Act of 1964, and the upholding of the 1954 *Brown vs. Board of Education* decision. In light of that belief, he shifted his attention to what he viewed as factors endemic to the African-American population.

6. Moynihan, *Negro Family*.

7. Ibid., chapter 2.

structures.[8] And this, in turn, he blamed upon the unnatural strength of African-American women, in other words, Black matriarchy. In Moynihan's view, then, the greatest cost of racist oppression was that Black families were forced into a matriarchal structure, in which the roles of husband and wife were reversed.[9] Indeed, even the Black church had become an overly matriarchal institution, especially in Northern urban areas where few men attended church.[10] Matriarchy, in turn, undermined male leadership and imposed "a crushing burden on the Negro male," resulting in educational underachievement, lack of discipline, poor work ethic, and a propensity toward immediate gratification.[11]

> The Black matriarchy thesis argued that African-American women who failed to fulfill their traditional "womanly" duties at home contributed to social problems in Black civil society. . . . Spending too much time away from home, these working mothers ostensibly could not properly supervise their children and thus were a major contributing factor to their children's failure at school. As overly aggressive, unfeminine women, Black matriarchs allegedly emasculated their lovers and husbands. These men, understandably, either deserted their partners or refused to marry the mothers of their children. From the dominant group's perspective, the matriarch represented a failed mammy, a negative stigma to be applied to African-American women who dared reject the image of the submissive, hardworking servant.[12]

Like recent scholars who argue that Black women are the new "model minority," Moynihan's assertion of Black matriarchy was based upon narrowly selected indicators of Black women's "success", including their higher educational achievement relative to Black men, the greater frequency with which they were primary wage earners relative to White women, and their greater representation in white collar occupations relative to Black men.[13] In other

8. Herbert Gans effectively points out numerous shortcomings in Moynihan's report. Moynihan provided little data to support his claims, ignoring the growing body of research on African-American families and social science findings that demonstrated that single parent families were not inherently instable. See Gans, "The Moynihan Report and Its Aftermaths."

9. Moynihan, *Negro Family*.

10. Ibid.

11. Ibid.

12. Collins, *Black Feminist Thought*, 75.

13. Moynihan, *Negro Family*.

words, Moynihan believed that Black women were too strong because they fared better than Black men and White women on some educational and occupational indices. Notably, he ignored Black women's higher rates of poverty and their overrepresentation in domestic service occupations relative to Black men and White women. Nor did he acknowledge women's lack of equal access to leadership opportunity within the supposedly matriarchal institution of the Black church.

The image of Black femininity portrayed in the Moynihan Report was not simply an abstract concept without relevance to the lives of African-American women. Deborah Gray White offers the following critique:

> The report was devastating to the black woman's image. It seemed to say that if only black women could be less dominant and domineering, the black man would have a chance. . . . Whatever else the report did it erased over seventy years of image-building on the part of black women's organizations. On top of the media's healthy dose of the "strong black woman"—the many portrayals of Mammy, and the Sapphire image made popular by the radio and television sitcom *Amos and Andy*—the Moynihan report legitimized the perception of black women as unnaturally strong and emasculating. The reverberations were disastrous.[14]

The report was particularly damaging in that it exposed, but did not challenge, a preexisting gender tension among African Americans. In her book *Sister Citizen: Shame, Stereotypes, and Black Women in America*, public scholar Melissa Harris-Perry argues that "the Moynihan Report did not create the angry black woman stereotype. It tapped into an existing framework and gave it a new, politically consequential name: the matriarch."[15] The Moynihan Report exacerbated an already existing gender tension among African Americans. The sentiments of the report had been expressed previously by African-American male leaders such as John Hope, who gave an indictment of black femininity in his 1898 Atlanta address before the National Association of Colored Women. A close friend of W. E. B. Du Bois and a fervent believer in full racial equality and self-help, the professor and subsequent first Black president of Atlanta Baptist College chastised the clubwomen's critical rhetoric of Black male leadership and admonished them for being too masculine. Hope believed that the race needed more manly men, an objective that could be accomplished only if women became

14. White, *Too Heavy a Load*, 199–200.
15. Harris-Perry, *Sister Citizen*, 94.

more womanly. "Women, thus, had to take less initiative, had to support their men as helpmates. To be more than that was to be emasculating."[16]

The Moynihan Report, then, lent substantial political authority to the criticism of Black women's strength. Thus, while the report received, and continues to elicit, considerable backlash from Black male activists and scholars, such criticism has predominantly centered upon Moynihan's negative portrayal of Black families rather than his treatment of Black women. Indeed, with the exception of the work of Black feminist scholar-activists, Moynihan's depiction of Black women as domineering was largely unchallenged and, in some cases, enthusiastically co-signed. Whereas white racist depictions of Black female hypersexuality traditionally incited stringent protest by Black male leaders, there was little outcry against Moynihan's depiction of the matriarch:

> No national organization defended black women against vilification for the role that racism has forced upon them. . . . [N]o national black women's organization explained that black women still predominated in domestic service and low-paying, nonsecure, service-sector jobs. Few Americans learned that black women were hardly represented in white-collar and professional occupations, that those in this sector were stuck in entry-level clerk and secretarial positions, or in the relatively low-paid, traditional female professions of teaching, nursing, and social work.[17]

Indeed, many Black men used his work to support what they already wanted to believe about Black women, namely, that Black women enjoyed educational, financial, and occupational advantages that they did not.[18]

> The construct of the emasculated, undervalued, beaten-down black man and the fecund, seductive, opportunistic black woman in slavery has been repeated so often that we have come to accept it as true. Rather than understand that women and men were equally oppressed during slavery, though in different ways, we have bought into the falsehood that black women were better off, and that the level of black men's brutalization was a result of this. To believe that black women "got over" during slavery at the expense of black men is to absolve white people of accountability for slavery and lay that responsibility at the feet of black women. This done, it is no stretch to believe that the role of black women

16. White, *Too Heavy a Load,* 57.

17. Ibid., 200–201.

18. Wallace, *Black Macho,* 109–10.

post-slavery is to repair the greater damage done to black men, to make up for our past imagined sins.[19]

The silence of Black women's organizations suggests that many African-American female leaders had also bought into the notion that Black women's success had come at the expense of Black men. Even organizations such as the National Council of Negro Women failed to repudiate the Moynihan Report. In fact, then president Dorothy Height confirmed Moynihan's emphasis of the importance of the paternal role in the family and was quoted in the report as identifying the status of Black men as the primary concern of Black women. In contrast to the leadership models of women such as Ida B. Wells and Mary Church Terrell, who organized and led opposition to public demonization of Black women, "Height and the Council lined up with those who blamed black women."[20]

The imprint of the Moynihan Report is particularly visible in the rhetoric of Black nationalism. In 1968, for example, just three years following the report's publication, Eldridge Cleaver published *Soul on Ice*, a collection of autobiographical essays on race and gender.[21] In "The Primeval Mitosis," Cleaver discusses the evolution of gender role norms, arguing that in class-based societies, God's original intent for a "Unitary Sexual Image" has been distorted, resulting not only in the distinct hemispheres of male and female, but in class-based images within each gender hemisphere.[22] Within the female hemisphere, he identified two fragmented sexual images, the Ultrafeminine and the Amazon. While Cleaver does not attribute a racial identity to either image, his description of the Amazon—strong, self-reliant, and domestic—clearly corresponds to the myth of the matriarch.[23]

> The Amazon is in a peculiar position. Just as her man has been deprived of his manhood, so she has been deprived of her full womanhood. Society has decreed that the Ultrafeminine, the woman of the elite, is the goddess on the pedestal. The Amazon is

19. Nelson, *Straight, No Chaser*, 97.

20. White, *Too Heavy a Load*, 201.

21. Cleaver, *Soul on Ice*.

22. Cleaver begins his chapter with an epigraph from Gen 2:21–23, suggesting that his understanding of a "Unitary Sexual Image" corresponds to the Adamic figure prior to the creation of woman in Gen 2:7 (ibid., 205).

23. In contrast, his description of the Ultrafeminine highly corresponds to the cult of true womanhood. Defined primarily by her relationship as partner to the privileged masculine figure, the "Omnipotent Administrator," the Ultrafeminine "achieves an image of frailty, weakness, helplessness, delicacy, daintiness" (ibid., 214).

the personification of the [elite woman's] rejected domestic component, the woman on whom "dishpan hands" seem not out of character.[24]

Cleaver employs a classic Black nationalist strategy for freeing African-American women from the tyranny of the matriarchal stereotype, namely, he advocates for a recovery of Black men's patriarchal role. His final chapter, "To All Black Women, from All Black Men," takes the form of an apology issued directly to Black women, whom he refers to using such illustrious terms as "Queen," "Daughter of Africa," and "Black Bride of My Passion."[25] Confessing Black men's impotence and abdication of their responsibilities as men, he places responsibility for the redemption of Black masculinity upon their female counterparts: "Flower of Africa, it is only through the liberating power of your re-love that my manhood can be redeemed. For it is in your eyes, before you, that my need is to be justified. Only, only, only you and only you can condemn me or set me free."[26]

Cleaver was not alone in his misogynist views. Black nationalism's assault on Black women was unrelenting. "African-American men, from Black Panther Eldridge Cleaver and sociologist Calvin Hernton, to psychiatrists William Grier and Price Cobbs, to ideologue Frantz Fanon, accused black women of harming and holding back the race."[27] Thus underwritten by "experts"—preeminent scholars and activists who were able to command the attention and influence the thinking of the masses—Black nationalism's misogyny was particularly pernicious in that it relied heavily upon Freudian psychology, thus giving it the appearance of intellectual and scientific merit.[28] The reassertion of patriarchy within the Black nationalist movement did not totally escape critique, especially from womanist scholar-activists. Jill Nelson, for example, argues that rather than taking gender issues seriously, the movement simply tried to put Black women on the same restricted pedestal that white women had occupied.

The black nationalist movement, in spite of its romanticized rhetoric about black women, was essentially anti-female, and attempted to relegate gender issues, once again and once and for all, to the very back of African America's political bus. Couched in

24. Ibid., 218.
25. Ibid., 236.
26. Ibid., 238.
27. White, *Too Heavy a Load,* 217.
28. Ibid.

the mythical legitimacy of some pseudo-African history in which all men were powerful Kings, most women powerless but adored Queens, and polygamy ruled the land, nationalism at its worst used bad history to justify the continued subordination of black women. . . . The seductive aspect of the black nationalist movement was that its rhetoric appeared to exalt and celebrate black women, to reverse erasure, make us visible, when in fact it was more about a uniform change, a little cosmetic makeover, brand-new packaging wrapped around the same old same old.[29]

Together with the preexisting stereotypes of African-American femininity that prevailed in popular culture and public discourse, the matriarchy thesis solidified the depiction of Black women as angry, domineering, and unnaturally strong. While the matriarch has little basis in the lived experiences of African-American women, it continues to dominate the U.S. popular imagination about the personalities and relationships of Black women. More than four decades following the publication of the Moynihan Report and *Soul on Ice*, it is this image that undergirds every Black male actor's decision to don a "fat suit" and a wig and to breathe life into the character of a dark-skinned, overweight, sharp-tongued Black woman—à la Flip Wilson's "Geraldine" in *The Flip Wilson Show*, Eddie Murphy's "Rasputia Latimore" in *Norbit*, Martin Lawrence's "Big Momma" in *Big Momma's House*, *Big Momma's House 2*, and *Big Mommas: Like Father, Like Son*, Tyler Perry's "Madea" character, and the numerous Black female characters played by Black men in drag on *Saturday Night Live*. Indeed, it would seem that impersonating the Black matriarch has become a rite of passage for Black male comedians. Meanwhile, as the roles for actual Black women continue to disappear on the small and large screens, these caricatures in drag disproportionately shape public perceptions about the lives of African-American women. While it is distinct from the StrongBlackWoman, the matriarch's shadow looms large over African-American women who struggle to live up to the cultural mandate of strength without being seen as excessively aggressive, dominating, and emasculating. For many, devoting much of their time to caring for the needs of others is viewed as the antidote to the negative depictions of the matriarch.

29. Nelson, *Straight, No Chaser*, 132.

Between Praise and Punishment

Over the past two decades, gospel theater has emerged as a chief proselytist in the gospel of Black women's strength. Once consisting primarily of stage plays derisively known as the "chitlin circuit," gospel theater is a cultural art form that combines Christian Scripture, music, and themes with stories of loss and triumph. Over the past decade the genre has made the leap to film, with producers routinely filming their staged productions for television and DVD release. Some producers, such as Tyler Perry, adapt their stage productions for film or create original films that retain the hallmark features of gospel plays. In 2005, Perry debuted his first film, *Diary of a Mad Black Woman*, based upon his play of the same name. The film stars Kimberly Elise as Helen McCarter, a woman forced to undergo a transformation in identity when her marriage to a successful attorney crumbles. *Diary of a Mad Black Woman* was also the first introduction of Perry's famous character, Madea, to the U.S. mainstream. Played by Perry in drag, Madea is the StrongBlackWoman on steroids: she is a gun-toting, no-nonsense, verbally and physically aggressive woman who readily provides shelter and food to anyone who needs it.

Throughout the film, Helen undergoes a radical transformation in identity. At the beginning of the film, she is a paradigm of the cult of true womanhood. A stay-at-home wife, she is utterly devoted to and dependent upon her husband, Charles. Her primary function is to take care of the couple's massive home and to maintain the public image of having a happy relationship, despite her husband's poor treatment and infidelity. She has never worked outside the home, has no meaningful job skills, and has no control over the couple's finances. She has no meaningful relationships with friends or family. Charles, she claims, has alienated her from her family, many of whom live in the same city, and has forced her to put her mother into a nursing home. Effectively, Helen has yielded full control of her life to him, a striking contrast to the StrongBlackWoman's high valuation on independence. Thus, when Charles evicts her from their home, Helen asks plaintively, "What am I supposed to do without you?" He, in turn, admonishes her to remain true to the silent submission of a true woman: "Now be a lady and leave quietly."

While *Diary of a Mad Black Woman* does not overtly mention the StrongBlackWoman, it reinforces the icon in several notable ways. First, each of the film's other female characters serve as countervailing images of

Helen's embodiment of womanhood. In addition to Madea's caricature of the StrongBlackWoman, there is Brenda, Charles' mistress and the mother of his two children. Brenda epitomizes the Jezebel stereotype; she dresses in a highly sexualized manner and has given birth to two children in an adulterous relationship. The film makes it clear that Brenda's actions are not born out of love. She is primarily interested in him for his money and abandons him when a gunshot renders him unable to work or to care for himself. Madea sums up Brenda's character effectively, calling her "a label hoe" and a "floozy." Another significant female character is Helen's cousin, Deborah, a drug addict who abandoned her husband and two children and who remains dependent upon Madea's charity to survive. Deborah is an example of what Patricia Hill Collins calls "the Bad Black Mother," a contemporary variation of the Jezebel stereotype who is typically abusive or neglectful of her children, either in utero or afterward.[30] Together with Helen's character at the film's beginning, these serve as object lessons of "bad" Black womanhood.

Second, several of the film's characters openly criticize Helen's weakness and encourage her to develop and embody the core features of the StrongBlackWoman. When Helen protests Charles' telling her that he's leaving her for Brenda, Brenda responds, "Please tell me you're not one of those weak, begging sisters." Even Helen's mother considers her daughter to be overindulged and weak; she blames herself for her daughter's lack of sufficiency. She tells Helen that she needs to learn how to "stand on [her] own two feet." While Madea's embodiment of the StrongBlackWoman is over-the-top, she encourages Helen to learn to express herself and to support herself. Under Madea's tutelage, Helen gets her first job and begins her transition to independence and to becoming a StrongBlackWoman. The film is particularly deliberate about distinguishing the ideal strength of Black women from the aggressiveness of Madea and the bitterness of the Angry Black Woman.[31] Helen's new love interest in the film expresses it cogently: "I also see a woman who's been hurt, a lot. And she's taught herself

30. Collins, *Black Sexual Politics*, 130–31. Drawing upon the language of hip-hop artists, who refer to women as "bitches" in ways that both reify and resist misogyny, Collins argues that "the sexualized bitch constitutes a modern version of the jezebel, repackaged for contemporary mass media" (ibid., 127–28). In media depictions and public discourse, Bad Black Mothers are typically portrayed as single, poor, young, and welfare dependent (ibid.,131).

31. When Helen returns home to care for Charles after his paralysis, she quickly turns brutal, repaying in equal measure the years of abuse that he dealt her.

how to be tough, real tough. But you know, the key is to be tough, not hard." That, in essence, is Perry's take-home message: Black women should be strong, but not too strong.

Gospel theater does not unilaterally affirm Black women's strength. Perry's work is also notable for its depiction of career-minded women as too strong. And other producers' treatments of the theme are downright vitriolic, such as the work of Tim Alexander. In 2008, Alexander released *Diary of a Mad Black Man*, seemingly in direct reaction to Perry's validation of the StrongBlackWoman. Whereas Perry's films have an obvious yet unstated didactic element, Alexander is more blunt. The film opens with the text, "This Is Not Just a Movie—It Is a Message; in the Name of Peace . . . Please Open Your Minds and Heart to It." Part scripted drama and part documentary, *Diary of a Mad Black Man* includes several "man on the street" segments in which people react to a three-minute video clip that Alexander describes as an Internet sensation that inspired the film. The clip, in actuality, is a scene starring Haitian actor Jimmy Jean-Louis, and it was produced as part of Alexander's film. The video clip opens at the home of Tonya, where she and three Black female friends sit relaxing and chatting in a living room, talking about their plans for the evening. The mood is light and filled with laughter, but quickly changes when a car pulls up driven by a Black man with a White woman in the passenger seat. The driver, James (played by Jean-Louis), is Tonya's ex-husband and has come to pick up their daughter. Tonya's friends immediately begin chiding her about James' companion: "Tell me that ain't James rollin' up with a White girl!" Another chimes in, "I know you not gonna let him disrespect you like that." Egged on by her friends, Tonya opens the door ready for confrontation with James: "You weak punk. You had to get a White girl. What's wrong? You couldn't find a sista who would lay down and let you walk over her?" One friend signifies from the sofa, "I hate Black men like you, too weak to deal with a strong black woman so you gotta go find a white girl to walk all over."

The film then traces the relationship between James and Tonya while also giving a view to relationships between other Black men and women. From its first few minutes, the film is painful to watch. James is depicted as the ideal Black man—a sensitive and supportive husband, father, financial provider, and man of faith (there is an allusion to him being a preacher). In contrast, Alexander depicts Black women as angry, abrasive, superficial, and unappreciative of "good" Black men. Some of the "word on the street' commentary is profoundly hostile toward Black women. Alexander, in his role as narrator and interviewer, reinforces negative messages about Black women while routinely interrupting the remarks of those who make supportive comments about Black women.

The film's message is stridently consistent: many Black girls are not raised by their fathers and thus have never learned how to respect a man. To make matters worse, their single mothers regularly demean their fathers and any traits in the children that are similar to the fathers. Consequently, when these girls grow up, then, they believe that men are "no good." This belief, in turns, leads them to date guys who are abusive, thus creating a self-fulfilling prophecy. Alexander's analysis strongly echoes that of Moynihan, in that he blames the conditions of African-American families upon the fact that most Black children are raised by single mothers. Importantly, Alexander's film has a clear conservative Christian undercurrent. Black women are criticized for their refusal to "submit" and for stepping away from their "natural roles." According to Alexander, then, Black women's strength is unnatural, unfaithful, and it is destroying Black relationships and families.

Alexander continued his assault in a 2011 film, *A Mother's Love*, described in the opening credits as "a gospel stage play in the format of a film . . . too big for the stage." Rolanda Watts stars as Regina Reynolds, whom the film's promotional materials describe as "a strong black woman in the truest sense," but who more closely approximates the sapphire/matriarch. Regina is the managing editor of a magazine (owned by another African-American woman) whose concerns with achievement and maintaining control cause her to become detached from her family. She is estranged from her family: her husband, Marcus, and her young adult daughter, Monica. The film is careful to underscore that her relationship problems are, in effect, her fault, the result of her pride, sharp tongue, materialism, and refusal to accept help from others. Despite Marcus' repeated assertions of his continuing devotion to her, Regina left him because she wanted to focus more upon her work. The message is clear: a StrongBlackWoman does not appreciate a good man. And while the rift with her daughter stemmed from Monica's drug addiction and theft, the film implies that Regina is a bad mother who has driven her daughter to substance abuse and who is more concerned with the material possessions that Monica has stolen from her.

As a photonegative of Regina's ambitious—and one-dimensional—independence is her mother, Georgia Nealy, who lives with her. Georgia is the family's primary caregiver and its source of wisdom. Whereas Regina has banned Monica from her home, Georgia sneaks her in and allows her to spend the night, later defending her actions to Regina: "She came to me asking for help and I'm not about to turn my back on her for stuff, anybody's stuff." She constantly encourages Regina to discover life's true priorities and to reconcile with her family. A deeply devout woman who quotes Scripture and prays throughout the film, Georgia admonishes Regina that her "foolish pride" and materialism have hindered her relationship with God: "You can't put things before family and expect to be blessed. That's the same as putting stuff before God." Regina rebukes her mother's appeals for her to trust God. She retorts, "Well, God better hurry up and fix me 'cause I'm getting weak and I'm about to snap."

And snap she does. At its climax, the film portrays Regina's autonomy and emotional detachment as maniacal, bordering on the point of mental illness. After a clash with her boss causes her to lose her job and subsequently most of her possessions, Regina deteriorates into a bitter, withdrawn, and self-obsessed woman. She does not care about others and resists any attempts by others to care for her, including her mother. Fortunately, though, just before she reaches the breaking point, she has a moment of "conversion," which she likens to Paul's experience on the Damascus Road.[32] Instantly, she reconciles with her family, gets her old job back, and recovers her possessions.

What is particularly striking about A Mother's Love is its resolution. Whereas the film is unrelentingly critical about Regina's independence and her strong achievement orientation, its resolution is not to decrease these features but rather to augment them with a greater concern for relationships. In a pivotal scene, Georgia chastises Regina's boss, Michelle, for not being sufficiently concerned about work. Indeed, the film depicts Michelle as another example of failed Black womanhood. Although she is the publisher and owner of a magazine, she is frivolous and overly focused upon romantic relationships. As the professional Black women in this film, Regina and Michelle are indeed betwixt and between: damned for working too hard and damned for not working hard enough. Further, in restoring Regina to both her job and her family, the film betrays the real motive behind its critical portrayal of Regina: "balancing" her emotional strength and her devotion to work with a greater emphasis on caregiving. It is not that Regina is supposed to be less successful or less strong; rather, she is also

32. Acts 1:19; 22:6–21; 26:12–18.

supposed to be more caregiving. The paradox of *A Mother's Love* is that it simultaneously derides African-American women's strength while firmly reinscribing the virtues of the StrongBlackWoman.

Unfortunately, this contradictory stance is highly common in gospel theater. Producers such as Perry and Alexander craft an ideal of Black femininity that places Black women upon a narrow pedestal in which they must be strong but not too strong, self-reliant and other-focused, and successful yet submissive. They must work equally hard inside and outside the home, ignore their own needs in order to serve others, and be uncritically supportive of Black men. They must be all things to all people at all times. And they must do all this without uttering a single complaint, lest they be accused of being bitter and angry.

Paging Dr. Bailey

In 2005, ABC premiered its award-winning medical drama series, *Grey's Anatomy*, which follows a cohort of surgical interns and residents at the fictional Seattle Grace Hospital. Created by Shonda Rhimes, an African-American woman who serves as the show's executive producer and is also its most frequent writer, *Grey's Anatomy* is frequently noted for its multicultural cast. When writing the script for the pilot, Rhimes did not specify the ethnicities, and in some cases the last names, of any of the characters. She utilized color-blind casting, in which actors auditioned for roles without consideration of their racial/ethnic background.[33] This does not mean, however, that the characters themselves were not based upon racial-gender archetypes. Perhaps nowhere is this more apparent than in the role of Dr. Miranda Bailey, a character reported to be inspired by Rhimes' mother, a college professor. Played by African-American actress Chandra Wilson, Bailey (as she is typically called on the show) fully embodies the three core features of the StrongBlackWoman.

Bailey's defining characteristic is her emotional toughness. She has a sharp tongue and a quick willingness to use it to chastise anyone who is out of line. Dubbed "the Nazi" by interns because of her no-nonsense approach, Bailey intimidates the interns, most of her fellow residents, and even many of the attending physicians to a degree directly inverse to her diminutive height of five feet.[34] She, in contrast, appears to be afraid of no

33. Fogel, "'Grey's Anatomy' Goes Colorblind."

34. The moniker itself became ironic—and was laid to rest—when Bailey had to

one, at one point boldly telling the Chief of Surgery, "I am not scared of you." For the first three seasons, Bailey's emotional range is limited between detachment and anger. On occasion, viewers catch a glimpse of her more vulnerable side, when she breaks down in tears over a particularly difficult loss or dances with joy after being promoted to chief resident. Yet in the guarded manner of StrongBlackWomen, she makes sure to keep both types of emotional displays hidden from her colleagues.

In addition to keeping her internal world concealed, the show reveals very little about Bailey's personal life, in stark contrast to the rest of the cast, whose personal (particularly romantic) lives are on continuous display. For the first three seasons, Bailey does not socialize with the other staff and has no discernible friendships among them. Whereas the other staff carry on illicit affairs that are known to everyone, no one is aware that Bailey is married until midway through the second season, when she becomes pregnant. Still, the first glimpse of her home life does not come until well into the fourth season, when the show depicts an argument with her husband; the theme of her conflicted marital relationship continues throughout the season.

Bailey's strength has a superhuman edge to it. Whereas the other physicians in Seattle Grace are driven by their libidos, Bailey evinces little, if any, physical needs and desires, including sex, physical touch, and even eating. Midway through the sixth season, one of the attending physicians remarks that in the entire time that he has worked at Seattle Grace, he has never seen Bailey eat. When during that same season, *Grey's Anatomy* introduces a romantic love interest for Bailey, the sexual aspect of her relationship has a cautious edge and is devoid of any semblance of the passion that characterizes her colleagues. Even within the confines of her home, she seems ill at ease with physical intimacy. It is not only Bailey, however, who is uncomfortable with sexuality; *Grey's Anatomy* itself seems torn about how to portray the sensual life of a professional, well-respected African-American woman. The show gives short shrift to her serial monogamy while exploring in-depth the roller-coaster romantic attachments of the other characters. And in an episode that is emblematic of the show's approach to Bailey's sexuality, the chief of surgery exempts her from filling out a form required of all personnel that discloses romantic relationships with colleagues. Bailey's sexuality is trapped, it seems, in the awkward liminal space between

---

save the life of a white supremacist whose stomach was emblazoned with a swastika in "Crash into Me—Part One" (season 4, episode 9, original air date November 22, 2007).

Jezebel and Mammy that characterizes the StrongBlackWoman. She is not quite asexual, but neither is she sensual.

In addition to her near asexuality, Bailey's seeming superhuman status is underscored by the show's depiction of her faith, which is a formidable basis for her strength. She is one of only two characters for whom religious belief plays an overt role (the other being Callie Torres, played by Latina actress Sara Ramirez). Consistent with its hands-off approach to her personal life, *Grey's Anatomy* provides little in the way of specificity about Bailey's religious beliefs. She is never shown going to church, talking about church, or reading the Bible. There are hints that she is a Christian or has been at some point in her life; she has an active prayer life and sings gospel hymns. Ultimately, though, Bailey's spiritual fortitude seems more deeply rooted in her personal relationship with God than in identification with a particular religion. Indeed, what is most noteworthy about her spirituality, especially as it relates to her embodiment as the StrongBlackWoman, is its openness and its effectiveness. This woman who is resistant to open displays of emotion—whether joy or sadness—is quick to talk openly—and aloud—to God, regardless of the place or the circumstances. And when she does, God responds. When, for example, a child cannot be revived during one procedure, Bailey looks upward and roars, "You give this boy back!" Instantly, the monitors beep and light up with signs of life. In a telling manner, Bailey responds with a nod of approbation directed upward. God is not simply the source of Bailey's strength; God answers to it.[35]

Despite her emotional toughness and her characterization as a "Nazi," Bailey has a significant caregiving role. She is a maternal figure to the interns and residents, and the wise sage to the attending physicians, despite the fact that she is only a few years older than the former and younger than the latter. When one resident comes to her with a plea to solve a problem, Bailey responds in frustration, "I am not your mother." The resident is swift to correct her: "You are our mother." Bailey is the person to whom everyone turns when a problem seems insurmountable, whether it is a professional or personal issue. When an attending physician gets cold feet on her wedding day and decides to cancel the nuptials, Bailey is dispatched to change her mind. She then proceeds to perform the ceremony since no ordained minister is willing to perform a wedding between two women.

---

35. This aspect of Bailey's character echoes Sheri Parks' description of the Strong-BlackWoman as a modern variant of the Wise Woman/Dark Feminine archetype (Parks, *Fierce Angels*, 3–33).

Moreover, throughout the series, Bailey's manner, responsibilities, and influence defy her rank. Her status as resident during the show's first four seasons ranks her midway in the hospital's pecking order between interns, who are fresh out of medical school, and attending physicians. Yet she appears to function as the "right-hand" of the chief of surgery. However, as is the case with many real-life StrongBlackWomen, her efforts are unrewarded. In the final episode of season three, she is passed over for the chief resident position. When the newly appointed chief resident proves unable to handle the role, Bailey steps up as an invisible assistant, essentially taking over the administrative functions of the role. When the chief of surgery finally figures it out, he offers the job to Bailey, saying, "You've been doing the lion's share of the chief resident's work. You've had all of the responsibility and none of the credit. You deserve the credit. You deserve the job. I should have given it to you in the first place. I hope you take it now. Because what you do and how you do it makes this hospital work." Bailey responds, "Well, it's about time you noticed," before breaking into tears and embracing the chief, one of her rare displays of emotional vulnerability.

Closely related to Bailey's emotional strength and caregiving is her independence. Even relative to her high-achieving colleagues, Bailey has a strong work ethic. As a resident, for example, she started a pro-bono clinic in the hospital with very little support or funding, simply willing it into existence and managing it in addition to her regular surgical duties. Strikingly, Bailey's independence and commitment to her career remain a recurring theme in her romantic relationships. Her husband's frustration with her demanding work schedule and his role as primary caregiver of the couple's son eventually leads to divorce. And when she later begins a relationship with a nurse who works in the hospital, he takes care to note who should be in charge in their romantic life: "Inside the hospital, you're the man. But out here, I'm the man."

It would seem obvious that being independent, self-reliant, and emotionally tough would be characteristics of any surgeon. For Bailey, however, these are the defining attributes of her personality. Thus, while *Grey's Anatomy* creator Rhimes may not have planned for the role of Dr. Miranda Bailey to be played by an African-American woman, throughout the life of the show, Bailey has consistently embodied the StrongBlackWoman, even when she struggles against it. Furthermore, the American public approves of this embodiment. Wilson, Rhimes, and the show have received little criticism about the stereotypical elements of the character.

In fact, Wilson has garnered numerous accolades for her performance as Bailey, including five Emmy nominations, three NAACP Image awards, one Peoples' Choice Award, and two Screen Actors Guild Awards. In the rare cases when bloggers and social commentators have taken the character to task, it is grudgingly. One blogger, for example, identifies Bailey as an embodiment of the StrongBlackWoman stereotype but just as quickly retracts the statement: "Perhaps Miranda is a manifestation of a new Black woman. Not the Mammy, not the strong black woman, but someone new altogether. I hesitate to go this far in saying that Miranda is a depiction of a new black woman because she seems stuck in 'Strongland.'"[36] More frequently, however, Bailey's character is celebrated by Black women. For example, Kimberly Foster, editor-in-chief of "For Harriet," a blog written by and about African-American women, identifies Bailey as "one of the most realistic Black female TV characters we've ever seen. Bailey isn't perfect, and that's what makes her great."[37]

Limping between Two Opinions

The opening epigraph to this chapter contains Elijah's rebuke to the people of ancient Israel, who wavered between worshipping YHWH and observing the cultic ritual practices of Baal (1 Kgs 18:16-40). In many ways, U.S. popular culture does the same with respect to the icon of the StrongBlackWoman, alternately (and sometimes simultaneously) revering and criticizing the archetype. Black women are expected and admonished to embody the icon's core features of emotional strength, caregiving, and independence. With the exception of variations of the Jezebel and sapphire/matriarch archetypes, the StrongBlackWoman is likely the most frequent image of African-American women in U.S. popular television, film, and music. Whether it is in television series, popular film, stage plays, or hip-hop and R&B song lyrics, America loves to depict African-American women as StrongBlackWomen. And women who fail to live up to these three features are judged lacking in their performance of Black femininity. Those who do not meet the threshold of independence and emotional strength are deemed "weak" and "begging" like Helen's character in *Diary of a Mad Black Woman*. And those who do not devote enough of their time and energy to caring for the needs of others are judged selfish, as is the case with the character of

36. Anonymous, "Bailey's Rum Cream."
37. Foster, "Best Black Female Characters in Television History."

Regina in *A Mother's Love*. These images not only shape Black women's aspirations, but they also shape the expectations of others. That is, because representations of the StrongBlackWoman dominate media portrayals of African-American women, society expects Black women to be strong. They expect Black women to be Dr. Bailey.

Paradoxically, society also seems deeply resentful of African-American women's strength. Thus, its praise of Black women's strength is leveled with an equal measure of criticism and hostility. From public policy to Black nationalism to Black gospel theater, the StrongBlackWoman is blamed almost singlehandedly for the supposed disintegration of Black marriages and families. Black women's strength is censured for the lowered educational and occupational achievement of Black males and the high rates of divorce, out-of-wedlock births, and single-parent families among African Americans. Images of too-strong African-American women are employed as formidable weapons of patriarchy, not only against Black women but also against women of all racial/ethnic backgrounds. Media depictions of the StrongBlackWoman as lonely, bitter, and struggling thus reinforce the cult of true womanhood and serve as formidable warnings for women of all races to embrace "appropriate" gender behavior.

Consequently, Black women are trapped in a classic double-bind scenario in that they receive several sets of contradictory messages about who American society expects them to be: strong but not too strong, independent and submissive, career-oriented and a consummate caregiver.

> Black women's lives are a series of negotiations that aim to reconcile the contradictions separating our own internally defined images of self as African-American women with our objectification as the Other. The struggle of living two lives . . . creates a peculiar tension to construct independent self-definitions within a context where Black womanhood remains routinely derogated.[38]

This "struggle of living two lives" is an impossibly narrow tightrope. Traversing it requires Black women to engage in constant self-appraisal and impression management, less they fail or deviate from the performance of strength and risk the criticism of others. As Christine Conrad Neuger explains, the effects of double-binding messages are particularly detrimental: "Although all narratives are formed out of a complex interaction of family life, body experience, social location, crises, networks of support, and so on, these kinds of double-binding messages make it difficult to develop

38. Ibid., 99–100.

narratives that are healthy and empowering."[39] Pastoral caregivers who minister to African-American women must be equipped to help them recognize and resist these paradoxical and disempowering messages. Yet unfortunately, as we will see in the next chapter, the church is often an active participant in reinforcing the double-bind.

Suggestions for Pastoral Practice

- Pastoral leaders who want to provide culturally competent care and counseling for African-American women must develop critical consciousness regarding issues of race and gender, particularly in popular media. Spend some time prayerfully and attentively watching television or movies that feature African-American female characters. What messages are being transmitted about African-American women? How do these portrayals differ from those of other racial or gender groups? In what ways do these portrayals evoke the icon of the StrongBlackWoman?

- Regularly read blogs about the intersection of race, gender, and popular culture, particularly those written from Black feminist/womanist perspectives, such as For Harriet (www.forharriet.com), The Feminist Wire (http://www.thefeministwire.com), Crunk Feminist Collective (http://crunkfeministcollective.wordpress.com), Racialicious (http://www.racialicious.com), and NewBlackMan (http://newblackman.blogspot.com). You may not agree with all that you read. In fact, you may be quite disturbed by some of it. However, the articles will help you view popular culture through the lens of an African-American feminist/womanist gaze and will alert you to some important subtexts and cultural issues that may otherwise go unnoticed.

- Consider developing a church-based media literacy program that helps youths and adults cultivate a more critical gaze from which to evaluate popular media. The Center for Media Literacy (http://www.medialit.org/) has media education curricula ranging from early childhood to young adulthood. The Women's Media Center (http://www.womensmediacenter.com) focuses specifically on raising awareness about issues of sexism in the media and has training programs for girls and women.

39. Neuger, *Counseling Women*, 46.

5

Must Black Women Bear the Yoke Alone?

The Church and the StrongBlackWoman

> Until there is a new understanding and regard for the full person-
> hood of all women with their gifts and talents in the church, we
> will not bear the yoke of Jesus. Instead, we will continue to bear
> the yoke of preserving patriarchal privilege. Must women bear the
> yoke alone, and all the men go free?[1]

In 2013, nine-year-old Quvenzhané Wallis made history when she became the youngest person ever nominated for an Academy Award for
Best Actress for her role in the film *Beasts of the Southern Wild*. Perhaps
appropriately for a young African-American girl, Wallis portrayed Hush-
puppy, a five-year-old who fends for herself while living with a dying father
in a fictional Louisiana bayou community isolated from civilization. The
morning after the Oscars were televised, the much-lauded Wallis became
the focal point of a different sort of attention when *The Onion*, a satirical
news organization, published the following Twitter post, reportedly intended to be a tongue-in-cheek denunciation of American celebrity culture:

1. Wood, "'Take My Yoke Upon You,'" 46.

"Everyone else seems afraid to say it, but that Quvenzhané Wallis is kind of a cunt, right?" Social media immediately erupted into a firestorm as activists, scholars, journalists, and clergy denounced *The Onion*, demanding an apology and the termination of the staff member who posted the crude tweet.

As I participated in the social media protest, I noticed a dominant trend among those who were involved: they were almost exclusively Black women. A few progressive Black men and White women, including clergy, chimed in. But there was scarcely any comment on the issue from women and men of other racial-ethnic groups. Even many of my progressive White allies were silent. Within a few days, I realized that the silence extended beyond my personal and professional networks. Predominantly White feminist organizations had barely mentioned the issue, despite public pressure from Black scholar-activists to do so.[2] A few days following the incident, there was not a single article about it on *Jezebel.com*, a highly popular feminist web magazine that could usually be counted on to address gender issues. The site did feature several upbeat articles about Wallis that had been posted following the Oscars. None, however, mentioned *The Onion* debacle; instead they described the correct way to say the young actress's name and reported that Wallis would play the title role in the upcoming remake of *Annie*.[3] When the site finally mentioned the issue, it was in an article entitled, "'Cunt' Should Not Be a Bad Word."[4]

As I watched the saga unfold, I felt that same sort of anxiety that I imagine Deborah Gray White experienced as she observed the response to Anita Hill's testimony during Clarence Thomas's Supreme Court confirmation hearings twenty years earlier: "Where were my advocates? Where were the people who were supposed to explain to the country who I was, to explain why I felt as I did, to deal with my conflicts? Why were they silent?"[5] Were progressive Christians of other racial-gender backgrounds silent because they did not view assaults against Black women's character—or in this case, a young Black girl's character—their issue? Had Wallis' portrayal of fierce independence conscripted her within the public imagination of the

2. For a more detailed analysis of the media coverage of this incident, see Cottom, "Did White Feminists Ignore Attacks?" and Savali, "Where Were White Feminists?"

3. Barr, "Quvenzhané Wallis Will Star as Annie"; Beck, "Is It Really that Hard to Say Quvenzhané?"

4. Baker, "'Cunt' Should Not Be a Bad Word."

5. White, *Too Heavy a Load*, 15.

StrongBlackWoman? Had she, like so many StrongBlackWomen, become the embodiment of the permissible victim whose suffering goes unnoticed by everyone, including the very institution that is supposed to care and to speak up for the "least of these"—the church? Frances Wood notes that

> The legendary strong Black woman has become the personification of the permissible victim. She is the sister whose solo on Sunday morning moves the congregation in a special way, despite her having been assaulted at home on Saturday night. In a younger version, she is the young teen who is an exemplary student and is being forced to keep secret the horrors of being molested. The woman is kept silent with a strong dose of Saint Paul; and the teenager, learning her lessons in being silenced, listens to a sermon on obedient children.[6]

In chapter 3, I reviewed the role that the church played in articulating and disseminating the ideology of the StrongBlackWoman. In this chapter, I demonstrate that the church maintains an active role in socializing African-American women and girls into the role.[7] Specifically, I focus upon church practices and theological teachings that encourage Black women to labor under the yoke of the StrongBlackWoman. Further, in anticipation of the strategic pastoral focus of the next chapter, I identify biblical and theological resources for healing African-American women's identities.

---

6. Wood, "'Take My Yoke Upon You,'" 40.

7. In this text, I utilize "the church" to describe the Christian church in the United States broadly. Given the racial stratification of U.S. congregations, it would be easy to target the Black church, in particular, as the primary culprit in the promulgation of the myth of Black women's strength. Indeed, because Black Christian women are overwhelmingly members of historically Black congregations, it is easier to identify and criticize the complicity of African-American churches and pastors in the construction and reinforcement of the ideology of the StrongBlackWoman. However, I am intentional in describing this issue as one that belongs to the church broadly. After all, the health epidemic that faces African-American women is not simply the responsibility of the Black church; it is the responsibility of the entire church, which is charged with caring for the poor and marginalized within society. The silence of predominantly White congregations on the suffering of Black women is just as sinful as that of Black congregations. Moreover, because the StrongBlackWoman developed as a direct response to White racist assaults on the personhood of African-American women, fully healing the identities of StrongBlack-Women necessitates White Christians reckoning with their own racial-gender ideals and the harm that these ideals have inflicted upon people of color.

Keeping Others' Vineyards

In the opening chapter of Song of Solomon, the female protagonist beseeches her audience:

> I am black and beautiful,
> O daughters of Jerusalem,
> like the tents of Kedar,
> like the curtains of Solomon.
> Do not gaze at me because I am dark,
> because the sun has gazed on me.
> My mother's sons were angry with me;
> they made me keeper of the vineyards,
> but my own vineyard I have not kept! (Song 1:5–6)

The modern church encourages African-American women to keep others' vineyards, while neglecting their own, in two ways: by venerating Black women's performance of strength and depending upon women's labor and financial support to maintain the church, without providing equal opportunity for Black women to exercise their gifts in ministerial leadership; and by distorting Scripture in a way that encourages suffering and self-sacrifice among Black women.

No Cross, No Crown

During my first year in seminary, students were required to attend a spiritual formation group. Under the guidance of an ordained clergyperson, eight to ten of us would meet for an hour each week to share our spiritual autobiographies and to pray together. The groups were intentionally designed to be racially diverse; in my group there were two African-American women, one African-American man, one Asian American man, and five White men and women, ranging in age from our twenties to our fifties. Midway into the semester, the other Black woman and I became very frustrated with the group. Among our concerns was our judgment that our classmates' spiritual autobiographies were inauthentic because they did not contain enough suffering. "Where's the 'test' in their testimony?," we asked. We both shared the view that Christian discipleship, and especially the call to ministry, was marked by suffering—a lot of suffering. When our peers failed to produce evidence to our satisfaction that they had withstood enough suffering, we questioned their fitness for ministry. In our minds, suffering and being a good Christian went hand in hand.

Unwittingly, my friend and I were endorsing the "no cross, no crown" thinking that Renita Weems has identified as widespread among African-American women.[8] In a 2004 article in *Essence* magazine, Weems described how a large number of African-American women believe that a good (in other words, faithful) woman is a self-sacrificing woman, one who "takes up her crown" and endures suffering and abuse because they believed that to do so was "natural, virtuous, even glorious."[9] It is not coincidental, then, that African-American women, more than Christians from any other racial-gender group, are frequently heard repeating religious platitudes such as the following: "God doesn't put more on you than you can bear"; "If He brought you to it, he'll bring you through it"; "This is my cross to bear"; "What doesn't kill you makes you stronger"; "Weeping may endure for a night but joy comes in the morning"; and "As long as I got King Jesus, I don't need nobody else." These sayings reveal two deeply held beliefs among African-American women: first, that suffering is ordained by God as a way of obtaining God's favor, and second, that we must stand alone in our suffering, relying only upon ourselves and refusing the support and assistance of others. As Bishop Teresa Snorton notes, the church explicitly reinforces these beliefs: "The [StrongBlackWoman] is often viewed as already having great spiritual strength and access to the spiritual resources for her own healing. She has many problems; however, traditions of faith and culture have taught her that her only recourse in this life is to look Godward."[10]

Snorton further identifies "affirming one's strength in the community of faith" as an aspect of the coping strategies of StrongBlackWomen.[11] Remember the case of Ms. Martha in chapter one? She was a woman who had suffered tremendous loss, but was praised by her pastor and several church members because she showed no signs of her losses. In her congregation, Ms. Martha was publicly affirmed as a woman of great spiritual and emotional strength. The church's veneration of Ms. Martha was likely to have two types of impact. First, it would encourage her to maintain the performance of strength even if she were crumbling beneath it. Having been exalted for her strength, she would be unlikely to risk disproving the congregation's view of her as an icon of faithful discipleship. Thus, she would be forced to stifle any overt signs of grief and unable to rely upon her pastor

8. Weems, "Sanctified and Suffering."

9. Ibid., 162.

10. Snorton, "Legacy of the African-American Matriarch," 53–54.

11. Ibid., 57.

and church family for support. Second, praising Ms. Martha's response to tragedy would teach (or remind) the congregation of the expectation that a faithful African-American woman is one who cares for others but who does not need or receive care from others.

Unfortunately, the case of Ms. Martha is not an isolated incident, based upon the testimonies of African-American scholars in theology and sociology. Karen Baker-Fletcher, for example, notes,

> Many of us know churchwomen who are close to death before they see a doctor (often for economic reasons) or the mother in the church whose commitment is so reliable that she returns to church less than a week after a heart attack, diabetic crisis, or some other major medical emergency. The preacher calls attention to this dedicated churchwoman, thanking God that she is alive and praising her commitment. In the meantime the church nurse is on hand to take her blood pressure and administer first-aid in case of an emergency. While such dedication is breathtaking and awe-inspiring, it is also dangerous. Such acts move beyond long-suffering to self-negligence and nihilism. They teach girls and young women to love their bodies little more than slave masters loved the bodies of Black foremothers when they commanded them back into the fields when seriously ill or within days of delivering babies. . . . For all the talk in churches about "tarrying on the Spirit" and "waiting on the Lord," church women could learn to "tarry on the Spirit" and "wait on the Lord" a little bit more for the sake of their own well-being and that of the church.[12]

Moreover, in her interviews with fifty-eight Black women about the concept of the StrongBlackWoman, sociologist Tamara Beauboeuf-Lafontant found that several participants pointed to the role of the church in reinforcing the notion that Black women are expected to be strong, regardless of the circumstances of their lives. One participant described her church's expectation that she would continue to serve the church while undergoing treatment for breast cancer and taking care of her two ailing parents:

> I'm tired. . . . So it's like I'm so *damned tired*. . . . But we don't get that time and it's like, if we don't *take* it, as women of color, we don't get it. No one allows us to rest. . . . And it's like, it's like they want to penalize you for just being human. And I know in my own church, when I found out that I had the lumps in my breast

12. Baker-Fletcher and Baker-Fletcher, *My Sister, My Brother*, 250.

> . . . *no one* comes to me and says, "How are you?" In fact, some
> people are actually insulted because I haven't accepted this or that
> responsibility in the church. They're like, "Oh well, you should just
> be superwoman and rise above it."[13]

Another participant noted that not only does the church expect African-American women to be strong, it expects their strength to benefit the church's male power structure: "Weakness is really someone who doesn't contribute to *men* the way, you know, *men* expect it to happen. And I see that especially in the church. You know, if you don't support men in the church, then, you know, what kind of woman are you?"[14]

This statement reveals a particularly insidious aspect of the church's veneration of the StrongBlackWoman. That is, the church reinforces Black women's performance of strength because it directly benefits from the labor of Black women. The church simultaneously depends upon women's labor and financial support while denying them equality of membership in the church. "Like its white counterpart, [the Black church] attracts a large female constituency, depends upon voluntary female labor, has a male-dominated clergy, and affirms traditional sex roles as biblically sanctioned in much of its preaching."[15] Women's labor and financial support are particularly critical in supporting the congregation and infrastructure of the church, and the church could not survive without the voluntary labor of women in their roles as "soloists, ushers, nurses, church mothers, Sunday school teachers, missionaries, pastor's aides, deaconesses, stewardesses, or prayer warriors."[16] W. E. B. Du Bois credited Black women with raising three-quarters of the property of Black churches.[17] Despite these contributions, the church has refused to allow African-American women unhindered access to ordination, the exercise of the preaching ministry, and the pastoral office.[18] And while there are many non-clergy roles within congregations that carry decision-making authority, these

13. Beauboeuf-Lafontant, *Behind the Mask,* 87–88.

14. Ibid., 85.

15. Wiggins, *Righteous Content,* 1.

16. Ibid., 2.

17. Du Bois, "Damnation of Women," 308.

18. While the number of Black women being ordained in traditionally Black denominations is growing, there remain stark patterns of gender inequity in the church. For more information, see Gilkes, *"If It Wasn't for the Women . . .",* and Wiggins, *Righteous Content,* as well as Lincoln and Mamiya's landmark text, *The Black Church in the African American Experience.*

roles—including that of the legendary church mother—frequently carry with them expectations of caregiver-based service that are neither expected nor required of men.

Discipleship or Martyrdom?

To be clear, it is true that teachings about the spiritual value of self-sacrifice are not limited to African-American women. A hallmark of contemporary Christian theology is its view that the fundamental sin of humanity is pride, that is, preoccupation with the self. In contrast, love, particularly Christian love, is assumed to be entirely self-giving and devoid of concern about the self. These teachings, however, bear a particular danger—that of martyrdom—for African-American women who are socialized to live, love, and labor under the weight of atoning for the "sins" of the race as imagined by White patriarchal racism.

Feminist theologian Valerie Saiving partially identified the problems inherent in the understanding of love as self-sacrifice in her groundbreaking article, first published in 1960, in which she identified and critiqued a masculine bias within theological anthropology, particularly as it is expressed in the writing of Reinhold Niebuhr.[19] Elizabeth Hinson-Hasty provides a concise summary of Niebuhr's understanding of sin and Saiving's challenge:

> Articulating the sin of pride as the misuse of freedom, Niebuhr stands squarely within the Augustinian tradition. According to Niebuhr, human beings experience anxiety as a result of living in a state of awareness of their own finitude and freedom; this anxiety creates the occasion for sin. Human beings misuse their freedoms when they allow themselves and their own projects, imaginations, abilities, and interests to become the center of the universe. Christ, for Niebuhr, is the ultimate response to human sin. Christ is the final norm for human nature in defining perfection through humble acts of sacrificial, self-emptying love. Saiving exposed the limitation of traditional views of sin as pride as products exclusively reflecting male experience. Pride could not be women's sin when women have been forced to stand at intersections created for them by men and have been deprived of the power and freedom to shape their own destinies, projects, and identities. Moreover, humility known only in acts of self-sacrificial love cannot be the

19. Saiving, "Human Situation."

means to redeem women's circumstances if women's freedoms have been taken from them.[20]

Specifically, Saiving argued that for most women, the far more common problem is not the sin of pride, that is, a form of idolatry in which the self is overvalued; rather, it is the sin of selflessness, a form of idolatry in which the self is underdeveloped and undervalued.[21] From early childhood, women are socialized to be in relationship with others. This becomes clear upon examination of the toy aisles in any major retailer. While infant toys are usually gender-neutral, by the preschool years, toys marketed toward girls almost unilaterally emphasize relational and caregiving activities such as grooming, cooking, and socializing. It is no wonder, then, that for Saiving, the primary problem of women is that of undifferentiation, including overdependence upon others for a sense of self and hypersensitivity to the feelings, moods, and opinions of others.[22] Thus, rather than an overinflated sense of self and a quest for power and prestige, women are much more likely to suffer from a form of idolatry that occurs from yielding one's identity to another, that is, worshipping the other. The primary temptations for women, then, are not pride, power, or selfishness. Rather, they are the

20. Hinson-Hasty, "Revisiting Feminist Discussions of Sin," 109–10.

21. Saiving, "Human Situation," 38.

22. Ibid., 32–33. Using childbearing and the mother-child attachment as her starting point, Saiving agrees with Niebuhr that separation is the defining characteristic of male identity, but argues that it is not the defining characteristic for female identity. Both male and female children must undergo a process of individuation relative to their mother (due to the close relationship between mother and infant), but the process varies for boys and girls. Girls learn that they are naturally supposed to be like their mothers, that they are, in fact, already women "in miniature" who must be protected against exploitation. Protection comes in the form of sticking close to the maternal figure. Boys, in contrast, learn that they are not women, nor are they yet men; they must prove themselves to be men, in the process differentiating themselves from their mothers. In the meantime, they do not need to be guarded in the same way as girls and are given greater freedom. Ironically, it is because of the mother-child relationship that women—and by extension, female theologians—are better able to identify the limits of self-giving love than are men: "A mother who rejoices in her maternal role—and most mothers do most of the time—knows the profound experience of self-transcending love. But she knows, too, that it is not the whole meaning of life. For she learns not only that it is impossible to sustain a perpetual I-Thou relationship but that the attempt to do so can be deadly. The moments, hours, and days of self-giving must be balanced by moments, hours, and days of withdrawal into, and enrichment of, her individual selfhood if she is to remain a whole person. She learns, too, that a woman can give too much of herself, so that nothing remains of her uniqueness; she can become merely an emptiness, almost a zero, without value to herself, to her fellow men, or, perhaps, even to God" (ibid.).

"specifically feminine sins" of "triviality, distractibility, and diffuseness; lack of an organizing center of focus; dependence on others for one's own self-definition; tolerance at the expense of standards of excellence; inability to respect the boundaries of privacy; sentimentality, gossipy sociability, and mistrust of reason—in short, underdevelopment or negation of the self."[23] In other words, the critical issue for women is servanthood at the expense of selfhood.

Drawing upon Saiving's critique, feminist pastoral theologian Brita Gill-Austern asserts that "the equation of love with self-sacrifice, self-denial, and self-abnegation in Christian theology is dangerous to women's psychological, spiritual, and physical health, and it is contrary to the real aim of Christian love."[24] She demonstrates that understanding love as self-sacrifice is common among women broadly, as a result of cultural teachings that emphasize that women's identities are defined by their relationships to and service for others.[25] By adolescence, females have internalized the notion that self-sacrifice is necessary in order to maintain relationships with others, which in turn forms the basis for self-worth. This is especially true for members of oppressed communities, for whom doing for others provides a sense of self-worth that is undermined by the larger culture. Gill-Austern posits,

> Women often behave in self-sacrificial ways because they believe they are less important, less valuable, and less essential than men. Low self-worth is endemic to people socialized in structures of domination and subordination; and they come to believe that they will feel better about themselves if they give. Because women often do not feel lovable, they settle for being needed. Women often feel they are worth something only if they do something for others.[26]

Women's tendencies toward self-sacrifice have several common consequences, including: loss of touch with one's own needs and desires; loss of one's sense of self and voice; eventual feelings of resentment, bitterness and anger; a continual outward focus that leads to a loss of self-esteem; a lack of capacity for genuine mutuality and intimacy; stress and role strain; reluctance and even refusal to use one's God-given gifts; and ultimately,

---

23. Ibid., 38.
24. Gill-Austern, "Love Understood as Self-Sacrifice," 304.
25. Ibid.
26. Ibid., 307.

the reinforcement of patterns of gender inequality.[27] Each of these are manifest among StrongBlackWomen. Like the women of Saiving's analysis, the StrongBlackWoman suffers from the form of idolatry that occurs from yielding one's identity to another. In addition to the problem of her identity being the creation of forces that seek her subjugation, the StrongBlack-Woman has little or no sense of self beyond that of caregiver, provider, and so forth.[28] Many African-American women have no problem identifying themselves as mother, daughter, sister, wife, worker, or church member. But like women of all races, they have difficulty identifying themselves beyond those roles. In working with groups of African-American women, I have often begun by asking women to describe themselves without any reference to a relational identity. Typically, the women struggle for several minutes before coming up with descriptors of their gifts, skills, or intrapersonal attributes; afterward, they often say that it is the first time that they have introduced themselves in that way.[29] In clinical settings, my African-American female clients have repeatedly described having dreams and goals that they sacrificed in order to support their spouses and families. They often experience an erosion in their sense of self and sense of voice that is very similar to that described by Saiving and Gill-Austern. Beauboeuf-Lafontant refers to this process as "the self that [is] submerged by strength."[30]

Womanist theologians have also extended Saiving's critique of servanthood as the exemplar of Christian discipleship, pointing out that in the context of intersecting oppression, not all servanthood is equal. Jacquelyn Grant frames the question in this way: "Could it be that women in general are believed to be, by nature, servants of men, and in the context of women's community, Black women are seen primarily as servants to all?"[31] She argues that the Christian concept of servanthood has been distorted by gender, race, and class oppression such that people of color have been relegated to be the servants of Whites and women have been relegated to be the servants of men.[32] Because of their location at the intersection of gen-

27. Ibid., 310–14.

28. Beauboeuf-Lafontant identifies selflessness as "a silencing and impending loss of the self—the eventual end to a complete identification with being strong" (*Behind the Mask*, 131).

29. This is not to say, however, that relational identities are unimportant. Rather, it is to say that they are not the whole.

30. Beauboeuf-Lafontant, *Behind the Mask*, 140.

31. Grant, "Sin of Servanthood," 199.

32. Ibid., 200.

der, race, and class, "African American women have been the 'servants of the servants,'" such that servitude, rather than service, is a more appropriate descriptor of the conditions of Black women's lives.[33] Theologians such as Grant and Williams caution African-American women against appropriating the language of servanthood in a way that socially coerced servanthood is made to look like Black women's freedom of choice.[34] The ideology of the StrongBlackWoman represents that very type of appropriation in that it teaches African-American women and girls that their humanity, racial/gender identity, and Christian discipleship must continually be proved through their service to others.

Moreover, the language of "strength" is seductive, implying that African-American women are gifted with suprahuman powers. Very often, the StrongBlackWoman has bought into what Marcia Riggs calls the "myth of personal exceptionalism," in which she strives to be seen as an exceptional Black person, woman, and disciple, in essence, to live up to her reputation as a suprahuman being.[35] As Baker-Fletcher notes, the societal belief that African-American women are *more* than human is just as dehumanizing as the suggestion that they are *less* than human.[36] With such high social rewards for African-American women who shoulder the burden of strength, and the attendant risk of disapprobation for those who do not, it is hard to refute the argument that African-American women do not don the mask of the StrongBlackWoman because they want to; they don it because they must. That is, African-American women's self-sacrificial behavior is not the result of individual neurosis but is rather conditioned by structural inequalities of gender. In a cultural context that penalizes women's autonomy and assertiveness, self-sacrifice becomes a socially sanctioned way for women to exercise power and control.[37]

33. Ibid., 200–201.

34. Williams, *Sisters in the Wilderness,* 182–83. Grant further argues, "We must resist the tendency of using language to camouflage oppressive reality, rather than eliminating the oppressive reality itself" (Grant, "Sin of Servanthood," 214).

35. Riggs identifies three social myths that have been internalized by African Americans: universal equality, personal exceptionalism, and abstract justice. Most relevant to the StrongBlackWoman is the myth of personal exceptionalism: "The social myth of personal exceptionalism derives from the notion of individualism, which is at the heart of liberalism and the concept of private property. For blacks, it has meant striving to be, or be labeled as, an exceptional black person standing apart from the larger mass of poorer black people" (Riggs, *Awake, Arise, and Act,* x).

36. Baker-Fletcher and Baker-Fletcher, *My Sister, My Brother,* 144.

37. Gill-Austern, "Love Understood as Self-Sacrifice," 307.

Christian theology plays a particularly pernicious role in shaping women's self-sacrificial tendencies. The dominant understanding of Christian love, whose defining attributes are self-denial and self-sacrifice, has been shaped by atonement theory, the understanding that the suffering, crucifixion, and death of Christ were required by God in order to atone for the sins of humanity. Womanist and feminist theologians have been particularly critical of atonement theory because of its impact upon the lives of women, who are already socialized to sacrifice their needs and desires for the sake of others.[38] As Gill-Austern notes, "When Jesus' passive victimization is seen as necessary to salvation, it is a small step to the belief that to be of value is to sacrifice self for others."[39] The Christian understanding of love as self-sacrifice and self-denial trains women for a form of "theological masochism," in which women learn to accept, submit to, and sometimes even welcome unjust suffering because such suffering is thought to be their divinely ordained role.[40] The church has romanticized Black women's suffering, failing to distinguish between suffering meant to temper the spirit and suffering meant to break the spirit or between suffering inflicted by those outside the church as a result of one's faith and suffering inflicted by those within the body of Christ.[41] Women's suffering has been silenced, ignored, dismissed, and even validated by appealing to the church fathers' notions of suffering as punishment for sin (particularly for women as a result of Eve's disobedience), as evidence of one's special standing in the sight of God, and as character-building.[42] Rather than helping African-American women to bear the yokes of racism, sexism, and classism, the church has lifted upon their necks a yoke of its own. Wood states that

> This yoke consists of silencing, ignoring, degrading, and dismissing women's experience, especially those experiences that reveal the nature and extent of oppression perpetrated against them

38. For a fuller womanist critique of atonement theory, see Townes, *Embracing the Spirit*, and Williams, *Sisters in the Wilderness*.

39. Gill-Austern, "Love Understood as Self-Sacrifice," 308.

40. Ibid., 308. Clinical psychologist Cheryl Thompson describes African-American women as suffering from "moral masochism . . . a level of excessive personal sacrifice that assumes pathological proportions. The moral masochist derives a sense of well-being or nonerotic pleasure from excessive sacrifice despite the pain of giving too much or giving to the point of personal depletion" (Thompson, "African American Women and Moral Masochism," 241).

41. Copeland, "'Wading through Many Sorrows,'" 118.

42. Wood, "'Take My Yoke Upon You,'" 37.

within the community. Idealization and romanticization of Black women's suffering is as insidious a habit in the African-American community as it has been historically in the dominant society. Elevating women's suffering to a form of martyrdom for the cause (of others) virtually guarantees that it will remain unexamined.[43]

Biblical teachings that reinforce the "no cross, no crown" mentality are targeted toward African-American women in a male-dominated church today in the same way that teachings about the virtues of servanthood were once selectively preached to enslaved Blacks on southern plantations. By framing suffering as the normative experience for African-American women, these teachings blind them to their own suffering, preventing them from recognizing it, searching for its causes, and working toward its end.

This emphasis upon suffering and sacrifice as the marker of genuine Christian love induces a sense of guilt in StrongBlackWomen who feel that they are not measuring up to the ideal. Many African-American women, having internalized the vicious propagandist messages that they have excelled at the expense of African-American men's success (and, implicitly, at the expense of "healthy" marriages) suffer from a form of survivor's guilt, a sense that they have somehow sinned by surviving difficult—often traumatic—circumstances. For upwardly mobile women who have internalized the ideology of the StrongBlackWoman, the sense of guilt is particularly pernicious. The middle-class StrongBlackWoman not only feels that she has to atone for her success but also that she has "no right" to complain about her physical and emotional distress given that her lot in life is vastly better than that of her female forbears. "If my momma and grandmothers never complained, then I shouldn't either" is the sentiment frequently expressed by successful African-American women who are suffering the physical and emotional fallout of being StrongBlackWomen.[44] Many StrongBlack-Women come to embody the role by emulating the strength and stoicism that they have witnessed in their mothers. Black mothers often hide expressions of vulnerability from their children; they cry only when in private, often leaving their children with the impression that they do not cry at all. Their daughters, as they grow into womanhoood, internalize the belief that a grown woman—a strong woman—does not cry.

43. Ibid., 39.

44. Thompson, "African American Women and Moral Masochism," 242. Thompson describes a similar pattern of guilt among successful African-American women.

> Because strong mothers establish the example of invulnerability by so carefully guarding the range of emotions they experience, a resulting disconnect emerges between a daughter's respect for her mother and the intimacy she feels with her role model.... Without evidence of their mothers' humanity, Black daughters are thereby left to question their own. Maturing into adulthood, they come to see their doubts, hurts, and worries as problematic weaknesses incongruent with these closely observed and highly revered models of Black female goodness.[45]

In the face of a theological worldview that encourages unmitigated submission to suffering, African-American women have little choice but to resort to stoicism—the suppression of emotion—as a coping strategy. African-American women are denied both the theological, systemic, and personal resources they need to transform and end their suffering, and the opportunity to lament their suffering. Where is the space for lamenting the suffering of African-American women in a theological and societal context that teaches them that their contemporary suffering is divinely ordained and is the salvation of the race? Absent the spiritual and social sanction to grieve, African-American women have no choice but to retreat to a position of stoicism, the form of emotional repression so common among StrongBlackWomen.[46]

Together, the church's emphasis on servanthood as the ideal standard for Christian love and discipleship and its lack of reciprocity with African-American women create a lethal ecclesiastical status quo. Weems explains it thus:

> Early biblical scholars, writing largely to male audiences, extolled self-denial over egocentricity, humility over pride, poverty over wealth, sacrifice over self-preservation. But it was women who would take these teachings to heart. And the church has benefited. The male hierarchy of the church, that is. As much as they bewail the relative absence of men in the church, male leaders enjoy having armies of humble, guilt-ridden women at their disposal who

---

45. Beauboeuf-Lafontant, *Behind the Mask,* 79.

46. Baker-Fletcher and Baker-Fletcher, *My Sister, My Brother,* 147. In contrast to the supposed "strength" of StrongBlackWomen, Baker-Fletcher distinguishes between stoicism and "genuine strength." Whereas stoicism accepts evil and suffering as unavoidable, true strength resists and transforms them.

feel it their Christian duty to deny themselves, take up their cross, and sacrifice for family and the church.[47]

Many StrongBlackWomen have carried their cross—and those of others—for so long without support that they have crossed the fine line from discipleship to martyrdom. In her text *Private Lives, Proper Relations*, Candice Jenkins identifies this tendency toward martyrdom as the "salvific wish," an outgrowth of the ideology of racial uplift and its attendant movements, including the women's club movement.[48] Jenkins defines the salvific wish as a primarily Black, female, and middle-class "longing to protect or save black women, and black communities more generally, from narratives of sexual and familial pathology, through the embrace of conventional bourgeois propriety in the areas of sexuality and domesticity . . . generally bound up with a call for self-control or self-denial."[49] As an extension of the salvific wish, the ideology of the StrongBlackWoman imprisons women in an endless cycle in which they must continually prove their self-worth through the unholy trinity of self-denial, suffering, and silence. Add to this the weighty, and frequently engendered, Christian admonition to take up one's cross, and the StrongBlackWoman becomes the modern sacrificial lamb, with her service and suffering offered up as atonement for her gender and her race.[50] Her martyrdom, coded in the language of "strength," is to be undertaken again and again, with only the promise of a long-distant resurrection in the hereafter. And the church unfortunately often functions as both the officiating priest and the altar of ungodly fire upon which African-American women are sacrificed.

From Self-Denial to Selfhood: A New Ethic for African-American Womanhood

Feminist/womanist critiques of suffering and self-sacrifice have not necessarily called for a rejection of these characteristics as elements of Christian discipleship. Rather, they call upon revised understandings of suffering and self-sacrifice that are contexualized against systemic issues of power and privilege. Gill-Austern, for example, notes that while humility and

47. Weems, "Sanctified and Suffering," 162.

48. Jenkins, *Private Lives, Proper Relations*, 12.

49. Ibid., 14.

50. Ibid., 13–14.

self-denial are important attributes for the powerful to learn, "women who experience little sense of power, who are victimized, who have not utilized their gifts, do not need to be preached self-denial as the central aspect of love."[51] In psychodynamic terms, extolling self-denial among those who lack a core sense of self is akin to trying to encourage the development of the superego in a person who lacks a healthy ego identity. No less is true for African-American women, for whom the interlocking experiences of gender, race, and class marginalization reinforce the messages of their servitude. From a pastoral perspective, what does it mean to preach suffering and self-denial to individuals who by virtue of their racial-ethnic identities are socialized to deny themselves to the point of martyrdom? How does a pastoral caregiver even approach the topic in a way that does not compound the struggles of African-American Christian women? Or to put it more pointedly, how can the church transition from an institution that further burdens StrongBlackWomen to a safe space where they can be liberated from the yoke of the ideology and freed for authentic selfhood? Baker-Fletcher provides a clue to the answer when she describes how many African-American women misinterpret the meaning and role of suffering in Christian discipleship:

> It is one thing to sacrifice the comfort of one's feet for a bus boycott. It is another to sacrifice one's health out of a sense of low self-esteem and lack of self-love. The first practice is a form of asceticism and prophetic action. The second practice implies that our bodies, minds, and spirits have less value than [those] of husbands, boyfriends, brothers, girlfriends, sisters, children, and friends; it presupposes, at an unconscious level, that others are worthy of the love, nurture, and compassion of God—oneself is not. The first practice, then, is a form of faithfulness. The second practice is a form of faithlessness.[52]

As Baker-Fletcher notes, for many African-American women, specifically those who have fallen prey to the ideology of the StrongBlackWoman, the impulse toward self-sacrifice usually stems not from an understanding of Christian discipleship that is based in a healthy sense of self, but rather from a lack of self-esteem and self-love. The StrongBlackWoman sacrifices herself because she has little sense of having a self-identity that should be cared for and protected. Healing, then, requires helping women develop a

51. Gill-Austern, "Love Understood as Self-Sacrifice," 309.
52. Baker-Fletcher and Baker-Fletcher, *My Sister, My Brother,* 148.

sense of authentic selfhood. Beauboeuf-Lafontant described this process as "coming to voice" whereby African-American women learned to redefine strength such as that is "predicated on self-care rather than self-neglect."[53] The critical question for pastoral theologians and caregivers is this: What are biblical and theological resources for redefining strength for African-American Christian women? The church, after all, functions as a source of both liberation and oppression for women.[54] Thus, despite the overt, and often unchallenged, racialized patriarchy within Christian congregations, African-American women are drawn to the church because it meets some of their basic needs and represents a sort of therapeutic community.[55] In the remainder of this chapter, then, I discuss biblical and theological resources that the church can draw upon to enrich its liberating potential for StrongBlackWomen and to help them move from selflessness to authentic selfhood.

The Trinitarian Model of Identity and Relationality

The Christian doctrine of the Trinity is an important theological resource for understanding the relationship between selfhood and self-giving, and thus is a good starting point for helping StrongBlackWomen to develop and maintain healthy self-identities. In *Exclusion and Embrace*, Miroslav Volf draws upon the image of the Trinity to articulate a relational model of gender identity.[56] Volf raises the question, "[How] can reflection on God be of any help in the discussions about gender identity?"[57] His analysis turns on *perichoresis*, the notion that the relationship between the three persons of the Trinity—the Father, the Son, and the Holy Spirit—is characterized by mutual indwelling, such that each fully contains and is contained by the other without being diminished by the other. Thus, he states, "the Son is the Son because the Father and the Spirit indwell him; without this interiority of the Father and the Spirit, there would be no Son. Every divine person *is* the other persons, but he is the other persons in his own particular way."[58] Mutual interiority, then, defines not only the relations between the three

53. Beauboeuf-Lafontant, *Behind the Mask*, 136.

54. Baker-Fletcher and Baker-Fletcher, *My Sister, My Brother*, 247.

55. Sheppard, *Self, Culture, and Others*, 27.

56. Volf, *Exclusion and Embrace*.

57. Ibid., 176.

58. Ibid., 128.

persons of the Trinity but also the identity of the three divine persons themselves.

Volf argues that the mutual indwelling of the Trinitarian persons provides the model for what he calls "nonself-enclosed identities," that is, identities in which each makes space for the other.[59] In pastoral theology, we might understand an individual with a nonself-enclosed identity as one who has permeable boundaries—that is, a person who has a clearly differentiated sense of self and who is also open to the risk of being changed through meaningful interactions with others. Volf notes that maintaining a balance between self-differentiation and relational intimacy is a particularly salient struggle for those who have experienced oppression:

> The struggle for survival, recognition, and domination, in which people are inescapably involved, helps forge self-enclosed identities, and such self-enclosed identities perpetuate and heighten that same struggle. This holds true for relations between genders no less than for relations between cultures. To find peace, people with self-enclosed identities need to open themselves for one another and give themselves to one another, yet without loss of the self or domination of the other.[60]

Clearly, the StrongBlackWoman meets Volf's description of a self-enclosed identity. As I and other scholars have argued, the StrongBlackWoman is akin to a psychological suit of armor that has evolved out of African-American women's need to defend themselves against the cultural assault of patriarchal racism. Individual and collective experience has taught StrongBlackWomen that physical and emotional survival depends, at least in part, upon adopting a stance of cynicism, in which one expects the worst to happen. In order to protect themselves, African-American women have effectively "walled themselves off" behind a façade of emotional distance and imperturbability. Snorton describes it as a "death-embracing ethos . . . [which] enables the [StrongBlackWoman] to stare in the face of death, sometimes with barely a tremble."[61] The StrongBlackWoman's frequently voiced declaration, "I don't need anyone," is less an expression of relational reality than it is an indicator of her fear of being disappointed, perhaps even taken advantage of, by others. Yet as Volf notes, this defensive maneuver has the effect of reinforcing the very problems that it was intended to

---

59. Ibid.

60. Ibid., 176.

61. Snorton, "Legacy of the African-American Matriarch," 57.

combat. In addition to the health consequences of living into this identity, lack of reciprocity conscripts StrongBlackWomen to the role of "servants of servants" who are emotionally isolated from others, ultimately perpetuating, rather than resisting, racial-gender domination.

In contrast to self-enclosed identities, nonself-enclosed identities are marked by complete self-giving and the complete presence of the self in the other.[62] Initially, this argument may seem to counter the critique that womanist and feminist scholars have leveled against the notion of love as self-denial. Volf, however, is careful to point out that such an argument does not reduce persons to relationships because personhood is reciprocal, rather than identical, to relationality. That is, we are not our relationships, but we are shaped by our relationships. Thus, mutual indwelling presupposes the preservation not only of the distinctness of the self, but also of the other. Indeed, Volf defines self-giving as "a self that can do the giving of itself and that can remain itself even after it has received the other."[63] Consequently, the self is not lost as it gives itself to the other; neither is the other lost or diminished by receiving the self.

Volf's argument is made clearer through Gill-Austern's analysis of how the doctrine of the Trinity provides a model of mutually self-giving love that is helpful for women. She argues that a proper understanding of Trinitarian relationality can help women understand that mutual self-giving, rather than self-denial and self-sacrifice, is the paradigm for Christian love:

> To be human is to care and to be cared for, to love and to be loved.
> . . . What is most distinctive about divine love is not first and foremost self-sacrifice but rather a total and mutual self-giving.
> . . . The Trinity offers important insights concerning the nature of divine love. First, self-giving is not about denial of self (there is no withholding of the self), but rather an offering up of one's very fullness. . . . Second, in the Trinity there is no pattern of domination or subordination, no quelling of individuality or uniqueness.
> . . . Third, the Trinity affirms persons' need for one another by showing us that wholeness is a relational concept, not something that one achieves on one's own. The God revealed to us here is a God who is needy and needs the other. At the heart of divine love is reciprocal giving.[64]

62. Volf, *Exclusion and Embrace*, 178.

63. Ibid., 180.

64. Gill-Austern, "Love Understood as Self-Sacrifice," 319.

Many StrongBlackWomen utterly lack relationships based upon mutuality and reciprocity, even among their close family and friends. Believing that radical autonomy is an ideal of adult development, they are often resistant to receiving support from others, including emotional, social, financial, and instrumental assistance. Understanding the centrality of mutual self-giving among the three persons of the Trinity can help StrongBlackWomen to understand not only that relationships of interdependency are valuable and helpful, but also that they are the paradigmatic expression of divine love. Understanding mutuality as the dominant paradigm of relationships teaches African-American women that good Christian disciples—indeed, genuinely strong Black women—are those who are capable of both giving and receiving love graciously and without resistance.

Further, Trinitarian doctrine models what relationships based upon mutuality look like, most importantly that they ought not result in a diminished sense of self. The concept of perichoresis enables and encourages us to imagine the Divine as three interconnected persons, each willing to risk loving and being loved by, knowing and being known by the Other. Yet even in their interdependency, they maintain fully intact boundaries such that each has a unique identity that is not diminished by being in relationship, but rather is supported and reinforced by it. Consequently, the Trinity stands in stark opposition to the StrongBlackWoman's tendency to give of herself until she has no self left to give, until her mind, body, and spirit are weakened by self-neglect and she is ravaged by disease to the point of death. In response to the health epidemic facing African-American women, the Trinity utters an emphatic NO! To be clear, this is not to say that African-American women are to engage in relationships only with individuals who are capable of reciprocating; after all, a critical element of Christian discipleship is giving to others who cannot reciprocate. Thus, Gill-Austern writes,

> A complex web of social forces compels women to sacrifice themselves in ways that can do great damage to their lives and the lives of the people they touch. Nevertheless, women need to resist the increasingly widespread tendency to condemn all forms of self-giving. Self-sacrifice is not pernicious by definition; it is not always a manifestation of codependency. Self-sacrifice can be an essential element of authentic, faithful love—the self-fulfilling self-transcendence to which Jesus calls us.[65]

65. Ibid., 315.

That is, rather than arguing for the rejection of self-giving, Gill-Austern suggests a revised understanding of self-denial as self-transcendence. She asserts that when one's sense of self is dependent upon receiving praise and admiration from others for one's service and giving—as it is in the case of StrongBlackWomen—self-denial "might require women to deny themselves the approval, the praise, and the sense of belonging that comes when we give up pleasing the other."[66] Self-transcendence requires us to transcend our base needs and desires (including the need for approval) in order that we might better align ourselves with God's will.[67] For African-American women, then, self-transcendence may require refusing to submit to the clutches of the StrongBlackWoman even when it means risking the disapprobation—and even condemnation—of others who judge one's performance of femininity as lacking, or worse yet, *weak*. It requires StrongBlackWomen to resist and reject the belief that they are not worthy of the attention, care, and support that they give to others. It necessitates that they subvert their own tendencies to take care of everyone else's needs at the expense of their own.

The Self-Love Assumption

In addition to the model of identity and relationality found in Trinitarian doctrine, pastoral caregivers who are committed to healing the identities of StrongBlackWomen can draw upon scriptural resources such as Luke 10:25–42. This pericope contains two incidents that occur in the context of what is commonly known as the Lucan travel narrative, a series of encounters occurring as Jesus and the disciples journey to Jerusalem: the first being Jesus' encounter with a Torah scholar (Luke 10:25–37); the second being Jesus' visit to the home of Martha and Mary (Luke 10:38–42). Together, these passages illuminate a tripartite vision of love in which devotion to God, love of self, and caring for one's neighbor are held in balance.

---

66. Ibid., 314.

67. Lyon makes a similar argument when she states, "Rightly understood, self-sacrifice involves acting contrary to our sinful desires, whatever those desires are. When this is kept in mind, the feminist concern that calling women to self-sacrifice will only reinforce their sinful tendencies becomes unwarranted. Rather than relegating women to a life of altruistic subservience, it is a call to the freedom of living into the full potential of a creature made in the image of God" (Lyon, "Pride and the Symptoms of Sin," 102).

The pericope begins when the Torah scholar poses the question, "What must I do to inherit eternal life?"[68] Christ immediately recognizes it as a disingenuous question, an attempt to challenge his knowledge and authority. Characteristically, he responds with a question of his own, forcing the impertinent scholar to concede the answer: "You shall love the Lord your God with all your heart, and with all your soul, and with all your mind; and your neighbor as yourself."[69] The scholar's response echoes Christ's Great Commandment.[70] Christian tradition has typically focused upon the first two elements of the response, namely that we are to love God and to love our neighbors. Little emphasis has been placed upon the final two words of the passage: "as yourself." Both here and in the Great Commandment, self-love is assumed. Further, while love of self appears as the final theme in the sentence, it is not seen as being less important than love of one's neighbor but is rather assumed to take place alongside, perhaps even in advance of, love of neighbor. That we are to love our neighbor in the same way that we love ourselves presumes that we already love ourselves. What is especially noteworthy in Luke's account is that self-love is implicated in one's salvation. The question posed by the scholar was not "What makes me a good person?" but rather "What must I do to inherit eternal life?"

Love of self, then, is a biblical injunction and is not to be equated with sinfulness or selfishness. The critical issue is how we understand the self. Moessner notes that "the loved self is a self-in-relationship-to God. Persons have absolute value because they have been created to receive God's presence. The absolute value of a person is based on God, who alone is wholly good."[71] This is a liberating message for the StrongBlackWoman. The biblical affirmation of self-love teaches us that StrongBlackWomen must be helped to know, express, and value their authentic selves. They must be freed to be who they are and to embrace their selves in fullness, including anger, joy, vulnerability, and frailty. It means no longer hiding their frailties, admitting that they cannot do it all and that they are in need of others. And it also means being freed to live into their God-given gifts and to exercise those gifts without apology on behalf of themselves and others.

Moessner argues effectively that Luke carries the love-of-self theme through the parable of the Good Samaritan. Dissatisfied with Christ's

---

68. Luke 10:25

69. Luke 10:27

70. Matt 22:34–40; Mark 12:28–31.

71. Moessner, "Preaching the Good Samaritan," 22.

subversion of his test, the Torah scholar pushes his challenge one step further. "Wanting to justify himself, he asked Jesus, 'And who is my neighbor?'"[72] Again, Jesus does not provide a direct answer but responds with a lesson and a question of his own. The merciful behavior of the Samaritan exemplifies the neighbor-love that is paradigmatic of Jesus' ministry and that he expects from his disciples.[73] However, as Moessner demonstrates, it is also about self-love. The idea that one's self is worthy of love and care is borne out in two characters in this pericope: that of the man who has been beaten by robbers and left to die, and that of the Samaritan who extends care to a person who has been abused and neglected by others. Moessner argues that in the moment of being cared for by the Samaritan, the beaten man realizes that he is loved by God:

> It is only from the periphery of the parable, from the side of the road, wounded and devalued, as one receives the mirroring of God's perfect love through the compassion of the Good Samaritan, that a person has a kairotic moment of understanding that she/ he is of cosmic concern and immense worth to God. This is the foundational understanding of a loved self. Love of self in this biblical sense is always interconnected with love of God and neighbor, thus avoiding the dangers of narcissism, ontological individualism, selfishness, utilitarian individualism, egotism, and romantic individualism which posits the isolated self as the only valid reality in the universe with the maximization of self-interest.[74]

Moessner's interpretation of the text underscores that Christian self-love is not narcissistic, but stems from the love that we receive from others out of their love of and obedience to God. The Samaritan, in tending the wounds of the beaten man, affirms that his bruised and broken body is worthy of love by God and by the neighbors who journey along the same road. What a powerful image for the StrongBlackWoman whose very personhood has been battered by a culture that teaches her that she must prove herself worthy of love by endlessly pouring herself out for others. It affirms Baker-Fletcher's assertion that "God does not demand that we be burnt-out workers. God provides grace and rest not only for others but for the self. It is important to love oneself, accepting God's love in one's own life, in order to remain alive long enough to share God's love with those who are within

---

72. Luke 10:29
73. Crowder, "Gospel of Luke," 170.
74. Moessner, "Preaching the Good Samaritan," 21.

reach of the full life-span God intends for us."[75] In submitting himself to be loved and cared for by another, the beaten man commits an act of radical self-love, refusing to acquiesce to the culture's expectation that he die.

Moessner further points out that the Samaritan also embodies self-love. She highlights an aspect of the parable that is particularly salient for women, namely, that the Samaritan finished his journey:

> The Samaritan finished his journey while meeting the need of a wounded and marginal person. The Samaritan did not give every-thing away; in this enigmatic parable, he did not injure, hurt, or neglect the self. He relied in a sense on the communal, on a type of teamwork as represented by the host at the inn. For women who have excelled at self-denial, self-abnegation, and self-sacrificial care of others, an understanding of the shared responsibility and the networking in pastoral care is a liberating perspective.[76]

Like the StrongBlackWoman, the Samaritan is marginalized by society. Perhaps because of his marginalization and his familiarity with experiences of physical and psychic brutalization, he can identify with the man in the ditch. In contrast to the priest and the Levite who crossed to the other side of the road so as to avoid encountering the beaten man, the Samaritan accepts the plight of the beaten man as his personal responsibility. Yet, he does not assume that he has to bear the entire responsibility for the man's care. He takes care of the man's most immediate needs and then places him in the hands of another before continuing on his journey. He does not assume that his own journey should stop. Remember, the Samaritan encounters the beaten man while traveling. Presumably, then he has a destination and goal in mind. By caring for the wounded man, he has delayed his journey. But he does not allow caring for another to bring his own journey to a halt. Neither does he assume that the man has become his long-term responsibility. His promise to return and repay the innkeeper demonstrates that he does not assume that the innkeeper should care for the man without reciprocity and that he expects the innkeeper's caregiving, like his own, to be time-limited. In other words, he expects the victimized man to resume his own journey.

Thus, the parable of the good Samaritan has several "journey mercies" that are instructive to the StrongBlackWoman: "The journey mercies that are received from the parable of the Samaritan in Luke 10 are these: love of self as interconnected with love of God and neighbor; shared responsibility

---

75. Baker-Fletcher and Baker-Fletcher, *My Sister, My Brother,* 250.

76. Moessner, "From Samaritan to Samaritan," 323.

and networking in pastoral care; the experience of community; and the finishing of one's journey while caring for others."[77] As the servant of servants, the StrongBlackWoman can learn from the Samaritan, who interrupts—but does not terminate—his life's journey in order to care for one who is wounded. The text teaches the StrongBlackWoman that she should not live only for others; she must live for herself. Just as in the Trinitarian model of mutual self-giving, the parable teaches the StrongBlackWoman that while her personal boundaries must be flexible and permeable enough to allow her life to be impacted by others, her care and love for others should not diminish her.

Following the encounter with the Torah scholar, Jesus and the disciples continue their journey, traveling to the home of Martha and her sister, Mary. There is a tendency among biblical scholars to treat these texts as though they are unrelated. Interpreters of Jesus' visit with Martha and Mary rarely focus upon the interaction between this pericope and the broader context of Luke's travel narrative. Several scholars, though, argue that the positioning of the narrative and its language indicate that it is closely connected to the rest of the chapter.[78] Luke's travel narrative starts with Jesus' commissioning the seventy-two disciples, providing these instructions:

> Carry no wallet, no bag, and no sandals. Don't even greet anyone along the way. Whenever you enter a house, first say, "May peace be on this house." If anyone there shares God's peace, then your peace will rest on that person. If not, your blessing will return to you. Remain in this house, eating and drinking whatever they set before you, for workers deserve their pay. Don't move from house to house. Whenever you enter a city and its people welcome you, eat what they set before you.[79]

77. Ibid.

78. Carter, for example, notes the continued used of several words that appear throughout the travel narrative, specifically πορεύομαι, "go," εἰσέρχομαι, "enter," and κώμη, "village" (Carter, "Getting Martha Out of the Kitchen," 267). Hutson further notes that whereas the transition to a different setting with different characters leads many interpreters to treat the story of Mary and Martha as unrelated to Jesus' encounter with the Torah scholar, Luke deliberately juxtaposes the two narratives such that the Mary and Martha story serves as further illustration of the themes in the encounter between Jesus and the Torah scholar (Hutson, "Martha's Choice," 143).

79. Luke 10:4–8. This is the second time in Luke's Gospel that Jesus provides such instructions to disciples as he commissions them for the journey, the first being the commissioning of the Twelve in Luke 9:1–6.

In welcoming Jesus into her home, then, Martha fulfills the type of hospitality that Jesus has instructed his disciples to expect.

The scene at the home of Martha and Mary is a familiar one for women, who simultaneously may experience it as justifying women's leadership roles in the church and critiquing women's traditional serving roles in the home. Jesus is a guest at the home of Martha and Mary. Martha, who appears to function as the head of household, is busy making preparations. The text does not specify what sort of preparations and there is debate over the exact nature of Martha's busyness. The traditional reading is that she is busy preparing a meal for Jesus, thus fulfilling her role as a woman and a host.[80] Other scholars reject this interpretation, noting that the text does not mention a meal and that, in fact, the language used to denote Martha's "serving" is that used to describe diaconal ministry.[81] Elisabeth Schüssler Fiorenza notes, "The text does not say that Martha is in the kitchen preparing and serving a meal but that she is preoccupied with *diakonia* and *diakonein*, terms that in Luke's time had already become technical terms for ecclesial leadership."[82]

But if Martha's activity epitomizes Good Samaritan service, as Sook Ja Chung claims, why does Jesus rebuke her when she requests that he direct Mary to help her?[83] Martha's plight is one with which many women can relate. The scene bears a striking resemblance to the holiday dinners in my own extended family, wherein the women do all the cooking, serving, and cleaning while the men sit and watch the football game. To be shouldered with the burden of taking care of the needs of others is tough enough; to be rebuked for doing what you have been taught makes you a good woman might be unbearable. Why, then, does Jesus affirm the responses of the scholar who is deliberately challenging and testing his authority, but reject the plea of Martha who opens her home to him and is providing suste-

80. For an example of this traditional reading of Martha's role, see Culpepper, "Luke."

81. Carter, for example, suggests that readers understand Martha's serving as a missional rather than domestic activity. He states, "The nature of the 'go-between' activity or agency which distracts Martha can be clarified by investigating the use of the noun διακονία in Luke-Acts. By the end of Acts, Luke's audience has encountered the noun διακονία eight times in contexts that concern not kitchen activity but participation with others in leadership and ministry on behalf of the Christian community" (Carter, "Getting Martha Out of the Kitchen," 270). For a similar interpretation, see Schaberg and Ringe, "Gospel of Luke," 507–9.

82. Schüssler Fiorenza, "Feminist Critical Interpretation for Liberation," 30.

83. Chung, "Women's Ways of Doing Mission," 12.

nance for his continued ministry? A possible response, as that made by Schüssler Fiorenza below, is that the text exhibits a patriarchal vacillation towards women's roles, perhaps setting the stage for society's praise-and-punishment of the StrongBlackWoman:

> This text is patriarchal because it reinforces the societal and ecclesiastical polarization of women. Its proclamation denigrates women's work while at the same time insisting that housework and hospitality are women's proper roles. It blames women for too much business but advocates at the same time women's "double role" as "super women." We ought to be not only good disciples but also good hostesses, not only good ministers but also good house-wives, not only well-paid professionals but also glamorous lovers.[84]

While I agree with Schüssler Fiorenza that this reading is possible, and unfortunately likely, in a patriarchal culture, I disagree that it is the text's intent. If we read Luke 10:38–42 as a continuation of the tripartite vision of love espoused in Jesus' encounter with the Torah scholar, we can discern a continuing interplay between devotion to God, love of self, and care for the neighbor. That is to say, Jesus does not rebuke Martha because she embodies Good Samaritan service; he rebukes her because she does not.

In contrast to the Good Samaritan's capacity to care for another while also remaining faithful to his own journey, Martha's caregiving results in a fragmented sense of self.[85] In her hospitality, Martha represents a faithful doer of the word and not merely a self-deceptive listener of the sort described in James 1:22. The problem, however, is that she is so consumed with *doing* that she is incapable of *listening*. She has failed to choose "the better part." Mary's acts of sitting and listening are not symbols of patriarchal submission as some scholars would claim. Rather, they are acts of radical self-care; in her seemingly passive act of devotion before Christ, Mary receives the physical rest and spiritual nourishment needed to sustain her ministry. Martha, in contrast, distracted from the very source of her life and ministry, becomes anxious and overwhelmed. And despite being in

84. Schüssler Fiorenza, "Feminist Critical Interpretation for Liberation," 33.

85. Doing a Jungian reading of Luke 10:38–42, Bumpus argues that "Martha and Mary represent two dimensions of the one Christian life, and both are essential for discipleship and transformation" (Bumpus, "Awaking Hidden Wholeness," 230). We experience fragmentation in personality and discipleship when we fail to integrate these two dimensions. The aim, then, from Jungian psychology is to draw these two components of the self together into a single, integrated sense of self, such that we can "experience the fullness of life promised by Jesus Christ" (ibid., 231).

the presence of both her kin and her Lord and Savior, she feels abandoned and alone. Her plight, thus, is not unlike that of the StrongBlackWoman, whose love of God, neighbor, and self perennially lean away from the latter, such that she becomes spiritually, physically, and emotionally ill-nourished while caring for the needs of others. Like the StrongBlackWoman, the remedy for Martha is to partake of the spiritual sustenance and physical rest that will help her to develop and maintain a coherent sense of self.

Summary

From the church's involvement in the Black women's club movement to its distorted understanding of self-love and women's leadership, the teachings and practices of Christian congregations have been complicit in the development and fortification of the ideology of the StrongBlackWoman. Yet the Christian tradition also contains rich resources for liberating African-American women from the yoke of the StrongBlackWoman. In particular, a rightful understanding of self-love and an emphasis upon mutual self-giving as the paradigm for Christian discipleship can free African-American women from the limitations of an identity circumscribed by emotional stoicism, self-sacrificial caregiving, and radical independence. Instead, we can set them on a path wherein their lives are characterized by acts of love that do not compromise their devotion to God and their love and care of self. And the church can become a true community that does not unduly burden them but helps to remove the heavy yoke from their necks and replace it with the yoke of love that is promised by Jesus Christ.

Suggestions for Pastoral Reflection and Practice

- This chapter begins by describing church practices and teachings that may inadvertently reinforce the ideology of the StrongBlackWoman. Prayerfully reflect upon the extent to which these practices and teachings are part of your congregational culture. How might these begin to be addressed?

- This chapter suggests two Christian resources for healing African-American women's identities, specifically the doctrine of the Trinity and Luke 10:25–42. What additional resources can you identify? Consider Scripture, hymns, and theological teachings.

- Using the theological and scriptural resources identified in this chapter or through your research, develop a sermon or teaching series on the StrongBlackWoman to be delivered during a worship service, Bible study, or small group series. Be prepared with referral resources for mental-health professionals for women who may need more intensive or specialized counseling than you may be prepared to give.

6

"For My Yoke Is Easy"

Liberating Black Women from the Burden of Strength[1]

> Come to me, all you that are weary and are carrying heavy burdens, and I will give you rest. Take my yoke upon you, and learn from me; for I am gentle and humble in heart, and you will find rest for your souls. For my yoke is easy, and my burden is light. (Matt 11:28–30)

In this text, I have argued that, as the hegemonic Black femininity, the StrongBlackWoman forces upon African-American women unrealistic expectations for emotional strength and regulation, caring for others at the expense of one's own needs, and radical self-sufficiency, which in turn increase stress, role strain, and poor self-care behaviors. Consequently, African-American women face a crisis of physical illness and emotional distress that reaches epidemic proportions, despite being routinely ignored by those who love to proclaim the good news of Black women's "success." If Black women are to be made whole, they must be liberated from the stronghold of the StrongBlackWoman. However, given the confluence of

---

1. Portions of this chapter, including the twelve-step model, were previously published on the author's blog at http://lovingblack.blogspot.com.

historical forces, popular culture, and Christian tradition in shaping and reinforcing the ideology of the StrongBlackWoman, the process of healing African-American women's identities is complex and requires navigating multiple challenges. In this chapter, I direct attention specifically to the task of healing African-American women's identities by addressing two questions: What does healing look like for the StrongBlackWoman, and how can pastoral caregivers facilitate the healing journey? Of course, an exhaustive response to these questions could fill a volume (if not several!). My goal here, then, is to outline a basic paradigm for liberatory pastoral care with StrongBlackWomen and to point to resources that can help pastoral caregivers respond compassionately and effectively to this population. "Pastoral care" in this chapter encompasses both generalized acts designed to support an individual's well-being as well as structured counseling that focuses upon specifically articulated needs and concerns. "Pastoral caregivers" includes ordained clergy and laity in specialized pastoral-care ministries who provide care and counseling to African-American women in congregational and nonprofit settings, institutional chaplaincy, and private practice. I begin by articulating the critical elements of a womanist framework for pastoral care with StrongBlackWomen. Then I proffer a twelve-step paradigm for facilitating self-recovery among StrongBlackWomen.

This chapter emerges, in part, out of my own search for healing. I come from a long line of StrongBlackWomen who have been my models for womanhood since birth. Having been consciously committed to my own healing for ten years has taught me firsthand the difficulty of the journey. It has not been a continuously forward movement, but has been full of fitful starts, stops, and occasional regressions. Yet in the midst of this journey I have found some powerful truths and tools for healing. At the time that I first became aware of my self-sacrificial tendencies, I began practicing mindfulness meditation. It was and continues to be the single most effective tool for my recovery. And conceptualizing the StrongBlackWoman as an addiction has been critical in teaching me to be continuously mindful of my recovery process on a day-to-day basis. And it has allowed me to forgive myself in moments of relapse. The twelve-step approach that I suggest here derives from my repetitive experiences of "falling off the wagon" and getting back on again. Like the man in the Hair Club for Men television commercials of the 1990s, when it comes to the StrongBlackWoman, I can state categorically, "I'm not only the president; I'm also a client."

A Womanist Framework for Pastoral Care
with the StrongBlackWoman

Effective pastoral care with the StrongBlackWoman begins by adopting a womanist approach to care. Like other forms of professional caregiving and mental health treatment, pastoral care to Black women has been shaped largely by the same presuppositions that inform care to White women, ignoring critical differences in Black women's social, political, psychological, and spiritual experiences.[2] Fortunately, a number of African-American female scholars and clinicians have highlighted the inadequacy of a one-size-fits-all professional approach, arguing that prevention and intervention efforts aimed at African-American women must be gender-specific and culturally relevant in order to have any real chance at effectiveness.[3] Marsha Foster Boyd defines "WomanistCare" as

> the intentional process of care giving and care receiving by African American women. It is the African American woman finding her place and her voice in this world. It is the bold expression of that woman caring circle. . . . [I]n this process, the focus is on holistic care of body, mind and spirit in order that healing and transformation occur for African American women and their circles of influence.[4]

Boyd's definition includes several important elements for healing the identities of African-American women, including the importance of empowering Black women's self-definition and the healing power of community, particularly relationships of mutual care among African-American women. Collins further describes the following as critical features of a Black feminist epistemology: lived experience as a criterion of meaning, the use of dialogue to assess knowledge claims, an ethic of caring, and an ethic of accountability.[5] And Baker-Fletcher identifies seven "gifts of power" that are part of the everyday faith experiences of African-American women and that can aid in revisioning Black womanhood: faith, voice, survival, vision,

2. Snorton, "Legacy of the African American Matriarch," 50. To date, the most comprehensive text on cultural issues and therapeutic approaches in treatment with African Americans is Jackson and Greene, *Psychotherapy with African American Women*.

3. Gaston, Porter, and Thomas, "Prime Time Sister Circles," 429; Townsend, Hawkins, and Batts, "Stress and Stress Reduction," 571.

4. Boyd, "WomanistCare," 198.

5. Collins, *Black Feminist Thought*, 257–69.

community building, regeneration, and liberation.[6] Below, I combine these approaches to elucidate six essential characteristics of a womanist approach to pastoral care with StrongBlackWomen: the credibility and accountability of the pastoral caregiver; honoring lived experience; empowerment for self-definition; cultivating critical consciousness; developing self-awareness; and community building.[7]

Pastoral Accountability and Credibility

A womanist approach to pastoral care with StrongBlackWomen begins with the personhood of the pastoral caregiver herself. Generally speaking, pastoral care and counseling is distinguished from other forms of professional caregiving, including secular therapeutic modalities, by its emphasis on the personhood of the caregiver. As Patton notes, the paradox of pastoral care is the notion that "full awareness of and care of the other require full awareness of oneself and what one is experiencing."[8] Thus, in contrast to traditional counseling, which stresses the importance of therapist affective and cognitive neutrality, the work of pastoral caregivers is firmly rooted within their life experience and their own sense of Christian identity and values. This does not mean, however, that the pastoral caregiver imposes her values upon others; rather, it means that she attempts to facilitate others' experience of growth out of her values.[9] Further, whereas traditional counseling places stringent limits on therapist self-disclosure, pastoral care and counseling recognizes that the relationship between the caregiver and the care recipient, rooted in their joint membership in the church universal, is bidirectional, such that each influences and is influenced by the other. Thus, while pastoral caregivers are careful to maintain an appropriate distance and focus upon the individuals and families to whom they provide care, their involvement in the lives of those same persons outside the counseling encounter modifies those boundaries. If as Patton notes, "pastoral

6. Baker-Fletcher and Baker-Fletcher, *My Sister, My Brother*, 148.

7. Notably, these elements are not unique to pastoral care and counseling relationships; they are applicable for therapeutic relationships with African-American women broadly.

8. Patton, *Pastoral Care*, 24.

9. The pastoral caregiver represents not only himself and his community of faith. "He is a reminder and re-presenter of God, faith, the church, and all that religion may represent to the person cared for" (ibid., 25).

care is the care of the whole person *in relationship*" (italics added), then it necessitates risk and vulnerability on the part of the caregiver.[10] Urias Beverly explains:

> The effective pastor does not hide behind his or her role as pastor, God's representative, the one who has it all together, or the strong one lending a helping hand to the weak. The successful pastor is willing to risk giving himself or herself away in relationship, so that he or she can be known as much as he or she knows and so that he or she can be transformed while he or she is transforming the other.[11]

A fundamental element of the pastoral care relationship, then, is reciprocity.[12]

A womanist approach to pastoral care further intensifies the demand for pastoral credibility and accountability in a way that has significant implications regarding who is most capable of providing effective pastoral care for StrongBlackWomen. As Snorton notes, "The pastoral relationship will be reflective of the larger world."[13] Thus, the caregiver's social identity—particularly her or his race, gender, and class—impacts the way in which she or he works with a StrongBlackWoman. "To be an effective pastoral caregiver requires one to step out of one's own culture and into that of the [StrongBlackWoman]."[14] It requires a willingness and capacity to educate oneself about the lives of StrongBlackWomen. A major impediment to help-seeking among African-American women is their perception of the lack of cultural competence among professional caregivers and their mistrust of what they view as a traditionally White field of mental health. Research on beliefs about treatment seeking among African-American women indicates that they express a consistent—and strong—preference

---

10. Ibid., 32.

11. Beverly, *Places You Go*, 14. Beverly is careful to note, however, that the caregiver's openness to transformation does not mean that that he or she "should dump his or her stuff on the parishioner or share all of his or her shortcomings, but it does mean that the pastor should *not* try to convey that he or she has all of the answers to life's situations" (ibid.).

12. For a fuller description of the role of reciprocity and vulnerability in pastoral care and counseling, see Switzer, *Pastoral Care Emergencies*, and Kornfeld, *Cultivating Wholeness*.

13. Snorton, "Legacy of the African American Matriarch," 59.

14. Ibid.

for African-American and female counselors.[15] For example, one African-American female participant in a community-based study of treatment-seeking preferences and barriers noted, "We want to relate to somebody when we talk about our own problems because we hold on to everything so tight. And then we get to talk to somebody of our own race, we open up a little bit more. We might let go a little bit more."[16] StrongBlackWomen need pastoral caregivers who understand the ideology, its familial and cultural transmission, and its stronghold on their lives to a sufficient degree that those receiving care are not forced into the position of having to educate the caregiver. They need pastoral caregivers who can contextualize, and thus normalize, their experiences of stress and role strain rather than treating their issues as evidence of individual pathology, and who can understand the tremendous difficulty of the healing journey.

Further, as Snorton notes, StrongBlackWomen need caregivers who are cognizant of, and guard against, the temptation toward role reversal, that is, the tendency "to want to receive strength from the black woman rather than to nurture her and critique her."[17] StrongBlackWomen need caregivers and counselors with the "courage to hear" the stories—including the stories of trauma and vulnerability—of their lives.[18] Credible pastoral care for the StrongBlackWoman is that which does not avoid, minimize, rationalize, or otherwise dismiss her experience, but is willing to "sit with" the discomfort of the realities of racism, sexism, and classism. It provides a safe space in which African-American women are freed from the pressure of protecting the caregiver by withholding information that they believe will cause distress to the caregiver. While this may be an especially pronounced risk with caregivers from other racial or gender backgrounds, it is a danger against which all pastoral caregivers must avoid.

Often, but not always, the requirements for pastoral credibility and accountability mean that the most effective pastoral caregivers for Strong-BlackWomen may be African-American women who have experienced the burden of the archetype and who have made sufficient progress in their healing journey. In other words, they may be wounded healers who are prepared to "make [their] wounds into a major source of [their] healing

---

15. Nicolaidis et al., "'You Don't Go Tell White People Nothing,'" 1473; Hunn and Craig, "Depression, Sociocultural Factors, and African American Women," 87.

16. Nicolaidis et al., "'You Don't Go Tell White People Nothing,'" 1473.

17. Snorton, "Legacy of the African American Matriarch," 59.

18. Daniel, "Courage to Hear."

power."[19] Using one's wounds as catalyst for one's healing ministry to others is the hallmark of personal testimony, one of the most cherished historic practices of African-American Christians. Regina Stoltzfus notes, "Testimony is the act of people speaking truthfully about what they have seen and experienced. . . . Testimony is more than just telling people what happened to you; it is a way of announcing your humanity in encounter with the divine. It is a way of edifying and encouraging one another."[20] Testimony, according to Stoltzfus, is confessional and transformative.[21] Its centrality within the Black church tradition teaches African-American Christian women that the best persons to care for them are those who know their struggles from firsthand experience. Thus, for many, if not most, Strong-BlackWomen, the most credible caregivers to accompany them on the healing journey are "those individuals who have lived through the experiences about which they claim to be experts . . . [rather] than those who have merely read or thought about such experiences."[22] Boyd refers to such caregivers as "empowered cojourners": "To envision oneself as an empowered cojourner, one understands that through one's life, through one's hurts, through one's victories, one has power to cojourn with others. . . . Cojourners are spiritual companions brought together on a common path for a particular time."[23]

The frequency with which African-American Christian female therapy clients express a preference for working with African-American Christian female therapists attests to the transformative power of the pastoral caregiver's appropriate self-disclosure of her lived experience. It is easy to dismiss this as reflecting cultural prejudices and even naiveté about the processes of counseling. Yet as several scholars note, it points to the possibility that these stated preferences are shorthand for a particular way of viewing the world, an epistemology in which the personhood and lived experience of the caregiver—and the caregiver's willingness to openly discuss these issues—are accorded as much, and possibly even more, importance as theoretical or general knowledge. Even for womanist pastoral caregivers, *knowing* about the StrongBlackWoman is not viewed as important as having *experienced* it.

19. Nouwen, *Wounded Healer*, 83.

20. Stoltzfus, "'Couldn't Keep It to Myself,'" 45.

21. Ibid., 47.

22. Collins, *Black Feminist Thought*, 257.

23. Boyd, "WomanistCare," 200. Boyd argues that the concept of the "empowered cojourner" is a more appropriate image for pastoral care with African-American women than Nouwen's "wounded healer," which she rejects because it places too much emphasis on Black women's woundedness and not enough emphasis on empowerment.

As Collins states, "To be credible in the eyes of [ordinary African-American women], Black feminist intellectuals must be personal advocates for their material, be accountable for the consequences of their work, have lived or experienced their material in some fashion, and be willing to engage in dialogues about their findings with ordinary, everyday people."[24] Because of the unrelenting mandate of strength that African-American girls and women receive from multiple social and cultural institutions, recognizing and critiquing the ideology of the StrongBlackWoman can be difficult without the companionship of an African-American woman whose lived experience can testify to the struggle. Notably, pastoral caregivers do not always have to fulfill this role; however, the healing ministry of pastoral caregivers who lack such direct experience would be enhanced by engaging in additional study and training (including self-awareness work) as well as by drawing upon the wisdom of lay women who can bear witness to the possibility of healing.

Honoring Lived Experience

Just as the pastoral caregiver's lived experience matters, equally if not more important is their capacity to honor the lived experience of those to whom they provide care. Indeed, in pastoral care broadly, clergy must subjugate their professional knowledge and personal experience to the lived realities of their congregants and counselees in order to avoid imposing their perspectives and values upon those to whom they minister. As Carroll Watkins Ali notes,

> A womanist approach to pastoral theology requires a paradigm shift in which the importance of contextuality is emphasized. Thus, theological reflection that begins with a focus on experience indigenous to the particular cultural context is a more appropriate point of departure for pastoral theological method. A womanist paradigm (1) gives primary consideration to theological questions that emerge from the experiences of those inhabiting the cultural context of ministry; and (2) the experience of the pastoral

---

24. Collins, *Black Feminist Thought*, 266. Teresa Fry Brown further points to the need for womanist scholars to remain connected to the lives of ordinary Black women both so that their work is relevant to the lives of these women, but also that scholars might themselves "avoid asphyxiation" (Brown, "Avoiding Asphyxiation," 76).

caregiver in relation to the needs of the cultural context becomes the secondary object of theological reflection.[25]

In other words, in the pastoral-care encounter, what the caregiver has known and experienced about the ideology of the StrongBlackWoman is relegated to the background so that the experiences, thoughts, and feelings of African-American women can dominate the foreground.[26] This is particularly important because a critical function of the StrongBlackWoman ideology is to shield from view the realities of Black women's lives, strains, and struggles. Further, the confluence of racism, sexism, and classism constantly undermines African-American women such that they are not believed when they narrate the realities of their lives. Thus, a crucial role of pastoral caregivers is to facilitate the storytelling, or "coming to voice," of StrongBlackWomen by providing an environment of unconditional positive regard in which they can narrate their lived experiences and by recognizing the influence of structural conditions in their struggles.[27] Pastoral caregivers must be careful not to label the StrongBlackWoman's experiences of excessive other-focus and role strain as indicators of codependency, enmeshment, or failure of boundaries.[28] These labels emphasize individual dysfunction and ignore the systemic realities that shape African-American women's ways of being in the world, including the cultural demands and expectations placed upon Black women by their families, churches, communities, and society.

Moreover, the pastoral caregiver should not underestimate the importance of communicating empathy and taking the time to develop the therapeutic alliance. Snorton notes that pastoral care with StrongBlack-Women requires a re-imagining of the role and meaning of vulnerability.

25. Ali, "Womanist Search for Sources," 63.

26. In her description of narrative therapy with women, Christie Cozad Neuger states, "The story heard has to be the counselee's story, not the counselor's projections or assumptions about the story" (Neuger, *Counseling Women*, 52).

27. "Coming to voice" is a frequent metaphor for women's healing processes. In her interview data, Beauboeuf-Lafontant found that in describing their journeys of self-recovery from the ideology of the StrongBlackWoman, participants used language and concepts that were consistent with feminist psychology's understanding of "coming to voice" (Beauboeuf-Lafontant, *Behind the Mask*, 135–50). Neuger integrates the term into her counseling framework, naming it as the first of four phases in narrative pastoral therapy with women, the other three being gaining clarity, making choices, and staying connected (Neuger, *Counseling Women*, 64).

28. Ali, *Survival and Liberation* 50, 59; West, "Mammy, Sapphire, and Jezebel," 461.

While vulnerability is a highly cherished value in pastoral care, it also poses a unique risk for the StrongBlackWoman, for whom the capacity to maintain one's guard is a necessary skill for survival outside of the pastoral-care moment.[29] Having been socialized against being emotionally vulnerable and discussing one's problems with others, the StrongBlackWoman will usually have difficulty relaxing her guard in the pastoral-care encounter. Even within the context of a pastoral-counseling session with a clergyperson whom she knows, she may fear being misunderstood, invalidated, and labeled deviant or pathological. She is likely to struggle with withholding information in an effort to maintain her self-presentation as calm and in control. Thus, Snorton states that effective pastoral care will strike a balance between trusting a StrongBlackWoman's narrative and questioning the reality that lies beneath the performance of strength:

> To do effective pastoral care means to engage in a meaning-making and reflecting process with our helpees, regardless of their race or gender. However, for the African-American woman, the process may look and feel different because of the impact of racism, sexism, and classism on her belief system. When the [StrongBlackWoman] says, "God will not place any more on you than you can bear," it is not enough to hear and admire how this woman has survived the various burdens and crises of her life, but also tantamount that the pastoral care provider engage with her around how this belief makes sense to her in view of the realities of discrimination, poverty, imprisonment, illness, premature death, and so forth, especially the ways in which these have been realities in her life. Healing will come through her struggle with making meaning out of the contradictions between her faith stance and her life experiences.[30]

A critical skill for pastoral care with African-American women is effective listening. Honoring the lived experiences of StrongBlackWomen, then, requires empathic listening that is designed to facilitate self-expression and to get at the deeper truths of their lives, truths about the struggles that

29. Snorton, "Legacy of the African American Matriarch," 60.

30. Ibid., 62. Snorton further advises that there are two beliefs about the Strong-BlackWoman that must be challenged for effective pastoral care with African-American women. First, practitioners must not take African-American women's self-presentation as the "overbearing, aggressive 'I can handle anything' woman" at face value. That is, they must question the reality that lies beneath the performance. Second, they must realize that what may seem to be expressions of profound faith can, in fact, reflect pastoral need in addition to spiritual strength (ibid., 54).

African-American women tend to repress and ignore. Without such truth-telling, healing is impossible.

Empowerment for Self-Definition

In academic, ministry, and personal contexts, the question that I have commonly been asked after discussing the problems with the ideology of the StrongBlackWoman is, "What is the alternative?" Women who struggle with the burden of being a StrongBlackWoman want to know what model of femininity ought to replace it (Oprah Winfrey and Michelle Obama are often suggested as champions for a new image of African-American femininity). But there is a problem inherent in searching for an alternative Black femininity: replacing the StrongBlackWoman with another fixed image will not destroy the yoke under which African-American women labor; it will simply replace it with a new yoke that may eventually prove to be just as dangerous. The goal of healing, then, is not a concrete image, a new monolithic Black womanhood; rather, the goal of healing is to embark on the journey of self-discovery and self-definition. Thus, the appropriate question that pastoral care should help StrongBlackWomen to answer is not "Who should *we* be?" but "How do *I* discover who *I* am?"

Self-discovery, in turn, is predicated upon liberation, both structurally and individually. Karen and Garth Kasimu Baker-Fletcher define liberation as "the act of reclaiming the power of freedom."[31] Carroll Watkins Ali notes that liberation includes "(1) total freedom from all kinds of oppression and (2) the ability to self-determine."[32] Total liberation for the StrongBlack-Woman is thus an eschatological reality, a now-and-not-yet. Ultimately, true freedom from the yoke of the StrongBlackWoman requires dismantling the structural systems of oppression and subordination that condition the ideology. Inasmuch as the church is concerned with the wholistic healing of God's people, it must also be concerned with the healing of identities that result from the structural sins of racism, sexism, and classism. The healing of the StrongBlackWoman, then, is not tangential to the church's evangelistic activity, but is central to its mission of reconciling people to God. Pastoral care for the StrongBlackWoman requires prophetic engagement with structural oppression, both within society at large and within the church itself. As Baker-Fletcher asserts, "The church must engage in

31. Baker-Fletcher and Baker-Fletcher, *My Sister, My Brother,* 158.
32. Ali, *Survival and Liberation,* 117.

radical societal criticism as well as radical self-criticism. Moreover, such societal criticism must be proactive, involving strategies for realizing *a new creation, the reign of empowering Spirit,* in the lives and entire environments of the dispossessed."[33] One concrete step that the church can take toward this aim is challenging and disrupting the socialization practices of families, churches, and popular culture that reinforce the archetype.

Liberation also occurs in pastoral care with individual African-American women. For the StrongBlackWoman, liberation encompasses two possibilities. The first possibility involves emancipation from the ideology such that one no longer ascribes to it. In other words, to discover who they are, African-American women must be free not to be the StrongBlackWoman. They must be freed to reject the demands for unyielding strength, constant caregiving, and radical independence, and freed to embrace self-definition that is based upon authenticity, giving and receiving hospitality, and mutual interdependence. They must be freed to embody the imago Dei within, rather than circumscribing their lives based upon who their families, churches, and society demand that they must be.

The second possibility of liberation for the StrongBlackWoman involves reclaiming freedom of choice, including the power to choose whether one wants to embody the archetype. This requires pastoral caregivers to be willing to relinquish control of a StrongBlackWoman's healing journey and to accept that the self-definition that women choose may not be what we would choose for them. Much of the destructive power of the ideology lies within African-American women's unconscious, and thus uncritical, acceptance of the identity. Liberation means that African-American women have the power to choose for themselves when and how to embody—or not—the characteristics of the StrongBlackWoman. In her foreword to Sheri Parks' *Fierce Angels,* founding editor of *Essence* magazine Marcia Gillespie reminds us that for many African-American women, the StrongBlackWoman has life-giving potential that can and should be galvanized:

> [Parks] reminds us to beware the one-size-fits-all cookie-cutter model of the strong black woman. And poses the question we Black women all need to ponder. Isn't it time for us to take charge of her? Take charge by embracing our power to change, not just our strength to bear. Take charge by claiming our right to take care of ourselves. Take charge by making our needs and those of our sisters a priority. Like those women who stand in our pantheon of

33. Baker-Fletcher and Baker-Fletcher, *My Sister, My Brother,* 247.

heroes, take charge by refusing to be taken for granted or bound by someone else's script. Take charge like media monarch Oprah and First Lady Michelle, women unafraid to be tough and tender, each marching to her own beat. Take charge by writing our own stories, telling our truths, owning our lives. Take charge by tending and listening close to our spirits. Take charge by embracing the Great Black She and heeding her eternal call to be fierce angels.[34]

Gillespie's statement resonates with many womanist theologians who affirm the need for African-American women's strength, provided that such strength does not prompt them to ignore their need to recieve care and nurture from themselves and others.[35] For example, Baker-Fletcher states, "It is good for Black women to be strong. But we need not be superwoman, a revision of the amazon myth which dehumanizes us by ignoring our need for equal opportunities of health and nurture."[36] And Cheryl Townsend Gilkes uses the term "holy boldness" to categorize Alice Walker's description of a womanist:

> A "womanist," according to Walker, was many things. She was a serious person, a loving person, and one who had a strong motivation to achieve and to contribute to the "survival and wholeness of entire people." Most of all, for our purposes, a womanist is one who has a very healthy personal cosmology. Besides being nurturant, celebrative, combative, communal, and self-loving, she "*loves* the Spirit."[37]

To the extent that African-American women find that oppression continues to render the StrongBlackWoman necessary, they must be empowered to choose—consciously, self-critically, and, perhaps most importantly, temporarily—its performance. The challenge for pastoral caregivers is to help African-American women appropriate the life-giving properties of the

34. Gillespie, foreword to *Fierce Angels*, x.

35. Copeland, for example, identifies one element of African-American women's strength, "sass," as a linguistic weapon of resistance. She asserts, "With motherwit, courage, sometimes their fists, and most often sass, Black women resisted the degradation of chattel slavery. Sass gave Black women a weapon of self-defense. With sass, Black women defined themselves and dismantled the images that had been used to control and demean them. With sass, Black women turned back the shame that others tried to put on them. With sass, Black women survived, even triumphed over emotional and psychic assault" (Copeland, "'Wading through Many Sorrows,'" 124).

36. Baker-Fletcher and Baker-Fletcher, *My Sister, My Brother*, 147–48.

37. Gilkes, "'Loves' and 'Troubles,'" 76.

StrongBlackWoman in a way that does not also activate its death-dealing attributes.

Cultivating Critical Consciousness

Pastoral caregivers who would provide liberatory pastoral care to Strong-BlackWomen would be remiss to exclusively focus attention upon individual complicity with the ideology. Pastoral care to African-American women cannot afford to be ahistorical. Those who minister to African-American women must themselves be familiar with the current and historical realities that shape the lives of Black women and their needs for pastoral care. They must cease to provide pastoral care as if the structural sin of patriarchal racism does not exist. Healing for StrongBlackWomen requires cultivating critical consciousness of the factors that lead to their impaired well-being in the first place, including recognition and understanding of the impact of racial-gender oppression. In other words, StrongBlackWomen must understand their lives in the context of a systemic pattern of injustice. Describing her support group process for African-American women, bell hooks writes,

> One important source of healing emerged when we got in touch with all the factors in our lives that were causing particular pain. For black females, and males too, that means learning about the myriad ways racism, sexism, class exploitation, homophobia, and various other structures of domination operate in our daily lives to undermine our capacity to be self-determining. Without knowing what factors have created certain problems in the first place we could not begin to develop meaningful strategies of personal and collective resistance.[38]

Thus, the StrongBlackWoman must develop critical consciousness of the ways in which African-American women are socialized to bear the yoke of strength. She must learn to critically observe and analyze the equivocal messages that are transmitted in popular culture, including secular and gospel music, scripted and reality television, and film. Further, she must assess the degree to which similar messages are codified and transmitted in her most proximate social networks, that is, her spouse/partner, family, friends, pastor, church family, supervisors, work colleagues, and community members. In other words, she must assess the degree to which the individuals and institutions with whom she interacts on a regular basis communicate the

38. hooks, *Sisters of the Yam*, 14.

expectation that African-American women are to be strong, independent caregivers. In what ways do they reinforce the notion that to be a good Black woman—a StrongBlackWoman—is to be stoic in the face of struggle, to devote oneself to taking care of others' needs at the expense of one's own, and to show no signs of needing support of any kind from others? She must learn to assess how these messages are communicated via the culture, practices, and social dynamics of her family, church, and workplace.

Pastoral caregivers need to assist this process by helping women to name the socialization practices and family and community dynamics that shape their embodiment of the StrongBlackWoman. This work begins with educating African-American women about the characteristics, etiology, and social reinforcement of the ideology. As Neuger notes,

> Many feminist counselors suggest that the most important first step in counseling is to help women counselees to see some of the value conflicts or injustices in their lives. This is in part an educative process, but it is also, more importantly, a tapping into the latent self-story within most women. . . . Therefore, it is helpful, not just for the counselor to do educational work, but to help this alternative narrative (with its strong ambivalences) to be voiced.[39]

The aim of this educative process, which Townes describes as "[practicing] a thorough hermeneutic of suspicion and . . . [sharpening] our critical tools," is to liberate African-American women from the traditional lenses of White patriarchal racism and to help them to locate their experiences of self, family, and world in a larger historical narrative of race, gender, and class inequality.[40] Moreover, education should help African-American women to craft an alternate lens of viewing the world that will enable them, at a minimum, to resist complicity in patterns of oppression. Patricia Hunter claims, "a systemic conspiracy has been at work to prevent women of color from knowing their power and passion. Demonic 'isms,' such as racism, sexism, classism, heterosexism, imperialism, have worked in concert against women of color claiming their divine privilege to be who God has created them to be."[41] Liberatory pastoral care is that which seeks to unmask the "demonic 'isms'" that operate within the lives of African-American women, to expose their death-dealing messages and subvert their powers of seduction.

39. Neuger, *Counseling Women*, 50–51.
40. Townes, "Living in the New Jerusalem," 88–89.
41. Hunter, "Women's Power—Women's Passion," 191.

Baker-Fletcher writes that this process requires memory: "the wisdom and knowledge required to make decisions that promote survival, healing, and liberation are dependent on the power of *memory.*"[42] Strong-BlackWomen in recovery must remember their individual and collective pasts, particularly the conditions that necessitated the creation (and their embodiment) of the ideology so that they can maintain an active position of resistance to its oppressive power.[43] Even when the ongoing reality of oppression leads African-American women to choose to function under the protective garb of the StrongBlackWoman, memory helps them to discern how and when to wear the armor. In particular, it serves as a corrective against the temptation to wear the armor permanently, calling to light the stories of women who succumbed to the death-dealing power inherent in embodying the role for too long. And it challenges not only African-American women but also the church universal to prophetic engagement against the systemic injustices that give rise to the StrongBlackWoman. Cultivating critical consciousness reminds the church that the burdens with which African-American women struggle are not of their own choosing; they are the consequence of the "powers and principalities" against which the church is called to be engaged. Challenging the church to "take seriously its prophetic role in regard to women's self-esteem," Gilkes argues that

> Refashioning social meanings and cultural definitions is an essential task for changing society. . . . The production of a humane cultural experience for all African-American women depends upon a radical cultural critique. The church must work to produce that humane experience. The uplift of the downtrodden involves an aggressive campaign to redefine those aspects of culture which demean and exclude and humiliate.[44]

Pastoral care that aims to cultivate critical consciousness reminds the church that the defense of African-American womanhood is not solely the responsibility of African-American women, or even of African-American churches. Rather, it is the call of the church universal to take up the burdens of African-American women.

42. Baker-Fletcher and Baker-Fletcher, *My Sister, My Brother,* 155.

43. Baker-Fletcher notes that "the power of resistance involves active unwillingness to perpetuate injustice. In my understanding, it involves subtle and explicit rebellious and insurrectionary acts against systems of oppression" (ibid., 157).

44. Gilkes, "'Loves' and 'Troubles,'" 208–9.

Developing Self-Awareness

In addition to helping African-American women develop a critical gaze with which to view the world around them, liberatory pastoral care with StrongBlackWomen teaches them to turn the gaze inward. It is not enough for the StrongBlackWoman to identify the socialization practices that encourage the embodiment of the archetype; she must also become aware of how these messages impact her self-understanding. That is, to what extent has she internalized these messages? How are they impacting her well-being and relationships? Pastoral care with the StrongBlackWoman must facilitate recognition of the myriad behaviors, thoughts, and emotional processes that keep her burdened by the yoke of strength. It must help her to recognize how, specifically, she embodies the archetype. How, for example, is she overcommitting herself and taking on roles and responsibilities that can, and often should, be assumed by others? To what degree does she notice something that needs to be done and automatically assume that she must be the person to do it? How often does she say yes to the requests of others for help because she feels obligated to do so, even as her inner voice may be resenting the request?

Further, the StrongBlackWoman must develop mindful awareness of the consequences of her excessive activity. She must learn to notice, rather than ignore or minimize, the signals of distress that her body and mind transmits—the fatigue, aches and pains, hypertension, weight gain/loss, problems sleeping, irritability, depression, anxiety, crying spells, and other stress-related health issues. And she must learn to view these signals with alarm, as symptoms that must be treated not only with medical/psychological intervention but also with radical changes in how she cares for herself. Finally, once she makes the commitment to self-care, she must be cognizant, on a moment-by-moment basis, of the internal and external messages that would tempt her to delay or deny the health-sustaining behaviors that she needs.

A critical element of self-awareness for StrongBlackWomen is learning to identify life-sustaining behaviors, activities, and ways of being, in other words, to identify mechanisms for self-love. For African-American women, survival in the culture of domination has meant wearing the mask of inordinate strength, pretending to be well when their bodies, minds, and spirits are crumbling. Focusing on the needs of others while ignoring their own needs eventually leads to women's incapacity to name their needs. "Dissimulation makes us dysfunctional. Since it encourages us to deny what we genuinely feel and experience, we lose our capacity to know who we really are and what we need and desire."[45] For the StrongBlackWoman, then, self-recovery requires developing truthful awareness of her feelings and needs. Many women view love of others and love of self as mutually exclusive options.[46] In my clinical, ministerial, and personal experience, I have repeatedly heard African-American women describe self-love as selfish. Making this distinction for women is an important part of the pastoral task of liberating StrongBlackWomen.

Pastoral caregivers must affirm the holiness of self-love as well as help African-American women name their needs for care both from others and from themselves. Jenkins asserts that

> *Naming* facilitates growth-enhancing relationships for African American women via acknowledging and validating all of their experience, thereby influencing authentic, positive, and differentiated connections to the self, others, and society-at-large. Naming also challenges the destructive superwoman image by increasing African American women's tolerance for "being held," comforted, and emotionally supported without confronting such needs with inadequacy/failure, weakness, or justification for exploitation.[47]

Naming has to do with the pastoral activity of helping women identify and name their concerns. A chief way in which the ideology of the StrongBlackWoman functions is to condition women to accept suffering and sacrifice as a way of life, such that they are disinclined to notice when their service exceeds the bounds of reasonable expectations or when they suffer. Much of the work of pastoral caregivers, then, is helping women to notice, identify, and name these experiences. The pastoral functions of listening, questioning, and confrontation are crucial here.

A particularly helpful intervention framework for cultivating self-awareness among StrongBlackWomen is mindfulness practice. Mindfulness has been defined in a number of ways. Perhaps most helpful for Christians is Symington and Symington's definition of mindfulness as "the process of keeping one's mind in the present moment, while staying

---

45. hooks, *Sisters of the Yam*, 24. Likewise, Gill-Austern notes, "Acculturation to their subordination to men often leads women to be silent about what they need. Even though women will go to great lengths to please others, they frequently do not know or attend to what pleases themselves" (Gill-Austern, "Love Understood as Self-Sacrifice," 310).

46. Gill-Austern, "Love Understood as Self-Sacrifice," 311.

47. Jenkins, "Stone Center Theoretical Approach," 77–78.

non-judgmentally detached from potentially destructive thoughts and feelings. . . . [The] discipline of mindfulness, which is a form of meditation, emphasizes attentiveness to activities of the body, sensations and feelings, and mental activities."[48] Many Christians avoid concepts and practices related to mindfulness and meditation because of their associations with Buddhism. And this may be especially true for African-American Christians. When teaching mindfulness practices in local churches and seminary courses, African-American Christians often describe having been taught that such practices were "un-Christian" and perhaps even dangerous. However, mindfulness, like prayer, is a spiritual practice that is not confined to a single religious tradition.[49] Symington and Symington, in particular, argue that a helpful model for pastoral caregivers to consider when appropriating mindfulness-based approaches is that of psychology, which has retained the goal and techniques of Buddhist philosophy that are consonant with psychology, while discarding discordant elements.

> Christians need to evaluate the adopted principles and practices of mindfulness from a Christian perspective rather than being distracted by its historical roots. Christians are free to extract and employ a truthful principle while not embracing the religious or philosophical tradition to which it is attached. . . . Both a Buddhist and a Christian can be engaged in a breath meditation, where he or she is following and focusing solely on the breath. . . . [H]owever, the Christian can use the exercise to draw near to God while the Buddhist uses the practice to embrace the impermanence of life.[50]

Arguing that mindfulness practice can and should be contextualized within the tradition of Christian contemplation, Symington and Symington propose a Christian model of mindfulness that is particularly applicable to pastoral care with the StrongBlackWoman. Based upon the three pillars of presence of mind, acceptance, and internal observation, their model

---

48. Symington and Symington, "Christian Model of Mindfulness," 71.

49. The field of health psychology has provided substantive support for the widespread applicability of mindfulness. In 1970s, Jon Kabat-Zinn pioneered mindfulness-based psychology when he introduced the practice into health psychology as a means of treating chronic pain. Over time, mindfulness-based treatments have gained strong empirical support for their effectiveness in treating a wide range of physical and psychological conditions, including depression, anxiety, borderline personality disorder, and eating disorders (see ibid.; Baer, "Mindfulness Training as a Clinical Intervention," 126).

50. Symington and Symington, "Christian Model of Mindfulness," 72.

aims to strengthen self-identity.[51] Presence of mind is a primary feature of mindfulness and is an antidote to the mindless drifting that typically characterizes the way that many people go through life. This state of mental drifting is a particular concern for the StrongBlackWoman, whose frequent responsibility and role juggling force her to remain "on the run" from the time she wakes up until the time that she goes to bed. She manages her multiple obligations by multitasking. Thus, she is rarely, if ever, focused upon one activity at a time. She lacks the mental "space" needed for self-reflection and ultimately for communion with God.

The second pillar, acceptance, involves learning "how to let go, accept, and not expend energy managing thoughts, feelings, and sensations that are beyond his or her control."[52] This is a powerful antidote to the StrongBlackWoman's tendency to manage distress by exerting tight control, or at least attempting to exert control, over her emotions and behaviors as well as those of others. It teaches the StrongBlackWoman to "let go" rather than "hold more tightly" when circumstances are beyond her control. And it encourages her to accept, rather than repress, feelings of vulnerability, loss, grief, and insufficiency.

The third pillar of Christian mindfulness is internal observation, the process whereby an individual learns to observe her internal sensations, including thoughts, feelings, and physiology.[53] Internal observation teaches the StrongBlackWoman to notice and name physiological, psychological, and emotional experiences that she has grown accustomed to ignoring, minimizing, or repressing, and to connect these symptoms to her tendencies toward excessive activity and responsibility. Further, it teaches her that her internal sensations are only part of who she is and that she may be capable of transcending or interrupting them. By recognizing the cycle between her hectic schedule and her physical and emotional distress, she is empowered to disrupt the cycle.

Several African-American female scholar-practitioners suggest that mindfulness practice would have significant benefits for African-American women. hooks, for example, identifies solitude and contemplation as essential to the work of self-recovery and self-definition. She argues that Black women "are so well socialized to push ourselves past healthy limits that we often do not know how to set protective boundaries that would eliminate

51. Ibid., 73.
52. Ibid.
53. Ibid., 74.

certain forms of stress in our lives."[54] Further, Woods-Giscombé and Black propose that mind-body interventions such as mindfulness practices may be effective in reducing health disparities among African-American women.[55] They write,

> The practice of mindfulness can enhance awareness of habitual patterns of responding to stress (e.g., worry, catastrophizing, rumination, and guilt) and can result in the interruption of psycho-physiological processes that result from chronic stress, as well as health behaviors that are used to cope (e.g., sedentary behavior as a means of resting from overexertion and tobacco or other substance use to numb undesirable emotions). Exercises in MBSR, such as sitting meditation and the body scan, can give African American women (who are often consumed by caring for the needs of others) a restorative and imperative time-out to quiet the mind and restore balance. . . . [T]he nonjudgmental awareness of emotions and thoughts emphasized in mindfulness practice can lead to an unbiased, nonjudgmental self-acceptance. The resulting cultivation of inner peace and personal fortification can lead to the embodiment of strength in ways that have more health promoting, rather than health deprecating, effects.[56]

An important mindfulness practice for StrongBlackWomen is learning to recognize one's healthy limits. In providing pastoral care to seminary students, I repeatedly encounter African-American female students who need challenge and assistance in recognizing a reasonable load. And my discussions with clinical pastoral education supervisors and seminary faculty and staff reveal that this is a common pattern. Since the problem of overextending oneself is common to women, to African Americans, and to clergy, it is not surprising that many supervisors, faculty, and staff routinely report concern about their overburdened African-American female seminarians, who routinely "add" seminary coursework onto already full loads of demanding full-time employment, marriage, raising children, caring for elderly relatives and other extended kin, and heavy church involvement. Mindfulness practice can help StrongBlackWomen to recognize the realistic "load" limits that they can bear while maintaining health-sustaining behaviors. This is an important element of self-awareness.

54. hooks, *Sisters of the Yam*, 55.
55. Woods-Giscombé and Black, "Mind-Body Interventions," 116–17.
56. Ibid., 122.

Community-Building

A primary responsibility of pastoral caregivers in caring for StrongBlack-Women is to cultivate safe spaces for nurturing women's consciousness and facilitating self-definition. The individual relationship with the pastoral care provider functions as one form of safe space. However, healing for many StrongBlackWomen requires more than this; it requires a community of support. Paradoxically, many StrongBlackWomen have strong community-building skills yet they lack community. That is, they have formidable social networks in which they nurture, assist, and sustain others; but they do not have relationships in which they receive emotional, social, and instrumental support. And they lack safe spaces in which they can freely examine the issues that concern them. In her explanation of community building, Baker-Fletcher references the "glue-like" capacities of African-American women, that is, their capacities to hold family, church, and community together.[57] Whereas African-American women have historically dedicated their community-building efforts to ensuring the stability and survival of familial and social institutions (including the church), healing African-American womanhood requires using the power of community for their own survival. In other words, what StrongBlackWomen need is *koinonia*.

Deborah van Deusen Hunsinger notes that the Greek noun *koinonia*, including its variants, occurs 119 times in Scripture and is most commonly translated as "communion," "community," and "fellowship."[58] She claims that *koinonia* is both the foundation and purpose of pastoral care in the Christian tradition. She asserts, "Koinonia is the fellowship that makes pastoral care possible. When koinonia flourishes, so does pastoral care."[59] And further: "Koinonia is the central purpose of Christian pastoral care. The loving communion of persons, both human and divine, is its telos. Being fully present to others, listening with care, and praying for their needs are ends in themselves. They are not a means to some other end."[60] Given the centrality of community in Christian theology and practice, the church represents the optimal site for cultivating community for StrongBlack-Women. For the StrongBlackWoman, the healing power of community within Christian congregations persists despite the church's involvement

57. Baker-Fletcher and Baker-Fletcher, *My Sister, My Brother*, 149.

58. Hunsinger, *Pray without Ceasing*, 2.

59. Ibid., 3.

60. Ibid., 13.

in the socialization of African-American women into the precepts of the ideology. Collins notes that despite problems of sexist oppression that often exist within African-American institutions, Black families, churches, and community organizations provide important social spaces where Black women can dialogue freely and resist objectification.[61] Likewise, Baker-Fletcher readily acknowledges the imperfections within the church but also asserts that "the church is vital for realizing the interrelatedness and interconnectedness of believers and the sacredness of life. It moves believers beyond an individualistic form of faith experience and activity to communal faith experience and activity."[62]

Women's friendships are generally viewed as important sites of building community and fostering healing in feminist pastoral care. Gill-Austern, for example, describes women's friendships as "resources that can help women move in [the] direction of life-giving love."[63] The same is true for African-American women, for whom community is often nurtured through friendships and small group settings, both within and outside the church. Indeed, womanist approaches to pastoral care frequently involve the use of small groups, sometimes known as "sister circles."[64] Spaces that are populated solely by African-American women provide emotional and spiritual sanctuary in which StrongBlackWomen feel safe enough to "dis-armor."[65] Several womanist scholars have written about the transformative power of support groups for African-American women, including bell hooks' *Sisters of the Yam* and Teresa Fry Brown's description of her S.W.E.E.T. support group model, a six-year project that reached at least five hundred women from various denominations, churches, and organizations in Denver.[66]

---

61. Collins, *Black Feminist Thought*, 100–101.

62. Baker-Fletcher and Baker-Fletcher, *My Sister, My Brother*, 245.

63. Gill-Austern, "Love Understood as Self-Sacrifice," 318.

64. Boyd, "WomanistCare," 198.

65. Collins notes that while "by definition, such spaces become less 'safe' if shared with those who were not Black and female," the goal of such exclusionary spaces is to work towards the creation of an inclusive and just society (Collins, *Black Feminist Thought*, 110).

66. Brown, "Avoiding Asphyxiation," 79–85. Notably, hooks initially organized her group as a response to needs among her Black female students, women who came from middle-class backgrounds but whose lives contained "the same problems that are so acutely visible among the black poor and underclass, problems that are usually seen by liberals in the larger society as rooted primarily in economics" (hooks, *Sisters of the Yam*, 12).

I have personally experienced the power of a small group in aiding my self-recovery from the ideology of the StrongBlackWoman. In the winter of 2002, I launched the SISTERS program at an African-American Baptist congregation in Durham, North Carolina.[67] The initial group of participants included twenty women, ranging in age from mid-twenties to late-forties, all of whom were members of the church; of that group, twelve became regular participants.[68] My original plan was to lead the group through a six-week self-care curriculum, which I developed.[69] But at the end of the six-week period, a bond had been established among the group, and the members did not want to disband. SISTERS continued to meet for approximately two years, weekly at first and eventually biweekly. The group's primary focus was to provide a safe space in which StrongBlackWomen could share life together. There was only one rule—confidentiality; whatever was shared in the context of the group was not to be repeated outside the group.[70] In the context of the group, there were no experts. I facilitated the group together with the congregation's women's ministry director. We began each meeting with prayer and "check-in" time, during which participants shared what was happening in their lives. For most meetings, there was no set agenda; we simply followed the Spirit's direction in the conversation, often directing most of our focus to whichever participant(s) seemed to have the most pressing needs. We listened to, affirmed, supported, and challenged each other's self-understanding. There were a few times when the group felt that a particular theme was resurfacing in our stories frequently enough that

67. SISTERS is an acronym for "Sustaining Imani Spirit through Experiencing Restorative Self-Care." *Imani* is the Swahili word for faith.

68. With the exception of the facilitator (me), the group was comprised of unmarried women. Many had never been married (particularly those in their twenties); others were divorced. Some had survived abusive relationships. The participants' education ranged from high school to graduate and professional degrees. About half were professionals with a bachelor's degree or higher; others worked as administrative assistants, in food service, or as laboratory technicians. Some were unemployed, and at least one received disability benefits. Two were licensed ministers; at least three others (including me) began to hear the call to ministry during the period in which the group met.

69. The following themes were addressed in the curriculum: assessing self-care strengths and weaknesses; using affirmations; practicing spiritual disciplines, including prayer, meditation, and journaling; balancing masculine and feminine energies; taking care of one's physical health; pursuing one's passion; and recognizing triggers for stress and self-care neglect.

70. Interestingly, several months into our meetings, the church's pastor marveled at how well participants maintained confidentiality. He expressed surprise at not hearing anyone discuss the content of our meetings.

we needed to devote a particular session to it. Notably, the most commonly reoccurring theme was problems in relationships with our mothers, many of whom could easily be identified as StrongBlackWomen.

My experience in SISTERS, as well as the shared experience of womanist pastoral caregivers, reveals that community serves several important functions for StrongBlackWomen. First, community provides space for the dialogue that is necessary for self-realization and self-definition. Within the context of community, StrongBlackWomen are given sanctuary and rest; they are released from their roles as caregivers and burden bearers. In "a nurturing, transformative, 'woman-space,'" African-American women do not have to worry about guarding against the pejorative images of the Jezebel, the Mammy, and the matriarch.[71] They are freed from bearing the responsibility for the lives of others and released from the obligation to appear as though they have it all under control. As they are able to focus their energies and attention upon themselves, they learn to express their needs, thoughts, and feelings, to name their suffering as well as their need for healing. In demonstrating compassion for one another, they learn to be compassionate toward themselves. In opening their inner lives to one another, StrongBlackWomen are empowered to discover their true identity as bearers of the image of God.[72] An excerpt from Audre Lorde's *Sister Outsider* provides an apt description of this process:

> We have to consciously study how to be tender with each other until it becomes a habit because what was native has been stolen from us, the love of Black women for each other. But we can practice being gentle with ourselves by being gentle with each other. We can practice being gentle with each other by being gentle with that piece of ourselves that is hardest to hold, by giving more to the brave bruised girlchild within each of us, by expecting a little less from her gargantuan efforts to excel. We can love her in the light

---

71. Brown writes, "Our sisters in family, church, and community need a safe place to begin the tedious transformation process of hearing new thoughts, working through the pain of ingesting fresh air, and processing how womanist theology and ethics may grow in their lives. . . . A nurturing, transformative 'woman-space' must be provided for women to think, refresh, rest, and rejuvenate. This space must be free of the distractions of societal definitions of roles of women and of our need to be what someone else wants us to be. It is hard to breathe when someone else is standing on your chest. Reaching the proper energy level for the liberation of struggle is hard if you are tired, have paralysis of the vocal folds, or have a collapsed lung due to the weight of oppression" (Brown, "Avoiding Asphyxiation," 78).

72. Hunsinger, *Pray without Ceasing*, 5.

as well as in the darkness, quiet her frenzy toward perfection and encourage her attentions toward fulfillment.[73]

This quotation illuminates a second function of community, namely, that it fosters interdependence. Hunsinger states, "In pastoral care, real interdependence becomes a reality when we reach out to one another in love."[74] As in the SISTERS experience, when StrongBlackWomen receive affirmation and support in the context of confidential relationships, they learn how to trust and depend upon others and how to receive hospitality. Further, within communal spaces women form relationships that model an important balance between relational engagement and healthy boundaries. In a well structured group, members affirm each other without enabling and they challenge each other without undermining or belittling, in turn teaching StrongBlackWomen how to give support and care to members of their social networks in ways that do not seek to control or diminish others. Finally, community provides accountability. When African-American women gather in supportive spaces that encourage them to tell the truth of their lives and to claim responsibility for their own well-being, they are also encouraged to accept responsibility for their own personhood and well-being. They become "women holding one another accountable for who we say we are and what we say we are about and, from that circle, moving forth to hold others accountable for who they say are and what they say they are about."[75] In the context of community, accountability results in the collective action necessary to effect true change in patterns of social domination.

The StrongBlackWoman's Twelve-Step Recovery Program

If this were a twelve-step meeting for StrongBlackWomen, I would begin by saying, *Hi, my name is Chanequa and I'm a StrongBlackWoman. I have been in recovery for over a decade now. But at most, I've probably only accrued a few weeks of being clean at once. I relapse constantly, maybe even daily. I don't know if I'll ever break free of this thing. But I'm here. And just for today, I will make at least one decision in favor of my physical, spiritual, emotional, and relational health. Just for today, I will try to let go of my need for control, to become aware of when I need help, and to ask for help when I need it. Just*

73. Lorde, *Sister Outsider,* 175.

74. Hunsinger, *Pray without Ceasing,* 27.

75. Boyd, "WomanistCare," 201.

for today, I give myself permission to cry when I'm sad, to scream when I'm frustrated, to smile and laugh when I'm happy, and to dance like I've got wings when the Spirit moves me. Just for today, I will reject the mandate to be a StrongBlackWoman. Just for today, I will simply be.

My personal healing journey, as well as my clinical work and ministry with African-American women who are burdened by the yoke of strength, have convinced me that being a StrongBlackWoman is an addiction, a force of habit ingrained in many African-American women from childhood. And given the high social demand for Black women to perform this role, the probability of relapse is high. Our healing, then, is not a one-time event, but rather a lifelong process. Thus, an appropriate model for pastoral care is one based upon twelve-step philosophy.

In *Hunger for Healing*, J. Keith Miller describes the twelve-step recovery model as an aid to authentic spiritual growth for Christians.[76] Within recovery communities, individuals in recovery bear witness to the healing work of God within the lives of others. And as they put themselves into the hands of God, they discover "firsthand the loving, redeeming, supporting, moral, and confronting nature of God."[77] The critical components of the programs resonate with several elements of the womanist framework for pastoral care described above. Miller reports that twelve-step programs are most effective when (1) they are worked out within the context of community rather than individually (i.e., *community building*); (2) they are worked out utilizing the support and guidance of a sponsor, that is, a leader whose authority stems from her personal experiences of recovery (i.e., *pastoral accountability and credibility*); (3) individuals educate themselves about their addiction and the recovery process (i.e., *cultivating critical consciousness*); (4) the disciplines of prayer and meditation are practiced regularly (i.e., *developing self-awareness*); and (5) individuals share their learning and recovery with others.[78]

The Twelve Steps

Below I describe and briefly explain each of the twelve steps.

76. Miller, *Hunger for Healing*, 1.

77. Ibid.

78. Ibid., 8.

Step One: We admit that we are powerless over our compulsion to be strong—that our physical, spiritual, emotional, and relational health are suffering. As in any twelve-step paradigm, the first step is the most critical for the StrongBlackWoman in recovery. It requires admission that our compulsions toward strength have gotten out of control and our lives have become unmanageable.[79] After all, it is easier to relinquish control once you realize that you are not really in control. Miller states, "Step One has to do with our inherent fear of turning loose our control over ourselves, others, and our futures enough to admit our own weakness and inability to fix life and to change the people, places, and things around us."[80] It aims to break through the StrongBlackWoman's denial and repression and to help her to recognize the systemic nature of her behaviors and experiences.

Step Two: We acknowledge that we are not the Divine, that there is a Power greater than ourselves who can restore us to right relationship with ourselves and others. Whereas the first step is designed to help the StrongBlack-Woman to face reality regarding the extent of her helplessness and distress, this step is designed to restore a sense of hope that healing is possible, but it does not rest within their sole power. Women who are actively involved in the life of the church may be tempted to move too quickly through this step. After all, their attendance and service at church would seem to prove their belief in the life-sustaining powers of God. However, the StrongBlack-Woman is typically so effective at repressing the anxiety and doubts that compel her performance of the archetype that she is utterly unaware of the extent to which she lacks trust in God. She does not realize that she believes that she has to do everything and that she cannot rely on anyone because, ultimately, she does not trust the provision of God's grace in her life and in the lives of others.[81] This step, thus, is a rallying point that encourages true humility, openness, and assurance in God's power to heal.[82]

---

79. Alcoholics Anonymous, *Twelve Steps and Twelve Traditions*, 23.

80. Miller, *Hunger for Healing*, 13.

81. Miller describes a similar process in his healing journey: "There was little doubt in my mind ever about the existence of God and the reality of Jesus Christ. And I was consciously committed to him with my whole life (as Lord and Savior). But at a certain point all my belief and commitment weren't effective in getting control of my life because I couldn't see my basic Sin—that in my denial I had put myself in the center where only God should be" (ibid., 33).

82. Alcoholics Anonymous, *Twelve Steps and Twelve Traditions*, 33.

Step Three: We make a decision to turn our will and our lives, and those of the people we care for, over to the care and protection of the Divine. The second step is about recognizing the power of God. In the third step, women must actively affirm their willingness to submit to that power. This step affirms that belief alone is insufficient to self-recovery; action—specifically changes in patterns of cognition, affect, and behavior—is necessary. "Like all the remaining steps, Step Three calls for affirmative action, for it is only by action that we can cut away the self-will which has always blocked the entry of God . . . into our lives."[83] In the third step, the StrongBlackWoman actively strives to conform her will to that of the Almighty and, particularly important, to relinquish control of those for whom she cares to the care and protection of God. She affirms once again that she is not God, she is not in control, and she does not need to be.

Step Four: We practice self-awareness, making a searching inventory of ourselves and our relationships. While mindfulness practice is helpful during each of the twelve steps, it is vital in the fourth step, conducting a fearless moral inventory. "Step Four is our vigorous and painstaking effort to discover what [the] liabilities in each of us have been, and are. We want to find exactly how, when, and where our natural desires have warped us. We wish to look squarely at the unhappiness this has caused others and ourselves."[84] With this step, the StrongBlackWoman must examine her behaviors, thoughts, and feelings to identify the ways in which she embodies the archetype and the harm that her embodiment has caused to herself and to others. Moreover, she attempts to identify the driving forces behind her compulsions of strength. For many women, this will be related to the desire to conform to social and family expectations; for others, experiences of trauma or neglect may have shaped a deep lack of trust and security in others. Because many of these processes may exist at the subconscious or unconscious level, it may be helpful for a woman at this step to work with a pastoral counselor or mental health clinician; at a minimum, a woman will need the compassion and accountability of a peer group or sponsor. Notably, conducting a moral inventory does not end with identifying one's negative traits; the second part of this step is identifying one's positive traits as well as one's needs, desires, and interests.[85] These latter elements form the

83. Ibid., 34.
84. Ibid., 42–43.
85. Miller, *Hunger for Healing*, 61.

basis of developing a healthier sense of selfhood, including skills in boundary setting and assertiveness.

Step Five: We admit to God, to ourselves, and to another human being the exact nature of our compulsions and the traumas and fears that drive them. The fifth step is an act of confession. This will be a difficult step for the StrongBlackWoman, who is accustomed to "keeping her own counsel," that is, withholding her thoughts and feelings from others. With this step, the StrongBlackWoman is required to reveal her most personal thoughts, feelings, and character defects to another human being. It will, of course, be tempting to her to avoid this step, to claim as many Christians do, "God knows my heart." But the soul-baring that is called for in this step—together with the radical truth-telling and accountability it demands—is necessary to the recovery process. Miller argues that "Step Five can be considered to be a spiritual filter for the toxic memories, thoughts, and behaviors of the past that continue to sabotage and poison our lives and relationships in the present."[86] In admitting the truth about herself to another person, the StrongBlackWoman is freed from the prison of isolation and loneliness in which she resides. She learns to receive hospitality and care, to trust and depend upon another, and to realize that her self-worth is not dependent upon her capacity for perfection. No longer invested in maintaining her image as the StrongBlackWoman, she is freed for intimacy. The role of the pastoral caregiver is especially important in this step, for she can serve as a confessor who creates an atmosphere of trust, confidentiality, respect, and love in which authentic self-expression can occur.

Step Six: We are ready to have the Holy One heal us. The sixth step would appear to repeat the content of Step Three, wherein the StrongBlackWoman submits herself and the lives of those under her care to the care and protection of God. This step utilizes a similar process, but this time in the aftermath of one's moral inventory. Having identified and confessed the specific nature of her character defects—including her anxieties, compulsions to control others, her lack of self-love, and even the behaviors that she has used to disguise the fact that she did not have it all together—the StrongBlackWoman becomes willing to seek God's healing for those defects. She is no longer content to wear the armor of the archetype to mask her pain. She wants to be made whole. As Miller describes, the work of Step Six requires the StrongBlackWoman to undertake a fundamental change in how

86. Ibid., 87.

she thinks about God, particularly God's willingness and power to effect change in her day-to-day life: "This attitude of readiness to let God reach into our lives and uncover and remove the things that make us spiritually and emotionally sick is paradoxically the doorway to active and effective change of specific lifelong habits and sins. But it means turning loose of control—even of our healing."[87]

Step Seven: We humbly ask the Almighty to remove our need for control and to nurture in us a commitment to self-care. The seventh step is a particularly challenging one for the StrongBlackWoman, who has learned that she should take care of everything herself in order not to be a burden or inconvenience to others. With this step, the StrongBlackWoman invites God's transforming power into her life. The humility required here involves recognizing her humanity and limitations, including her inability to "fix" herself. In other words, this step involves the humble admission that she is not in control of her recovery and that she needs to turn her defects completely over to the care and control of God.[88] Importantly, in working Step Seven, the StrongBlackWoman is asking not just to have her behaviors changed, but also her relationships. She becomes more aware of the unrealistic nature of the demands that she is trying to meet. In embracing humility, she embraces her limitations and finitude. Paradoxically, as she releases control over the outcomes of her life and others' lives, she begins to develop a more secure and genuine sense of selfhood. Miller states, "A paradoxical discovery is that when we admit our powerlessness, we can discover the latent power that God has put in us. . . . This personal power of authenticity develops as we continue to let go and center our lives in this relationship with God."[89] Thus, in letting go of the masked self, she begins to recognize and appreciate her authentic self, including her true strengths and gifts.[90] And out of this genuine self-love, she becomes truly capable of loving her neighbor.

Step Eight: We make a list of all persons we have harmed and continue to harm through our excessive caretaking, and we become willing to make amends to them all. Step Eight, together with Step Nine, is about healing the relational brokenness that usually affect the StrongBlackWoman. To

87. Ibid., 113.
88. Ibid., 116.
89. Ibid., 121.
90. Ibid.

some degree, the process of making amends begins as soon as a woman embarks upon her healing journey. From the moment of recognition of her role as a StrongBlackWoman, she is likely to begin making changes in her personal relationships, perhaps even confessing her tendencies to those with whom she has close relationships. In Step Eight, however, she makes a list of specific persons to whom she needs to make direct amends. Twelve-step philosophy categorizes these into three groups: (1) persons to whom amends ought to be made as soon as possible once a person feels relatively secure about maintaining her recovery; (2) persons to whom only partial restitution is necessary because full disclosure might do them more harm than good; and (3) persons to whom restitution must be delayed or may even be impossible.[91] Some women may have difficulty seeing just how their performance of the archetype adversely affects others, particularly given its deleterious effects on their own health and well-being. In some cases, a woman's overcommitment may cause her to neglect her most intimate and family relationships. In others, the StrongBlackWoman's sense of responsibility for others is so great that it actually hinders the capacity of others to take responsibility for their own lives; that is, it interferes with their self-development. And some women may have been active in reinforcing others' performance of the archetype, particularly their daughters. As the StrongBlackWoman develops genuine trust in God's love and care and a more secure sense of self, she begins to develop the courage to make amends to others. In working Step Eight, she conducts an inventory of her relationships in order to determine what damage she has done, to prepare to ask for forgiveness and make restitution when needed, and to forgive those who have taken advantage of her tendencies toward excessive responsibility. Notably, her task here is not to assume full responsibility for others' lack of selfhood or for their healing journey; this step is undertaken for her recovery, not to change others. Thus, she must only accept responsibility for her contribution to the problem and prepare to rectify that part of the relationship over which she has control.

Step Nine: We make direct amends to such people wherever possible by allowing them to assume responsibility for their own lives. In Step Nine, the woman begins making direct amends to those whom she has identified in Step Eight. As an act of reconciliation, this step is critical not only to recovery for

91. Alcoholics Anonymous, *Twelve Steps and Twelve Traditions*, 83. Miller further characterizes specific family members, friends, and business associates as a separate category (Miller, *Hunger for Healing*, 149).

the StrongBlackWoman but also to Christian discipleship. Scripture, after all, tells us that if as we come to the altar, we remember that our sister or brother has anything against us, we are to leave our gift at the altar and to go and be reconciled.[92] Likewise, the StrongBlackWoman, as she prepares to offer God and the world the gift of her newly developed healthy sense of self, must be reconciled to those whom she has harmed. This is not an easy task; it involves a great degree of discomfort and embarrassment. After all, it requires the StrongBlackWoman to look honestly at her relationships and to go in humble contrition before those whom she believes she has hurt and to ask for forgiveness. It is a risky task; there is no guarantee that her attempts at reconciliation will be accepted, rather than scorned or rejected. But in the context of a secure trust in God and a healthy respect for one's personal boundaries, the StrongBlackWoman in recovery possesses the courage and psychospiritual fortitude to accept, and cope with, this risk.[93] She understands that her healing does not depend upon another's willingness to recognize or accept it. It is for this reason that the intentional work of making amends requires working through eight other steps first! Moreover, having a healthy sense of self is critical to making sure that this step is one with sensitivity, humility, and compassion. Miller states,

> Before going out to make amends, you will need to gain humility and to release your pain and anger about what others have done to you. This comes through forgiving them. . . . Forgiveness in this sense means simply that we release our need to punish, to get even, to make the other person apologize or do anything. We release our need to continue to be hurt or be angry about what they did.[94]

Thus, to ensure that Step Nine is not used as exercise in blaming, scapegoating, justification, or manipulation, it is imperative that the StrongBlackWoman first forgives those to whom she needs to make amends. After all, "it does not lighten our burden when we recklessly make the crosses of others heavier."[95]

Step Ten: We continue to practice self-awareness, and when we relapse we promptly admit and correct it. The last three steps of a twelve-step program are generally designed to maintain change and to "give away" what one

92. Matt 5:24–26
93. Miller, *Hunger for Healing*, 148.
94. Ibid., 143.
95. Alcoholics Anonymous, *Twelve Steps and Twelve Traditions*, 86.

has found.[96] Step Ten, in particular, is designed to guard against and cope with relapse. Relapse is an unavoidable part of the recovery process for the StrongBlackWoman for two reasons: first, because she is usually so conditioned to acting out the role that it has become her primary way of being in the world; and second, because entire social and cultural institutions are dependent upon her strength. Liberation for the StrongBlackWoman does not come without a cost. Wood states, "As is true in any paradigm of oppression, whenever the alleged inferior group seeks, as womanists have, to define itself on its own terms or, in any other way, shift the status quo, a backlash ensues. Whatever forms it takes, backlash is intended to keep a group 'in their place.'"[97] As a perpetual caretaker who constantly focuses on the needs of others to the exclusion of her own, the StrongBlackWoman fails to develop her full selfhood and instead is forced into the role of the "rescuer" of dependent others. The individuals and institutions who benefit from her care often develop an unhealthy dependency upon her labor and care and will resist her attempts to recover herself. Often, this means that her efforts to withdraw her excessive caretaking will be met with chaos; that is, just as she tries to convince herself that everything will not fall apart if she does not take care of it, everything does indeed fall apart! Without self-awareness, the StrongBlackWoman in recovery will return to her former self, stepping in to restore order and to reduce her anxiety. But continued practice of mindfulness during crisis empowers her to maintain the changes that she has instituted in her life and reveals her "growing edges," the personal liabilities that predispose her to donning the armor once again. It reminds her that she is not God, that others are capable of accepting responsibility for their own lives, and that she can and should "stay the course." And in the event that she does momentarily relapse, self-awareness prompts her to get back on track and begin working her program once again.

Step Eleven: We seek through prayer, meditation, and journaling to nurture our connection with the Divine, praying for knowledge of God's will for our lives and for faith in God's protection and care. Spiritual disciplines such as prayer, meditation, and journaling are important throughout the recovery process for the StrongBlackWoman. In Step Eleven, they become essential strategies for the maintenance of one's recovery and for relapse prevention.

96. Miller, *Hunger for Healing*, 164.
97. Wood, "'Take My Yoke Upon You,'" 39.

Miller notes that within twelve-step programs broadly, regular practices of prayer and meditation are often identified as characteristics of individuals who "work good programs"; these disciplines are not merely reduced to strategies for health but are also practiced out of gratitude and awe that the God they love is invested in their healing.[98] For the StrongBlackWoman in recovery, these practices foster the connection with God and self-examination that are necessary for continued healthy self-development. They help her to become aware of her temptations to "play God," both in her own life as well as in those of others. They strengthen her capacity to find and maintain peace in the midst of chaos and uncertainty, thus lessening her proclivity to "fall back" on her typical anxiety-reducing methods of over-activity and excessive control. They remind her who and whose she is, that she is not an unfeeling, self-sacrificing cultural trope, but that she is a much beloved child of the triune God, who holds her in loving arms of protection and care.

Step Twelve: We try to carry this message to the StrongBlackWomen in our lives and to embody these principles as an example to them and to the generations that follow us. Consistent with a womanist framework, the StrongBlack-Woman in recovery is not interested solely in her personal liberation; she is "committed to survival and wholeness of entire people, male *and* female."[99] This commitment is embedded in Boyd's description of WomanistCare:

> WomanistCare involves a confrontation between and among African American women and, as a result of those confrontations, a confrontation of structures and the strictures in our world. The purpose of confrontation in which African American women are called to engage is bridge building, so that those who come behind us will not have to go through what we have had to go through. The coming generation is to stand on our shoulders.[100]

Step Twelve, then, which involves sharing one's learning and recovery process with others, commits women in recovery to the education and healing of other StrongBlackWomen. It is a practice that Baker-Fletcher labels "re-generation [which] is the power to pass on wisdom, knowledge, and Black women's cultural heritage from generation to generation."[101] As an act of

98. Miller, *Hunger for Healing*, 180.

99. Walker, *In Search of Our Mothers' Gardens*, xi.

100. Boyd, "WomanistCare," 201.

101. Baker-Fletcher and Baker-Fletcher, *My Sister, My Brother*, 154.

re-socialization that challenges the unrelenting messages of Black women's strength that are transmitted by popular culture, by families, and by the church, Step Twelve seeks to undo—or at the very least, interrupt—the messages that have conscripted generations of African-American women and girls into the legacy of strength. Notably, as the StrongBlackWoman spreads the message of liberation, she is further empowered to continue her own recovery process. No longer alone, she is gifted with companions for the journey. Her decision to choose wellness becomes an act of communal liberation and political resistance.[102]

Using the Twelve Steps in Pastoral Care

Pastoral caregivers who utilize the twelve-step approach in facilitating the healing journey of StrongBlackWomen should keep in mind that there is no fixed timeline for the healing process. Depending upon the strength of the socialization practices that have conditioned a person to embody the StrongBlackWoman, working the program could take two or more years. And during that time, there may be several occasions of relapse. Yet with intentional focus and effort upon one's recovery, African-American women can indeed be freed from the burden of strength. They can experience the joy and lightness of being that comes from laying their burdens down.

> I feel better, so much better,
> since I laid my burden down.
> I feel better, so much better,
> since I laid my burden down.[103]

Suggestions for Pastoral Practice

- If you are an African-American female who personally struggles with the StrongBlackWoman, work through the twelve-step program, using J. Keith Miller's *A Hunger for Healing* as a companion text. You may need to solicit the help of a pastoral counselor or spiritual director who can serve as a source of support or accountability as you work the program.

102. hooks, *Sisters of the Yam,* 14.
103. "Glory, Glory, Hallelujah."

- If you provide pastoral care in a setting that includes African-American women, consider establishing a support group for StrongBlackWomen. The group should meet at least twice monthly. Ideally, the facilitator will be an African American woman with training and experience in group facilitation and exceptional cultural and gender competency. Each session should include prayer, mindfulness practice, personal check-in time, and discussion of one of the twelve steps. Free or low-cost childcare should be provided.

- Even if you do not fall into either of the above two categories, the likelihood is high that you know someone who does. Consider gifting them with a copy of this book. Pray about how you can serve as a support to them during their healing journey or their ministry to StrongBlackWomen.

The StrongBlackWoman's Twelve-Step Recovery Program

Step One. We admit that we are powerless over our compulsion to be strong—that our physical, spiritual, emotional, and relational health are suffering.

Step Two. We acknowledge that we are not the Divine, that there is a Power greater than ourselves who can restore us to right relationship with ourselves and others.

Step Three. We make a decision to turn our will and our lives, and those of the people we care for, over to the care and protection of the Divine.

Step Four. We practice self-awareness, making a searching inventory of ourselves and our relationships.

Step Five. We admit to God, to ourselves, and to another human being the exact nature of our compulsions and the traumas and fears that drive them.

Step Six. We are ready to have the Holy One heal us.

Step Seven. We humbly ask the Almighty to remove our need for control and to nurture in us a commitment to self-care.

Step Eight. We make a list of all persons we have harmed and continue to harm through our excessive caretaking, and we become willing to make amends to them all.

Step Nine. We make direct amends to such people wherever possible by allowing them to assume responsibility for their own lives.

Step Ten. We continue to practice self-awareness, and when we relapse we promptly admit and correct it.

Step Eleven. We seek through prayer, meditation, and journaling to nurture our connection with the Divine, praying for knowledge of God's will for our lives and for faith in God's protection and care.

Step Twelve. We try to carry this message to the StrongBlackWomen in our lives and to embody these principles as an example to them and to the generations that follow us.

Bibliography

Alcoholics Anonymous. *Twelve Steps and Twelve Traditions.* New York: Alcoholics Anonymous World Services, 1981.

Ali, Carroll A. Watkins. *Survival and Liberation: Pastoral Theology in African American Context.* St. Louis: Chalice, 1999.

———. "A Womanist Search for Sources." In *Feminist and Womanist Pastoral Theology,* edited by Bonnie J. Miller-McLemore and Brita L. Gill-Austern, 51–64. Nashville: Abingdon, 1999.

American Cancer Society. *Cancer Facts & Figures for African Americans 2007–2008.* Atlanta: American Cancer Society, 2007.

American Psychiatric Association. *Diagnostic and Statistical Manual of Mental Disorders.* 4th ed., text revision. Washington, DC: American Psychiatric Association, 2000.

Anderson, Victor. *Beyond Ontological Blackness: An Essay on African American Religious and Cultural Criticism.* New York: Continuum, 1995.

Anonymous. "Bailey's Rum Cream: Pass Her a Glass STAT!" *WhatBlackWomenThinkAbout,* April 12, 2011, http://whatblackwomenthinkabout.wordpress.com/2011/04/12/baileys-rum-cream-pass-her-a-glass-stat/.

Baer, Ruth A. "Mindfulness Training as a Clinical Intervention: A Conceptual and Empirical Review." *Clinical Psychology: Science and Practice* 10 (2003) 125–43.

Baker, Katie J. M. "'Cunt' Should Not Be a Bad Word." *Jezebel.com,* February 27, 2013, http://jezebel.com/5987317/cunt-is-not-a-bad-word.

Baker-Fletcher, Karen, and Garth KASIMU Baker-Fletcher. *My Sister, My Brother: Womanist and Xodus God-Talk.* Maryknoll, NY: Orbis, 1997.

Barbee, Evelyn L. "African American Women and Depression: A Review and Critique of the Literature." *Archives of Psychiatric Nursing* 6 (1992) 257–65.

Barr, Doug. "Quvenzhané Wallis Will Star as Annie in a New Annie Movie by *Easy A* Director." *Jezebel.com,* February 24, 2013, http://jezebel.com/5986551/quvenzhane-wallis-will-star-as-annie-in-a-new-annie-movie-by-easy-a-director.

Beauboeuf-Lafontant, Tamara. *Behind the Mask of the Strong Black Woman: Voice and the Embodiment of a Costly Performance.* Philadelphia: Temple University Press, 2009.

———. "You Have to Show Strength: An Exploration of Gender, Race, and Depression." *Gender and Society* 21 (2007) 28–51.

Beck, Laura. "Is It Really that Hard to Say Quvenzhané?" *Jezebel.com,* February 25, 2013, http://jezebel.com/5986852/is-it-really-that-hard-to-say-quvenzhane.

Beverly, Urias. *The Places You Go: Caring for Your Congregation Monday through Saturday.* Nashville: Abingdon, 2003.

Black Women's Health Imperative. "The Impact of Psychosocial Factors on Health: A Study of African American Women." http://nbwhp.convio.net/site/PageServer?pagename=RS_ourresearch#minimal.

Boyd, Marsha Foster. "WomanistCare: Some Reflections on the Pastoral Care and the Transformation of African American Women." In *Embracing the Spirit: Womanist Perspectives on Hope, Salvation and Transformation*, edited by Emilie M. Townes, 197–202. Maryknoll, NY: Orbis, 1997.

Brown, Diane R., and Verna M. Keith. "The Epidemiology of Mental Disorders and Mental Health among African American Women." In *In and Out of Our Right Minds: The Mental Health of African American Women*, edited by Diane R. Brown and Verna M. Keith, 23–58. New York: Columbia University Press, 2003.

Brown, Teresa L. Fry. "Avoiding Asphyxiation: A Womanist Perspective on Intrapersonal and Interpersonal Transformation." In *Embracing the Spirit: Womanist Perspectives on Hope, Salvation and Transformation*, edited by Emilie M. Townes, 72–94. Maryknoll, NY: Orbis, 1997.

Bumpus, Mary Rose. "Awakening Hidden Wholeness: A Jungian View of Luke 10:38–42." *Journal of Psychology and Christianity* 29 (2010) 229–39.

Carby, Hazel V. *Reconstructing Womanhood: The Emergence of the Afro-American Woman Novelist*. New York: Oxford University Press, 1987.

Carter, Warren. "Getting Martha Out of the Kitchen: Luke 10:38–42 Again." *Catholic Biblical Quarterly* 58 (1996) 264–80.

Centers for Disease Control and Prevention. *Age-Adjusted Percentage of Civilian, Noninstitutionalized Population with Diagnosed Diabetes, by Race and Sex, United States, 1980–2010*. http://www.cdc.gov/diabetes/statistics/prev/national/figraceethsex.htm.

———. *HIV Among African Americans*. http://www.cdc.gov/hiv/topics/aa/PDF/aa.pdf.

———. *HIV Among Women*. http://www.cdc.gov/hiv/topics/women/pdf/women.pdf.

———. *National Diabetes Fact Sheet: National Estimates and General Information on Diabetes and Prediabetes in the United States, 2011*. http://www.cdc.gov/diabetes/pubs/pdf/ndfs_2011.pdf.

———. *Sexual Violence: Facts at a Glance*. http://www.cdc.gov/ViolencePrevention/pdf/SV-DataSheet-a.pdf.

Chung, Sook Ja. "Bible Study: Women's Ways of Doing Mission in the Story of Mary and Martha." *International Review of Mission* 93 (2004) 9–16.

Cleaver, Eldridge. *Soul on Ice*. 1968. Reprint, New York: Delta, 1991.

Clinton, Catherine. "Caught in the Web of the Big House: Women and Slavery." In *The Web of Southern Social Relations: Women, Family, and Education*, edited by Walter J. Fraser, R. Frank Saunders Jr., and Jon L. Wakelyn, 19–33. Athens: University of Georgia Press, 1985.

———. "'With a Whip in His Hand': Rape, Memory, and African-American Women." In *History and Memory in African-American Culture*, edited by Geneviève Fabre and Robert O'Meally, 205–18. New York: Oxford University Press, 1994.

Collins, Patricia Hill. *Black Feminist Thought: Knowledge, Consciousness, and the Politics of Empowerment*. 2nd ed. New York: Routledge, 2000.

———. *Black Sexual Politics: African Americans, Gender, and the New Racism*. New York: Routledge, 2005.

Cooper-White, Pamela. *Many Voices: Pastoral Psychotherapy in Relational and Theological Perspective*. Minneapolis: Fortress, 2007.

Copeland, M. Shawn. "'Wading through Many Sorrows': Toward a Theology of Suffering in Womanist Perspective." In *A Troubling in My Soul: Womanist Perspectives on Evil and Suffering*, edited by Emilie M. Townes, 109–29. Maryknoll, NY: Orbis, 1993.

Cose, Ellis. "The Black Gender Gap." *Newsweek*, March 3, 2003, 48–51.

Cottom, Tressie McMillan. "Did White Feminists Ignore Attacks on Quvenzhané Wallis? That's an Empirical Question." *Tressiemc.com*, February 28, 2013, http://tressiemc.com/2013/02/28/did-white-feminists-ignore-attacks-on-quvenzhane-wallis-thats-an-empirical-question/.

Crowder, Stephanie Buckhanon. "The Gospel of Luke." In *True to Our Native Land: An African American New Testament Commentary*, edited by Brian K. Blount et al., 158–85. Minneapolis: Fortress, 2007.

Culpepper, R. Alan. "Luke." In *The New Interpreter's Bible*, 9:230–32. Nashville: Abingdon, 1995.

Daniel, Jessica Henderson. "The Courage to Hear: African American Women's Memories of Racial Trauma." In *Psychotherapy with African American Women: Innovations in Psychodynamic Perspectives and Practice*, edited by Leslie C. Jackson and Beverly Greene, 126–44. New York: Guilford, 2000.

Danquah, Meri Nana-Ama. *Willow Weep for Me: A Black Woman's Journey through Depression*. New York: One World, 1998.

Du Bois, W. E. B. "The Damnation of Women." In *W. E. B. Du Bois: A Reader*, edited by David Levering Lewis, 299–312. New York: Henry Holt, 1995.

———. "The Talented Tenth." In *The Negro Problem: A Series of Articles by Representative Negroes of To-day*. New York: J. Pott, 1903.

Edge, Dawn, and Anne Rogers. "Dealing with It: Black Caribbean Women's Response to Adversity and Psychological Distress Associated with Pregnancy, Childbirth, and Early Motherhood." *Social Science and Medicine* 61 (2005) 15–25.

Field, Craig A., and Raul Caetano. "Longitudinal Model Predicting Partner Violence among White, Black, and Hispanic Couples in the United States." *Alcoholism: Clinical & Experimental Research* 27 (2003) 1451–58.

Fogel, Matthew. "'Grey's Anatomy' Goes Colorblind." *New York Times*, May 8, 2005, http://www.nytimes.com/2005/05/08/arts/television/08foge.html?_r=1&pagewanted=all.

Foster, Kimberly. "The Best Black Female Characters in Television History." *ForHarriet.com*, September 13, 2010, http://www.forharriet.com/2010/09/best-black-female-characters-in.html.

Gaines, Kevin K. "Racial Uplift Ideology in the Era of 'the Negro Problem.'" *Freedom's Story, TeacherServe©. National Humanities Center*. http://nationalhumanitiescenter.org/tserve/freedom/1865-1917/essays/racialuplift.htm.

Gans, Herbert J. "The Moynihan Report and Its Aftermaths: A Critical Analysis." *Du Bois Review* 8 (2011) 315–27.

Gaston, Marilyn Hughes, Gayle K. Porter, and Veronica G. Thomas. "Prime Time Sister Circles: Evaluating a Gender-Specific, Culturally Relevant Health Intervention to Decrease Major Risk Factors in Mid-life African-American Women." *Journal of the National Medical Association* 99 (2007) 428–38.

Giddings, Paula. *When and Where I Enter: The Impact of Black Women on Race and Sex in America*. 1984. Reprint, New York: Perennial, 2001.

Gilkes, Cheryl Townsend. *"If It Wasn't for the Women . . .": Black Women's Experience and Womanist Culture in Church and Community*. Maryknoll, NY: Orbis, 2001.

———. "The 'Loves' and 'Troubles' of African-American Women's Bodies: The Womanist Challenge to Cultural Humiliation and Community Ambivalence." In *A Troubling in My Soul: Womanist Perspectives on Evil and Suffering*, edited by Emilie M. Townes, 232–49. Maryknoll, NY: Orbis, 1993.

Gill-Austern, Brita L. "Love Understood as Self-Sacrifice and Self-Denial: What Does It Do to Women?" In *Through the Eyes of Women: Insights for Pastoral Care*, edited by Jeanne Stevenson Moessner, 304–21. Minneapolis: Fortress, 1996.

"Glory, Glory, Hallelujah." In *Lift Every Voice and Sing II: An African American Hymnal*, 130. New York: Church Publishing, 1993.

Grant, Jacquelyn. "The Sin of Servanthood and the Deliverance of Discipleship." In *A Troubling in My Soul: Womanist Perspectives on Evil and Suffering*, edited by Emilie M. Townes, 199–218. Maryknoll, NY: Orbis, 1993.

Harrington, Ellen F., Janis H. Crowther, and Jillian C. Shipherd. "Trauma, Binge Eating, and the 'Strong Black Woman.'" *Journal of Consulting and Clinical Psychology* 78 (2010) 469–79.

Harris-Perry, Melissa. *Sister Citizen: Shame, Stereotypes, and Black Women in America.* New Haven: Yale University Press, 2011.

Head, John. *Standing in the Shadows: Understanding and Overcoming Depression in Black Men.* New York: Broadway, 2004.

Higginbotham, Evelyn Brooks. *Righteous Discontent: The Women's Movement in the Black Baptist Church, 1880–1920.* Cambridge: Harvard University Press, 1993.

Hinson-Hasty, Elizabeth L. "Revisiting Feminist Discussions of Sin and Genuine Humility." *Journal of Feminist Studies* 28 (2012) 108–14.

hooks, bell. *Black Looks: Race and Representation.* Boston: South End, 1992.

———. *Sisters of the Yam: Black Women and Self-Recovery.* Boston: South End, 1993.

Hunn, Vanessa Lynn, and Carlton David Craig. "Depression, Sociocultural Factors, and African American Women." *Journal of Multicultural Counseling and Development* 37 (2009) 83–93.

Hunsinger, Deborah van Deusen. *Pray without Ceasing: Revitalizing Pastoral Care.* Grand Rapids: Eerdsmans, 2006.

Hunter, Patricia L. "Women's Power—Women's Passion: And God Said, 'That's Good.'" In *A Troubling in My Soul: Womanist Perspectives on Evil and Suffering*, edited by Emilie M. Townes, 189–98. Maryknoll, NY: Orbis, 1993.

Hutson, Christopher R. "Martha's Choice: A Pastorally Sensitive Reading of Luke 10: 38–42." *Restoration Quarterly* 45 (2003) 139–50.

Jack, Dana Crowley. *Silencing the Self: Women and Depression.* New York: HarperCollins, 1991.

Jackson, Leslie C., and Beverly Greene, eds. *Psychotherapy with African American Women: Innovations in Psychodynamic Perspectives and Practice.* New York: Guilford, 2000.

Jacobs, Harriet A. *Incidents in the Life of a Slave Girl*, edited by Jean Fagan Yellin. Cambridge: Harvard University Press, 1987.

James, Sherman A. "John Henryism and the Health of African Americans." *Culture, Medicine, and Psychiatry* 18 (1994) 163–82.

Jenkins, Candice. *Private Lives, Proper Relations: Regulating Black Intimacy.* Minneapolis: University of Minnesota Press, 2007.

Jenkins, Yvonne M. "The Stone Center Theoretical Approach Revisited: Applications for African American Women." In *Psychotherapy with African American Women:*

Innovations in Psychodynamic Perspectives and Practice, edited by Leslie C. Jackson and Beverly Greene, 62–81. New York: Guilford, 2000.

Jones, Cherisse, and Kumea Shorter-Gooden. *Shifting: The Double Lives of Black Women in America*. New York: HarperCollins, 2003.

Kaba, Amadu Jacky. "Race, Gender, and Progress: Are Black American Women the New Model Minority?" *Journal of African American Studies* 12 (2008) 309–35.

Katzmarzyk, Peter T., et al. "Ethnic-Specific BMI and Waist Circumference Thresholds." *Obesity* 19 (2011) 1272–78. http://www.nature.com/oby/journal/v19/n6/full/oby2010319a.html.

Kerrigan, Deanna, et al. "Staying Strong: Gender Ideologies among African-American Adolescents and the Implications for HIV/STI Prevention." *Journal of Sex Research* 44 (2007) 172–80.

Kirmayer, Laurence J., and Allan Young. "Culture and Somatization: Clinical, Epidemiological, and Ethnographic Perspectives." *Psychosomatic Medicine* 60 (1998) 420–30.

Kornfeld, Margaret. *Cultivating Wholeness: A Guide to Care and Counseling in Faith Communities*. New York: Continuum, 2011.

Krieger, Nancy. "Embodiment: A Conceptual Glossary for Epidemiology." *Journal of Epidemiology and Community Health* 59 (2005) 350–55.

Lincoln, C. Eric, and Lawrence H. Mamiya. *The Black Church in the African American Experience*. Durham: Duke University Press, 1990.

Lorde, Audre. *Sister Outsider: Essays and Speeches*. Freedom, CA: Crossing, 1984.

Lynch, Cheryl, et al. "Obese African-American Women's Perspectives on Weight Loss and Bariatric Surgery." *Journal of General Internal Medicine* 22 (2007) 908–14. http://www.ncbi.nlm.nih.gov/pmc/articles/PMC2583799/.

Lyon, Jodie L. "Pride and the Symptoms of Sin." *Journal of Feminist Studies in Religion* 28 (2012) 96–102.

Mayou, Richard, et al. "Somatoform Disorders: Time for a New Approach in DSM-V." *American Journal of Psychiatry* 162 (2005) 847–55.

Miller, J. Keith. *A Hunger for Healing: The Twelve Steps as a Classic Model for Christian Spiritual Growth*. New York: HarperCollins, 1991.

Moessner, Jeanne Stevenson. "From Samaritan to Samaritan: Journey Mercies." In *Through the Eyes of Women: Insights for Pastoral Care*, edited by Jeanne Stevenson Moessner, 322–33. Minneapolis: Fortress, 1996.

———. "Preaching the Good Samaritan: A Feminist Perspective." *Journal for Preachers* 19 (1995) 21–25.

Morgan, Joan. *When Chickenheads Come Home to Roost: A Hip-Hop Feminist Breaks It Down*. New York: Simon and Schuster, 1999.

Moynihan, Daniel Patrick. *The Negro Family: The Case for National Action*. Washington, DC: United States Department of Labor, Office of Policy Planning and Research, March 1965. http://www.dol.gov/oasam/programs/history/webid-meynihan.htm.

National Institute of Mental Health. *Epidemiologic Catchment Area Study, 1980–1985*. Rockville, MD: U.S. Department of Health and Human Services, National Institute of Mental Health 1992.

Neal, Mark Anthony. *New Black Man*. New York: Routledge, 2006.

Neal-Barnett, Angela, and Janis H. Crowther. "To Be Female, Middle Class, Anxious, and Black." *Psychology of Women Quarterly* 24 (2000) 129–36.

Nelson, Jill. *Straight, No Chaser: How I Became a Grown-Up Black Woman*. New York: Putnam's, 1997.

Neuger, Christie Cozad. *Counseling Women: A Narrative, Pastoral Approach*. Minneapolis: Fortress, 2001.

Nicolaidis, Christina, et al. "'You Don't Go Tell White People Nothing': African American Women's Perspectives on the Influence of Violence and Race on Depression and Depression Care." *American Journal of Public Health* 100 (2010) 1470–76.

Nouwen, Henri. *The Wounded Healer*. New York: Doubleday, 1972.

Parker, Lonnae O'Neal. "Black Women Heavier and Happier with Their Bodies than White Women, Poll Finds." *The Washington Post*, February 27, 2012, http://www.washingtonpost.com/lifestyle/style/black-women-heavier-and-happier-with-their-bodies-than-white-women-poll-finds/2012/02/22/gIQAPmcHeR_story.html.

Parks, Sheri. *Fierce Angels: The Strong Black Woman in American Life and Culture*. New York: Ballantine, 2010.

Patton, John. *Pastoral Care: An Essential Guide*. Nashville: Abingdon, 2005.

Pleis, John R., and Margaret Lethbridge-Çejku. *Summary Health Statistics for U.S. Adults: National Health Interview Survey, 2005*. Atlanta, GA: Centers for Disease Control and Prevention, 2006.

Poussaint, Alvin F., and Amy Alexander. *Lay My Burden Down: Suicide and the Mental Health Crisis among African-Americans*. Boston: Beacon, 2000.

Randall, Alice. "Black Women and Fat." *New York Times*, May 5, 2012, http://www.nytimes.com/2012/05/06/opinion/sunday/why-black-women-are-fat.html?_r=1.

Riggs, Marcia Y. *Awake, Arise, and Act: A Womanist Call for Black Liberation*. Cleveland: Pilgrim, 1994.

———. "'A Clarion Call to Awake! Arise! Act!': The Response of the Black Women's Club Movement to Institutionalized Moral Evil." In *A Troubling in My Soul: Womanist Perspectives on Evil and Suffering*, edited by Emilie M. Townes, 67–77. Maryknoll, NY: Orbis, 1993.

Romero, Regina E. "The Icon of the Strong Black Woman: The Paradox of Strength." In *Psychotherapy with African American Women: Innovations in Psychodynamic Perspectives and Practice*, edited by Leslie C. Jackson and Beverly A. Greene, 225–38. New York: Guilford, 2000.

Saiving, Valerie. "The Human Situation: A Feminine Viewpoint." *Pastoral Psychology* 17 (1966) 29–42.

Savali, Kirsten West. "Where Were White Feminists Speaking Out for Quvenzhané Wallis?" *ClutchMagOnline.com*, February 28, 2013, http://www.clutchmagonline.com/2013/02/quvenzhane-wallis-white-feminism/.

Scarinci, Isabel C., et al. "Depression, Socioeconomic Status, Age, and Marital Status in Black Women: A National Study." *Ethnicity and Disease* 12 (2002) 421–28.

Schaberg, Jane D., and Sharon H. Ringe. "Gospel of Luke." In *Women's Bible Commentary*, 3rd ed., edited by Carol A. Newsom, Sharon H. Ringe, and Jacqueline E. Lapsley, 493–511. Louisville: Westminster John Knox, 2012.

Schüssler Fiorenza, Elisabeth. "A Feminist Critical Interpretation for Liberation: Martha and Mary: Lk. 10:38–42." *Religion & Intellectual Life* 3 (1986) 21–36.

Scott, Kesho. *The Habit of Surviving: Black Women's Strategies for Life*. New Brunswick: Rutgers University Press, 1991.

Sheppard, Phillis Isabella. *Self, Culture, and Others in Womanist Practical Theology*. New York: Palgrave, 2012.

Snorton, Teresa E. "The Legacy of the African-American Matriarch: New Perspectives for Pastoral Care." In *Through the Eyes of Women: Insights for Pastoral Care,* edited by Jeanette Stevenson Moessner, 50–65. Minneapolis: Fortress, 1996.

Stoltzfus, Regina Shands. "'Couldn't Keep It to Myself': Testimony in the Black Church Tradition." *Vision* 10 (2009) 43–49.

Switzer, David K. *Pastoral Care Emergencies.* Minneapolis: Fortress, 2000.

Symington, Scott H., and Melissa F. Symington. "A Christian Model of Mindfulness: Using Mindfulness Principles to Support Psychological Well-Being, Value-Based Behavior, and the Christian Spiritual Journey." *Journal of Psychology and Christianity* 31 (2012) 71–77.

Thompson, Cheryl L. "African American Women and Moral Masochism: When There Is Too Much of a Good Thing." In *Psychotherapy with African American Women: Innovations in Psychodynamic Perspectives and Practice,* edited by Leslie C. Jackson and Beverly Green, 239–50. New York: Guilford, 2000.

Townes, Emilie. *Breaking the Fine Rain of Death: African American Health Issues and a Womanist Ethic of Care.* New York: Continuum, 1998.

———. "Living in the New Jerusalem: The Rhetoric and Movement of Liberation in the House of Evil." In *A Troubling in My Soul: Womanist Perspectives on Evil and Suffering,* edited by Emilie M. Townes, 78–91. Maryknoll, NY: Orbis, 1993.

Townsend, Tiffany G., Stephanie R. Hawkins, and Ayonda Lanier Batts. "Stress and Stress Reduction among African American Women: A Brief Report." *Journal of Primary Prevention* 28 (2007) 569–82.

"Unique Monument for Commemorating Virtues of 'Mammy' Is Projected." *The Sunday Oregonian,* March 11, 1923.

U.S. Census Bureau, "Expectation of Life at Birth, 1970 to 2007, and Projections, 2010 to 2020." http://www.census.gov/compendia/statab/2011/tables/11s0103.pdf.

———. "Occupation of the Civilian Employed Population 16 Years and Over by Sex, for Black Alone and White Alone, Not Hispanic: 2010." *Current Population Survey, Annual Social and Economic Supplement,* 2010. http://www.census.gov/population/race/data/ppl-ba10.html.

———. "Table 3. Educational Attainment of the Population 25 Years and Over by Sex, for Black Alone and White Alone, Not Hispanic: 2010." *Current Population Survey, Annual Social and Economic Supplement,* 2010. http://www.census.gov/population/race/data/ppl-ba10.html.

———. "Table 10. Projected Life Expectancy at Birth by Sex, Race, and Hispanic Origin for the United States: 2010 to 2050." http://www.census.gov/population/projections/files/summary/np2008-t10.xls.

———. "Table 11. Earnings of Full-Time, Year-Round Workers 15 Years and Over by Sex, for Black Alone and White Alone, Not Hispanic: 2009." *Current Population Survey, Annual Social and Economic Supplement,* 2010. http://www.census.gov/population/race/data/ppl-ba10.html.

———. "Table 13. Poverty Status of the Population by Sex and Age, for Black Alone and White Alone, Not Hispanic: 2009." *Current Population Survey, Annual Social and Economic Supplement,* 2010. http://www.census.gov/population/race/data/ppl-ba10.html.

———. "Table 102. Expectation of Life at Birth, 1970 to 2007, and Projections, 2010 to 2020." *Statistical Abstract of the United States: 2012.* http://www.census.gov/compendia/statab/2011/tables/11s0103.pdf.

———. "Table 238. Years of School Completed by Race, Sex, and Spanish Origin: 1960 to 1979." *Statistical Abstract of the United States*, 1970. http://www.census.gov/prod/www/abs/statab1951-1994.htm.

Volf, Miroslav. *Exclusion and Embrace: A Theological Exploration of Identity, Otherness, and Reconciliation*. Nashville: Abingdon, 1996.

Waite, Roberta, and Priscilla Killian. "Health Beliefs about Depression among African American Women." *Perspectives in Psychiatric Care* 44 (2008) 185–95.

Walker, Alice. *In Search of Our Mothers' Gardens: Womanist Prose*. New York: Harcourt Brace Jovanovich, 1983.

Walker-Barnes, Chanequa. "The Burden of the Strong Black Woman." *Journal of Pastoral Theology* 19 (2009) 1–21.

Wallace, Beverly. "A Womanist Legacy of Trauma, Grief, and Loss: Reframing the Notion of the Strong Black Woman Icon." In *Women Out of Order: Risking Change and Creating Care in a Multicultural World*, edited by Jeanne Stevenson-Moessner and Teresa Snorton, 43–56. Minneapolis: Fortress, 2010.

Wallace, Michele. *Black Macho and the Myth of the Superwoman*. 1979. Reprint, New York: Verso, 1990.

Wallace-Sanders, Kimberly. *Mammy: A Century of Race, Gender, and Southern Memory*. Ann Arbor: University of Michigan Press, 2008.

Ward, Earlise C., and Susan M. Heidrich. "African American Women's Beliefs about Mental Illness, Stigma, and Preferred Coping Behaviors." *Research Nursing Health* (2010) 480–92. http://www.ncbi.nlm.nih.gov/pubmed/19650070.

The Washington Post. "Washington Post-Kaiser Family Foundation Poll of Black Women in America." http://www.washingtonpost.com/wp-srv/special/nation/black-women-in-america/.

Weems, Renita J. "Sanctified and Suffering." *Essence*, December 2004, 160–64.

Welter, Barbara. "The Cult of True Womanhood: 1820–1860." *American Quarterly* 18 (1966) 151–74.

West, Carolyn M. "Mammy, Sapphire, and Jezebel: Historical Images of Black Women and the Implications for Psychotherapy." *Psychotherapy* 32 (1995) 458–66.

Westcott, Diane Nilsen. "Blacks in the 1970s: Did They Scale the Job Ladder?" *Monthly Labor Review* 105 (1982) 29–38.

White, Deborah Gray. *Too Heavy a Load: Black Women in Defense of Themselves, 1894–1994*. New York: Norton, 1999.

Wiggins, Daphne C. *Righteous Content: Black Women's Perspectives of Church and Faith*. New York: New York University Press, 2005.

Williams, Delores S. *Sisters in the Wilderness: The Challenge of Womanist God-Talk*. Maryknoll, NY: Orbis, 1993.

Williams, Dorothy, and Kathleen A. Lawler. "Stress and Illness in Low-Income Women: The Roles of Hardiness, John Henryism, and Race." *Women and Health* 32 (2001) 61–75.

Williams, Terrie. *Black Pain: It Just Looks Like We're Not Hurting*. New York: Scribner, 2008.

Wood, Frances E. "'Take My Yoke Upon You': The Role of the Church in the Oppression of African-American Women." In *A Troubling in My Soul: Womanist Perspectives on Evil and Suffering*, edited by Emilie M. Townes, 37–47. Maryknoll, NY: Orbis, 1993.

Woods-Giscombé, Cheryl L. "Superwoman Schema: African American Women's Views on Stress, Strength, and Health." *Qualitative Health Research* 20 (2010) 668–83. http://www.ncbi.nlm.nih.gov/pmc/articles/PMC3072704/pdf/nihms279491.pdf.

Woods-Giscombé, Cheryl L., and Angela R. Black. "Mind-Body Interventions to Reduce Risk for Health Disparities Related to Stress and Strength among African American Women: The Potential of Mindfulness-Based Stress Reduction, Loving-Kindness, and the NTU Therapeutic Framework." *Complementary Health Practice Review* 15 (2010) 115–31.

Scripture Index

1 Kings

18:15–46	83
18:16–40	127
18:21	109
18:4	83
21:1–16	83
21:25	83

2 Kings

9:30–37	84

Song of Solomon

1:5–6	133

Matthew

11:28–30	160
5:24–26	192

Luke

10:25–42	151
10:38–42	157
10:4–8	155

Philippians

4:6	60

James

1:22	157

Subject Index

A

acceptance, in mindfulness practice, 179
accountability, community and, 185
achievements, frustration at praise of, 17
addiction, being StrongBlackWoman as, 186
affect regulation, 69
African-American actresses, 86
African-American families, 28, 121
African-American women. *See also* Black women
    church universal taking burdens of, 175
    freedom of choice, 171
    negative stereotypes, 18
African-Americans, gender tension among, 113
agoraphobia, 59
Ahab, 83
AIDS, 48–49
Alexander, Tim, *Diary of a Mad Black Man*, 120–23
Ali, Carroll Watkins, 167, 170
Amazon sexual image, 115–16
amends, making to those harmed, 190–91
Anderson, Victor, 95
anger, 22
antisocial personality disorder, 53
anxiety disorders, 53, 58–60
    resistance to disclosing, 60
arthritic conditions, 49
authentic relationships, loss of, 71
authenticity
    vs. stereotypes, 57
    StrongBlackWoman and, 34

B

Bailey (*Grey's Anatomy* character)
    faith depiction, 125
    StrongBlackWoman features in, 123–27
Baker-Fletcher, Garth Kasimu, 170–71
Baker-Fletcher, Karen, 153, 170–171, 194
    on Black women not seeking help, 135
    on church role in community-building, 182
    on community building, 181
    gifts of power identified, 162
    on misinterpreting role of suffering, 146
    on power of memory, 175
Beasts of the Southern Wild (film), 130–32
Beauboeuf-Lafontant, Tamara, 4n3, 70, 71, 135, 147, 168n27
    on breakdowns, 72
beauty products, 70
Beverly, Urias, 164
binge eating, 69–70, 77–79
The Birth of a Nation (film), 82
births, out-of-wedlock, 111
Black, Angela R., 180
Black, 2n2
Black church
    and Black women's club movement, 101–2
    hymns of, 39
    racial ideology and, 102
    women, 105
Black femininity, 170
Black Feminist Thought (Collins), 82

Black girls
  raised by single mothers, 121
  socialization of, 35
*Black Macho and the Myth of the
  Superwoman* (Wallace), 6
Black men, impact of matriarch
  image on, 114–15
Black nadir, 98*n*68
Black nationalism, rhetoric of, 115
Black progress, factors jeopardizing,
  111
Black racial identity, 95
Black women
  attacks on moral integrity, 98
  justification for brutal treatment,
    87
  myth of strength, 1
  as permissible victim, 132
  physical labor of, 19
  racism's cultural assault against,
    81–94
Black women's clubs, 98–101
views on Black men, 99*n*74
"blame-the-victim" approach, 64
blogs, on race, gender, and popular
  culture, 129
Boyd, Marsha Foster, 162, 166, 194
breakdown, 72
  return to functioning after, 73–74
  secrecy of, 74
breast cancer, 47
Brotherhood of Sleeping Car Porters,
  Ladies Auxiliary, 97
Brown, Teresa Fry, 182, 184*n*71
Burroughs, Nannie Helen, 105
busyness, of Martha, 156

C

cancer, 46–48
Carby, Hazel, 19*n*7, 91
career-minding women, in Perry's
  work, 120
caregiving, 25–29
  by Bailey, 125
  dependency of others on, 193
  self-sacrifice and, 133

stress from, 66
view of infinite resources for, 28
of White family by slave, 85
caretaking tendencies, 2
categorical racism, 95
Center for Disease Control and
  Prevention, 45–46
Center for Media Literacy, 129
cervical cancer, 47
children
  abuse of, 61
  individuation by, 138*n*22
  Mammy as caregiver, 85
  responsibilities, 26
Christ. *See* Jesus Christ
Christian love, 149
  suffering and sacrifice as marker,
    143
Christian theology, and women's self-
  sacrificial tendencies, 142
Christians, and mindfulness
  practices, 178
chronic pain, 49–51
Chung, Sook Ja, 156
church, 132*n*7. *See also* Black church
  Black women and, 5–6
  discipleship vs. martyrdom,
    137–45
  involvement in
    StrongBlackWoman
    development, 158
  leadership roles in, 27
  male hierarchy, 144
  radical societal criticism by,
    170–71
  role in socializing African-
    American women and girls,
    132
  role in women's self-esteem, 175
church functions, role in, 26
circulatory diseases, 46
Civil Rights Act of 1964, 42, 110
Cleaver, Eldridge, *Soul on Ice*, 115
clichés, about mental illness, 55
cojourners, 166
college-educated Black women,
  median income, 42

Collins, Patricia Hill, 81, 86, 89, 162, 182
Black Feminist Thought, 82
on matriarch image, 90
color-blind casting, 123
colorectal cancer, 47
"coming to voice," 168*n*27
commitments, reassessing, 37
confession, 189
confidentiality, in small groups, 183
consciousness, cultivating, 173–75
contextuality, paradigm shift for, 167
control, crying as loss of, 22
Cooper, Anna Julia, 99*n*74
Cose, Ellis, 42
cosmetics, 70
counselors
ability to listen to trauma and vulnerabilities stories, 165
traditional vs. pastoral caregivers, 163
credibility, in pastoral care, 163–67
Crowther, Janis H., 77–78
Crunk Feminist Collective (blog), 129
crying, 15, 37
avoidance of, 21
as failure, 21–22
hiding, 143
cult of Black genius, 95
cult of true womanhood, 90–93, 96, 118
and public activism, 104

D

daily living, difficulties with activities, 50
Danquah, Meri Nana-Ama, 55
daughters
learning to guard emotions, 144
socialization of, 71
David and Goliath, 36
defense mechanisms
coping with stress, 23
StrongBlackWoman as, 81
delay in seeking help, 74

demonic "isms," 174
denial, 67*n*109
depression, 54–58
from chronic stress, case example, 23–25
hidden symptoms, 74
unnoticed in StrongBlackWomen, 58
Destiny's Child, 31
"Independent Women, Part 1," 29–30
devaluation, protection from threat of, 35
diabetes, 45–46
Diagnostic Interview Schedule (NIMH DIS), 52
diakonia, 156
Diary of a Mad Black Man (Alexander), 120–123
Diary of a Mad Black Woman (Perry), 118–20, 127
dirty laundry phenomenon, 63
discipleship, vs. martyrdom, 137–45
distress, 53–54
noticing signals, 176
proactivity in identifying, 78–79
domesticity, in true womanhood, 92
double-binding messages, 128–29
drifting, 179
Du Bois, W.E.B., 88–89, 95, 136
"The Damnation of Women," 89*n*26
dysthymia, 16, 24
racial-gender differences in, 56

E

eating practicies, 69–70
Economic Opportunity Act of 1964, 111*n*5
economic self-sufficiency, as Black women's goal, 100*n*79
education, of African-American women, 42
embodiment of stress, 66–67
emotional distress, and physical ailments, 62
emotional intimacy, reducing, 25

emotional stoicism, 4
emotions
 awareness of, 177
 control of, 101
 learning to guard, 144
empathy, communicating, 168
enjoyment, 28
Epidemiologic Catchment Area
 (ECA) Study, 52
 and depression, 55
equality, myth of universal, 141n35
European racial ideology, 95
excessive activity, awareness of
 consequences, 176
Exclusion and Embrace (Volf),
 147–48
expectations of others, 128
experience, honoring, 167–70
extended kinship structures, 28

F

failure, perception of, 73
faith, 4, 17, 73
family relationships,
 StrongBlackWoman in, 76
feelings. *See* emotions
female-headed households, 111
"female Talented Tenth," 103
femininity, 100
Feminist Wire (blog), 129
fight-or-flight mode, 37
film industry, women of color in,
 20–21
financial autonomy, and
 independence, 30–31
financial support, of church, from
 women, 136
For Harriet (blog), 129
Foster, Kimberly, 127
Frazier, E. Franklin, 88–89
freedom of choice, 171
friendships of women, 182
functional impairment, 49–51

G

Gans, Herbert, 112n
gender
 blogs on, 129
 tension among African
 Americans, 113
gender identity, relational model of,
 147
gender role norms, 115–16
generalized anxiety disorder, 59
gifts of power, 162
Gilkes, Cheryl, 101, 103n90, 175
Gill-Austern, Brita, 139–40, 142,
 145–46, 149, 150–51, 182
Gillespie, Marcia, 171–72
God, 122
 acknowledging as greater than
 ourselves, 187
 Bailey's interaction with, 125
 connection with, 193–94
 inviting transforming power, 190
 recognizing power of, 188
 as women's primary priority, 105
Godey's Lady's Book, 91
Goldberg, Whoopi, *Star Trek: The
 Next Generation*, 20
Good Samaritan, love-of-self theme
 in, 152–54
gospel theater, 118–23
Grant, Jacquelyn, 140–141
Great Commandment, 152
Greene, Beverly, *Psychotherapy with
 African American Women*, 7
Grey's Anatomy (TV show), 123–27
grief, 16
Griffith, D.W., 82

H

Harper, Frances Ellen Watkins, 99n74
Harrington, Ellen F., 77–78
Harris-Perry, Melissa, 84, 86, 96
 on matriarch, 89
*Sister Citizen: Shame, Stereotypes, and
 Black Women in America*, 113

healing
    appearance, 161
    goal of, 170
    readiness for, 189
    search for, 161
health
    of Black women in U.S., 36
    cycle in StrongBlackWoman,
        63–78
health crisis
    for Black women, 5
    from StrongBlackWoman, 106
heart disease, 46
Height, Dorothy, 115
help, 38
    difficulty asking for, 32, 33
    resistance to, 150
    StrongBlackWoman need for, 17
    willingness to provide, 4
heterosexual relationships, matriarch
        stereotype and, 90
Higginbotham, Evelyn, 101, 102, 103
Hinson-Hasty, Elizabeth, 137
HIV/AIDS, 48–49
holy boldness, 172
home, women confined to, 92
hooks, bell, 173, 179
    Sisters of the Yam, 182
Hope, John, 113
hopelessness, 56
humility, 190
    and making amends, 192
A Hunger for Healing (Miller), 186,
        195
Hunter, Patricia, 174
hymns of Black church, 39
hypersexuality, 84
    myths about Black women, 82
hypertension, 46

I

idealization, of Black women's
        suffering, 143
identity, Trinity as model, 147–51
"I'm Happy with Jesus Alone," 39

Incidents in the Life of a Slave Girl
    (Jacobs), 19
independence, 29–34
    of Bailey, 126
    as Western ideal, 34
individualism, 80–81
    as Western ideal, 34
individuation, by children, 138n22
interdependence, community and,
        185
internal observation, in Christian
        mindfulness, 179
intimacy, 35
"isms," 174
isolation, 189

J

Jack, Dana Crowley, 57
Jacks, James, 98
Jackson, Leslie, *Psychotherapy with
        African American Women*, 7
Jacobs, Harriet, *Incidents in the Life of
        a Slave Girl*, 19
Jean-Louis, Jimmy, 120
Jenkins, Candice, 177
    Private Lives, Proper Relations, 145
Jesus Christ
    commissioning of disciples, 155
    Good Samaritan parable, 152–54
    Niebuhr on, 137
    Torah scholar and, 152
    visit to Martha and Mary, 151,
        155–58
Jezebel stereotype, 82, 83–85
    continuation, 109
Jim Crow segregation, 88, 94
Jones, Charisse, *Shifting: The Double
        Lives of Black Women in
        America*, 57, 70
journaling, 193–94
justice, myth of, 141n35

K

Kaba, Amadu, 42–43
Kaiser Family Foundation, telephone
        survey, 45

Kerrigan, Deanna, 48–49
kinship, extended structures, 28
koinonia, 181

L

labor of church women, 136
Ladies Auxiliary of the Brotherhood
    of Sleeping Car Porters, 97
ladyhood of upper class, 91
lament
    rituals of, 78–79
    of suffering, 144
leisure, social standing and, 100
liberation of Black women, 160–62,
    193
life expectancies
    of Black women, 51
    of enslaved women, 86
limits, recognizing healthy, 180
listening
    Martha and Mary, 157
    in pastoral care, 169
lived experience, honoring, 167–70
loneliness, 189
"Long as I Got King Jesus," 39
Lorde, Audre, *Sister Outsider*, 184–85
love, and self-sacrifice, 137, 139–40
Lucan travel narrative, 151, 155–58
lung cancer, 47
Lyon, Cheryl, 151n67

M

male identity, separation as defining
    characteristic, 138n22
*Mammy: A Century of Race, Gender,
    and Southern Memory*
    (Wallace-Sanders), 87
Mammy archetype, 82, 85–86
    continuation, 109
    legacy of, 28
Manpower Development and
    Training Act of 1962, 111n5
Martha and Mary, Jesus' visit to, 151,
    155–58
martyrdom, vs. discipleship, 137–45

mask, vs. personality, 4
matriarch, 82, 88–90
    actor impersonating, 117
    impact of image on Black men,
        114–15
    myth of Black, 110–17
    in U.S. popular imagination, 117
media literacy program, development
    of church-based, 129
meditation, 193–94
memory, power of, 175
mental health care, mistrust of
    perceived White field of,
    164–65
mental health of Black women, 52–63
    anxiety disorders, 58–60
    barriers to treatment, 63
    depression, 54–58
    emotional distress, 62, 160
    somatization, 62–63
    stress and distress, 53–54
    violence and trauma, 61
middle-class values, Black Christian
    women dissemination of,
    103–4
migraines, 49
Miller, J. Keith, 189, 190, 194
A Hunger for Healing, 186, 195
mindfulness meditation, 161, 188
    for cultivating self-awareness,
        177–79
model minority, 43
Moessner, Jeanne Stevenson, 152–54
mood disorders, 53
moral masochism, 142
Morgan, Joan, *When Chickenheads
    Come Home to Roost*, 7
mortality, from racial differences in
    cancer, 48
mother-child relationship, 138n22
mother-daughter relationship, 71
A Mother's Love (film), 121–23, 128
Moynihan Report, 89, 110–15
    damage from, 113–14
multitasking, 4
music, independence theme in, 29
mutual interiority, 147–48

mutual self-giving, 149
mutuality, 150
myth
    of Black matriarchy, 110–17
    of justice, 141*n*35
    of personal exceptionalism, 141
    of strength, 1, 3–4
    of universal equality, 141*n*35

N

naming needs for care, 177
National Association of Colored
    Women (NACW), 97
National Baptist Convention, U.S.A.
    Woman's Convention, 97–98
    women of, 102–3
National Baptist Union, 105
National Comorbidity Survey (NCS),
    52
    and depression, 55
    phobic conditions, 59
National Council of Negro Women,
    97, 115
National Health Interview Survey
    (NHIS), 44*n*8, 50
National Institute of Mental Health
    (NIMH), 52
National Mental Health Association,
    54
Ne-Yo, 30, 31
needs of StrongBlackWoman, 32–33
negative emotions, failre to
    acknowledge, 23
*The Negro Family: The Case for
    National Action*, 110–15
    damage from, 110–15
Nelson, Jill, 116
nervousness, 60
Neuger, Christine Conrad, 128, 174
NewBlackMan (blog), 129
Newsweek, 42
Niebuhr, Reinhold, 137
nonself-enclosed identities, 148, 149

O

obesity, 44–45, 64
The Onion, 130–31
ontological blackness, 95
oppositional gaze, 93*n*51
oppression, dismantling structural
    systems of, 170
ordained ministry
    church approval of candidacy, 38
    limitations on women, 136
out-of-wedlock births, 111
over-commitment, 4
overactivity, as normal, 2

P

pain
    chronic, 49–51
    of StrongBlackWoman, 41–43
panic disorder, 60*n*82
pastoral care. *See also* womanist
    framework to pastoral care
    for StrongBlackWoman
    accountability and credibility,
        163–67
    facilitating storytelling, 168
    healing facilitated by, 161
    individual relationship with
        provider, 181
    proactivity in identifying distress,
        78
    suggestions, 13
pastoral theology, womanist, 10
pastors, 17
    impressions of African-American
        women, 41–42
patriarchy
    and Martha's role, 157
    Wallace critique of, 6
Patton, John, 163
perichoresis, 147, 150
Perry, Tyler, *Diary of a Mad Black
    Woman*, 118–20, 127
personal exceptionalism, myth of,
    141
personality, vs. mask, 4
phobia, 59

physical appearance, emphasis on, 71
physical distress, ignoring symptoms
    of, 67
physical health of Black women,
    43–51
    cancer, 46–48
    chronic pain and functional
      impairment, 49–51
    diabetes and circulatory diseases,
      45–46
    emotional distress and, 62
    HIV/AIDS, 48–49
    illness crisis, 160
    obesity and physical activity,
      44–45
physical labor of Black women, 19
politics of responsibility, 95
popular culture
    blogs on, 129
    and StrongBlackWomen identity,
      127
posttraumatic stress disorder (PTSD),
    61
poverty, African-American women
    in, 42
power, gifts of, 162
praise, vs. punishment, 118–23
praxeological method, 10*n*11
prayer, 193–94
pride, 137
Private Lives, Proper Relations
    (Jenkins), 145
pseudo recovery, 73
*Psychotherapy with African American
    Women* (Jackson and
    Greene), 7
public activism, and cult of true
    womanhood, 104
punishment, vs. praise, 118–23
purity, in true womanhood, 92

R

race, blogs on, 129
racial discrimination, 111
racial ideology, Black churches and,
    102

racial uplift movement, 94–96
Racialicious (blog), 129
racism, 96
    cultural assault against Black
      women, 81–94
Randall, Alice, 64
rape, 61
reconciliation, 192
recovery program. *See*
    StrongBlackWoman's twelve-
    step recovery program
relapse, 192–93
relationality, Trinity as model, 147–51
relationships, 122, 149, 191
    friendships, 182
    individual with pastoral care
      provider, 181
    inventory of, 188
    mutuality and reciprocity in, 150
religious identity, StrongBlackWoman
    as, 39
religious piety, in true womanhood,
    91
repression, 67*n*109
respect, of girls for men, 121
respectability, 95–96
responsibility, 2
    freedom from bearing, 184
    Good Samaritan limits, 154–55
    of others for own lives, 191–92
    politics of, 95
restlessness, 60
Rhimes, Shonda, 123
Riggs, Marcia, 101, 141
myths internalized by African
    Americans, 141*n*35
rituals of lament, 78–79
role reversal, caregivers guarding
    against, 165
romantic relationships, 71
romanticization, of Black women's
    suffering, 143

S

sadness, 56
Saiving, Valerie, 137

sapphire, 88
  continuation, 109
sass, 172*n*35
Schüssler Fiorenza, Elisabeth, 156, 157
Scott, Kesho, 22
secrecy of breakdowns and health crises, 74
self-awareness, 192–93
  developing, 176–80
  mindfulness meditation for cultivating, 177–79
self-care
  neglect, 2
  postponement of, 76
self-definition, empowerment for, 170–73
self-denial
  in Christian love, 142
  transition to selfhood, 145–58
self-description, 140
self-disclosure, in pastoral care, 163–64
self-discovery, 170–71
self-expression, 35
self-giving, 149
  mutual, 149
self-identity, low sense of, 146
self-image, control and, 74
self-love, 151–58
  Good Samaritan and, 154
  vs. love of others, 177
self-recovery, 177
self-reliance, independence and, 29
self-sacrifice, 4, 141, 146, 150
  caregiving and, 133
  in Christian love, 142
  and love, 139–40
self-transcendence, 151
selfhood, self-denial transition to, 145–58
selfishness, 28
selflessness, 138
separation, as defining characteristic of male identity, 138*n*22
servanthood, 140
  church emphasis on, 144

sexual abuse, of enslaved Black women, 82
sharecropping, 88
Shifting: The Double Lives of Black Women in America (Jones and Shorter-Gooden), 57, 70
Shipherd, Jillian C., 77–78
Shorter-Gooden, Kumea, *Shifting: The Double Lives of Black Women in America*, 57, 70
silence of churches, on suffering of Black women, 132*n*7
"sister circles," 182–85
Sister Citizen: Shame, Stereotypes, and Black Women in America (Harris-Perry), 113
Sister Outsider (Lorde), 184–85
Sisterella complex, 57–58, 70*n*123
Sisters of the Yam (hooks), 182
slavery, 19*n*7, 82, 88
  life expectancies of women, 86
sleeping, guilt over, 76
small groups, 182–85
  confidentiality in, 183
Snorton, Teresa, 134, 164, 168
social phobia, 59
socialization
  of Black girls, 35, 66
  critical consciousness of, 173–74
society
  Black women's usefulness to, 88
  contradictory messages for Black women, 128
  and StrongBlackWomen identity, 37
socioemotional autonomy, 32
somatization, 62–63, 68
Sophia characters, 20–21
Soul on Ice (Cleaver), 115
spiritual discipline, 193–94
spiritual formation group, 133
spouses, StrongBlackWoman financial independence from, 31
Star Trek: The Next Generation (Goldberg), 20

stereotypes, 81
  about mental illness, 55
  vs. authenticity, 57
  of Black feminity, 83
  development, 90
  function as controlling images,
    106–7
  Jezebel, 82, 83–85
  Mammy, 82, 85–86
  matriarch, 82, 88–90
Stewart, Maria, 100*n*79
stoicism, 144
Stolzfus, Regina, 166
stomach cancer, 47
strength, 73
  admission of compulsions
    toward, 187
  Black women and, 15
  of Black women as backhanded
    compliment, 20
  church expectations for African-
    American women, 134–35,
    136
  connotation with dangerous
    consequences, 21
  emotional, 18–25
  freedom from burden, 195
  illusion of, 1
  myth of, 1, 3–4
  resentment of African-American
    women's, 128
stress, 2, 53–54
  negative health outcomes, 67
  from role as caregiver, 16
  of StrongBlackWoman, 66
stroke, 46
StrongBlackWoman
  alternative, 170
  birth of, 94–97
  child responsibilities, 1–2
  church involvement in
    development, 158
  core features of, 18–34
  in *Diary of a Mad Black Woman*,
    118–20
  ecosocial model of health
    connection, 65–74

  expectations of others, 38
  factors shaping as model of
    identity, 81
  and Good Samaritan, 155
  health crisis from, 106
  health cycle in, 63–78
  ideological ancestry, 6–8
  instruction in, 66
  negative consequences, 5–6, 76
  pain of, 41–43
  pastoral care for, 165, 170
  politics of respectability and,
    95–96
  portrait of, 14–17
  refusing to submit to image, 151
  relaxation of guard in pastoral-
    care encounter, 169
  and self-enclosed identity, 148
  societal reactions to, 109–10
  and suit of armor, 34–39
  themes central to, 75
  unrealistic expectations, 160
  use of phrase, 3–4
StrongBlackWoman's twelve-step
    recovery program, 185–95
  admission of compulsions toward
    strength, 187, 189
  decision to turn to care and
    protection of Divine, 188
  God, acknowledging as greater
    than ourselves, 187
  invitation of God's transforming
    power, 190
  making amends to those harmed,
    190–91
  practicing self-awareness, 188
  prayer, meditation, and
    journaling, 193–94
  readiness for healing, 189
  self-awareness and relapse,
    192–93
  summary, 197–98
  use in pastoral care, 195
submissiveness, 92–93
substance use disorders, 53

suffering, 142
    church silence on Black women's,
        132n7
    idealization and romanicization
        of, 143
    misinterpreting meaning and
        role, 146
    role in Christian life, 133–37
    strength and, 21
    StrongBlackWoman identity
        defined by, 97
Superwoman, 6
support from others. *See* help
survivor's guilt, 143
Symington, Melissa F., 177–79
Symington, Scott H., 177–79

T

tears. *See* crying
television industry
    Grey's Anatomy, 123–27
    women of color in, 20–21
Terrell, Mary Church, 99–100, 115
testimony, 166
therapist self-disclosure, in pastoral
    care, 163–64
Thompson, Cheryl, 142
Torah scholar, Jesus and, 152
Townes, Emilie, 19n7, 174
trauma, impact of, 76–77
Trinity as model
    of identity and relationality,
        147–51
    of mutually self-giving love, 149

U

Ultrafeminine sexual image, 115–16
undifferentiation, as women's
    problem, 138
U.S. Department of Labor, *The Negro
    Family: The Case for National
    Action*, 110–15
universal equality, myth of, 141n35
uterine cancer, 47

V

value conflicts, counseling to help
    see, 174
van Deusen Hunsinger, Deborah, 181
vicarious stress, 54
victims, African-American women
    as, 61
Volf, Miroslav, 149
    Exclusion and Embrace, 147–48
vulnerability, 168–69
    fear of, 22, 25
    hiding expressions of, 143
    repressing feelings of, 57

W

Walker, Alice, 9, 109–110, 172
Wallace, Michele, *Black Macho and
    the Myth of the Superwoman*,
    6
Wallace-Sanders, Kimberly, *Mammy:
    A Century of Race, Gender,
    and Southern Memory*, 87
Wallis, Quvenzhané, 130–32
Warhol, Andy, *Myth* series, 86
Washington Post, telephone survey, 45
Watts, Rolanda, 121
weakness, avoiding appearance of,
    101
Webbie, 31
"Independent," 30
Weems, Renita, 134, 144
Wells, Ida B., 115
Welter, Barbara, 91
*When Chickenheads Come Home to
    Roost* (Morgan), 7
White, Deborah Gray, 98, 113
White culture, assumptions on
women's capabilities, 19n7
White racism, and negative
    stereotypes, 81
White women
    cultural constructions of, 90
    image of weakness, 93–94
    in post-World War II era, 90
wholeness, 149

Wilson, Chandra, 123
    awards for performance as Bailey,
       127
womanist, 172
    definition, 9
womanist framework for pastoral
    care with StrongBlackWoman,
    162–85
    community-building, 181–85
    cultivating critical consciousness,
       173–75
    developing self-awareness,
       176–80
    empowerment for self-definition,
       170–73
    honoring lived experience,
       167–70
    pastoral accountability and
       credibility, 163–67
womanist pastoral theology, 10

WomanistCare, 194
Woman's Convention of the National
    Baptist Convention, U.S.A.,
    97–98
women
    behavior boundaries, 91
    Black Christian women on roles
       of, 104
    fallen and true, 90–94
    primary temptations, 138–39
women of color, "isms" impacting,
    174
Women's Media Center, 129
Wood, Frances, 132, 193
Woods-Giscombé, Cheryl, 71, 72,
    75, 180
work ethic, 30, 32
work, missing due to injury or illness,
    51
worthlessness, 56

60911795R00140

Made in the USA
Lexington, KY
22 February 2017